THE FOUR GEORGES

THE FOUR GEORGES

*Top, left—*George I, after the portrait by Sir Godfrey Kneller. *Right—*
George II, from the studio of Charles Jervais. *Below, left—*George III, in
his Coronation Robes, from the picture by Allan Ramsay. *Right—*
George IV, by Sir Thomas Lawrence. *Reproduced by permission from the*
National Portrait Gallery

THE FOUR GEORGES

A Revaluation of the period from 1714–1830

by

SIR CHARLES PETRIE

KENNIKAT PRESS
Port Washington, N. Y./London

THE FOUR GEORGES

First published in 1935
Reissued in 1971 by Kennikat Press
Library of Congress Catalog Card No: 72-118496
ISBN 0-8046-1244-7

Manufactured by Taylor Publishing Company   Dallas, Texas

PREFACE

THIS volume in no way claims to narrate the political, social, and economic history of England from the accession of George I to the death of George IV. It is solely concerned with those events which during that period changed the whole face of our national life, and with such movements and scenes as illustrate the attitude of our ancestors on various occasions during the reigns of the first four Georges. Wherever contemporary evidence of a tolerably reliable nature is available it has been quoted, for the aim throughout has been to show how the men and women of the eighteenth century lived, and how they regarded the problems that confronted them. In these circumstances it was inevitable that some events which occupy much space in modern history books should receive scant attention, and that others should be omitted altogether.

No effort has been made to depict the period as romantic. Every age appears romantic or otherwise according to the angle from which it is regarded, but none has the monopoly of romance. The Highland charge at Prestonpans, or the death of Byron at Missolonghi, will for some invest the Hanoverian era with a halo of romance, which will not be apparent to those who are concerned with the victims of the Enclosure Acts and the Industrial Revolution. My object has been to show the period as it was by allowing the facts to speak for themselves.

I should like to take this opportunity of expressing my deep gratitude to Mr. Douglas Jerrold for his criticism and advice on innumerable occasions, and also to Mr. John Boyd-Carpenter for help in respect of several points of law: neither, of course, is in any way responsible for the views put forward in these pages. 43821

v

Thanks are also due to the British Museum for permission to reproduce the caricatures of John Wilkes and the Gillray cartoon; to the National Portrait Gallery for the portraits of the Four Georges and of Canning; and to the William Salt Library, Stafford, for the print of the execution of Lord Ferrers. I must also thank Messrs. B. T. Batsford, Ltd. for the loan of the volumes of Ackermann's *Microcosm*, Pyne's *Royal Residences*, and H. D. Roberts's *The Royal Pavilion at Brighton*, from which the illustrations of Brooks's, Carlton House and the Royal Pavilion at Brighton are taken.

CHARLES PETRIE

CONTENTS

ILLUSTRATIONS

CHAPTER I

THE SETTING

A FEW minutes after seven o'clock on the morning of Sunday, August 1st, 1714, there died at Kensington Palace the last Stuart to rule in Great Britain, Queen Anne, and with her death the eighteenth century began. Nearly a hundred and sixteen years later, on June 26th, 1830, also in the early hours of the morning, passed away the First Gentleman of Europe, at Windsor, and the eighteenth century was ended. Superficially, the world appeared much the same on both occasions. The Most Christian King reigned in Paris, as did his Most Catholic brother in Madrid; whole provinces of Italy acknowledged the temporal sovereignty of the Vicar of Christ; and the Crescent still confronted the Cross on the frontiers of Hungary. Men travelled along the roads in horse-drawn vehicles, or across the sea in sailing-ships; Parliament was unreformed, and the crumbling ruins of Old Sarum returned two members to the House of Commons; and a prisoner charged with felony was denied counsel.[1] Yet this resemblance was in appearance alone; in the closing years of Anne men were still thinking in terms of the Civil War, while in those of George IV their gaze was directed towards the age of Victoria.

The past was very real to the men and women of the early eighteenth century, and this explains much that would otherwise be obscure. What M. Jacques Bainville says of his own country is equally true of England, *"ce grand siècle n'est devenu celui de l'ordre qu'après avoir passé par le désordre"*.[2] Those who were still young men when Anne died could remember

---

[1] Since 1695 prisoners accused of treason and misprison of treason had been allowed counsel, but in the case of those accused of felony counsel could only argue points of law on their behalf.

[2] *Histoire de France*, p. 209.

the Revolution of 1688; those in middle age had no difficulty in recalling the horrors of the Popish Plot and Monmouth's rebellion; while there must have been a few survivors of an earlier generation who had stood beneath the scaffold in Whitehall that January afternoon when a King of England was done to death. Many, too, during the spring and early summer of 1714 must have recalled the stories their parents had told them of those March days over a century before when another Queen lay dying at Richmond, and the succession was in doubt. It takes a long while either to settle or to unsettle a nation. During the reigns of the early Stuarts the memory of the relative calm of the Elizabethan era was still vivid, and many years elapsed before the continued constitutional crises engendered a feeling of insecurity in the mind of the ordinary citizen. Conversely the same was true in the early eighteenth century, and it was not until after the Forty-five that a sense of stability began to return. "The dominating impression of life in eighteenth-century London, from the standpoint of the individual, is one of uncertainty and insecurity."[1] With the accession of George III an attitude of increasing complacency is to be observed, which not even the loss of the American colonies and the French Revolution was able seriously to disturb. After Waterloo feeling changed again, but such apprehension as existed then was caused by the unknown terrors of the future rather than by fear of a repetition of the troubles of the past.

One or two generations usually elapse before the full effect of political changes is felt in the social sphere, and the reigns of Anne and George I are examples of this. Land was still the main source of wealth, but it had of late been changing hands to no inconsiderable extent. Many of the old families had become impoverished in the Civil War, and they gradually began to decline before those which had risen on the proceeds of the Reformation. It was not until the second half of the seventeenth century that the latter class began to grasp at political power, but when they did so it was with no uncertain hand, and it was they who precipitated the Revolution. During

[1] George, M. D.: *London Life in the XVIIIth Century*, p. 269.

the Commonwealth the egalitarian doctrines of the more extreme Puritans had kept them moderate Royalist, and Charles II had proved too clever for them, but his successor gave them their chance. By then, too, they had permeated not only the higher offices of the State, but of the Church as well: a notable example of this was Henry Compton, who was Bishop of London from 1675 to 1714, and was largely instrumental in bringing about the Revolution; he was a younger son of the second Earl of Northampton. Such was the origin of that "Venetian oligarchy", to quote Disraeli, which ruled England politically during the reigns of the first two Georges, and socially until the death of George IV.

Since the Restoration a new middle-class had come into existence, and this was to prove a factor of increasing importance. England has rarely been so prosperous as she was under Charles II. The Protectorate had been responsible for an economic crisis of the first magnitude,[1] but there was a marked revival after 1660. The value of exports and imports rose from 7,750,000 in 1662-63 to some 11,500,000 by the date of the Revolution, while the increase in national savings during the same period was estimated at 100 per cent.[2] The receipts from the customs duties rose from £260,000 in 1661 to nearly £600,000 in 1785. Between 1658 and 1677 inclusive the East India Company divided 130 per cent in dividends, and in 1681 there were 181 holders of £1,000 or more in East India stock. Imports of bullion averaged £372,000 per annum from 1666 to 1680, as against £60,000 from 1660 to 1666. There had always, of course, been the burghers in the towns, but what was new about the class now coming up was that it was no longer content to live over its counting-house. Defoe, in particular, bears testimony to this development, and in his account of a tour of Essex in the reign of George I he says:

"It is observable, that in this part of the country, there are several very considerable estates purchased, and now

[1] cf. James, M.: *Social Problems and Policy during the Puritan Revolution, 1640–1660*, pp. 71–77.
[2] cf. Feiling, K.: *British Foreign Policy, 1660–1672*, pp. 14–15.

enjoyed by citizens of London, merchants and tradesmen. . . .
I mention this to observe how the present increase of wealth
in the city of London, spreads itself into the country, and
plants families and fortunes, who in another age will equal
the families of the ancient gentry, who perhaps were bought
out."[1]

It was not until the end of the century that this class began
to make its weight felt in politics to any great extent, and the
situation arose when it was possible to say of a Canning that
he was "long kept down by the plebeian aristocracy of Mr.
Pitt as an adventurer".[2] In the meantime it was content to
follow the lead of the Whig magnates, not necessarily because
it loved the House of Hanover, but because it disliked change:
it would equally have supported James III had he been the
monarch in possession.

When Anne died England was an overwhelmingly agricultural country, and the brilliant social life of the capital
must not be allowed to obscure the fact that the vast majority
of the population lived on and by the land. Difficulty of
communication set a wider gulf between town and country
then than has been the case since, and contemporary literature
is full of jokes at the expense of the countryman who came to
London for the first time. He was considered fair game, and
Hogarth in Plate I of *The Harlot's Progress* shows the fate that
might await the young girl who came up in a wagon to find
employment in domestic service. Even rich squires, like
Squire Western, spoke with the dialect of their own county,
and their manners, if not their morals, left much to be desired
when compared with those of equal position in London. By
the death of George IV the improved means of communication
had effected a revolution, but in 1714 the position was what
it had been for centuries. What kept England, and still more
Scotland and Ireland, apart was that which should have bound
them together, namely, the roads. When the Crown exercised
real power these, together with the bridges, had been its
responsibility, but the change from monarchy to oligarchy had

---

[1] *A Tour through England and Wales.*   [2] Disraeli, B.: *Sybil*, Bk. I, Ch. III.

resulted in the gentry omitting to discharge their obligations since there was no longer anyone to compel them to do so. Defoe gives many instances of the incredible badness of the roads, but one or two of these will suffice.

"Going to church at a country village, not far from Lewes, I saw an ancient lady, and a lady of very good quality, I assure you, drawn to church in her coach with six oxen; nor was it done in frolic or humour, but mere necessity, the way being so still and deep, that no horses could go in it."[1]

Sussex roads were particularly bad, for in another place Defoe refers to that

"which was formerly a Roman work, called Stony Street or Stone-Street: Mr. Camden mentions it as going from Leatherhead to Dorking, and through Dorking churchyard, then cross a terrible deep country, called the Holmwood, and so to Petworth and Arundel: but we see nothing of it now; and the country indeed remains in the utmost distress for want of good roads".[2]

The remedy applied to this state of affairs was the characteristically English one of farming out the roads to joint-stock companies, who erected turnpike gates, and recouped the "shareholders out of tolls levied on all who rode or drove along what had once been the King's highway".[3] This system was also calculated, though it would be unfair to suggest that such was the original intention, to prevent the poor moving about at all.

A century before there had been a strong yeoman and peasant class with property of its own. It is difficult to say how many people thus possessed the land upon which they lived, but it has been estimated that half the nation was in this position.[4] The holdings varied from a hundred to two hundred acres, down to those of the cottager with his four or five. Some of these smallholders had to pay dues to the squire, but so long as they did so they could not be dispossessed.

[1] *Op. cit.*   [2] *Op. cit.*   [3] John, E.: *King Charles I*, p. 70.
[4] *cf.* Belloc, H.: *Charles the First*, p. 24; also Jerrold, D.: *England*, pp. 65–66.

By 1714 this state of affairs was already becoming a memory, and the rich were getting richer while the poor were getting poorer. To quote Mr. Evan John once again:

> "The physical presence of the poor (except of those trained and adorned for domestic serfdom) grew distasteful to the rich man, whose ancestors had eaten and made merry at the long board of the Elizabethan manor."[1]

The eighteenth century was to see the completion of the process by which the rich became masters of the land; but the Enclosure Acts were only the logical results of the victory of the vested interests over the nation, as represented by the monarchy, in the Civil War and at the Revolution. Once the rich had been checked by the Prerogative Courts such as the Star Chamber and the Council for the North,[2] but now the same people made the laws as M.P.s, and administered them as J.P.s. It was becoming impossible for the poor to obtain justice at all when they came into conflict with those who governed the country, and this explains why Jacobitism drew so much of its strength from what are now called the working classes.[3]

Nevertheless, when Guelph succeeded Stuart much of the old England of the sixteenth and seventeenth centuries still survived, and the subjects of George I lived rather in the manner of those of James I than in that of their descendants under George IV. The inns, for example, had not yet begun to change their character. There were no bars, no set dinners, and no dining-rooms, for these innovations did not come until the reign of George III. Travellers of any social distinction ordered what they liked, or rather what the house could supply, in their own rooms, which had names, such as "Blenheim" or "Rose", not numbers as to-day. Moreover, no charge was made for the use of the room, as the landlord reckoned to recoup himself out of the food and drink consumed, and the

---

[1] *Op. cit.*, p. 72.

[2] These were far from being the organs of oppression the Whig historian would have us believe; cf. Reid, R. R.: *The King's Council for the North*, passim.

[3] Bates, C. J.: *History of Northumberland*, pp. 265–266: "The attachment of the working classes to the Stuart cause was much deeper than might now be supposed."

stabling. Poorer people, such as those who travelled in the carrier's wagon, gravitated towards the kitchen. What the latter was like may be gathered from the opening paragraph of Smollett's *Sir Lancelot Greaves:*

"It was on the great northern road from York to London, about the beginning of October, and about the hour of eight in the evening, that four travellers were, by a violent shower of rain, driven for shelter into a little public-house on the side of the highway, distinguished by a sign which was said to exhibit the figure of a black lion. The kitchen, in which they were assembled, was the only room for entertainment in the house, paved with red bricks, remarkably clean, furnished with three or four Windsor chairs, adorned with shining plates of pewter, and copper saucepans nicely scoured, that even dazzled the eyes of the beholder; while a cheerful fire of sea-coal blazed in the chimney."

Sometimes the landlord made a mistake in his estimate of the social position of an arrival, and when Tom Jones arrived at the inn at Upton-on-Severn with the half-naked Mrs. Waters it was assumed by the landlady that he wanted a room for the purpose for which rooms are often engaged even in the twentieth century. This explained, if it did not excuse, the landlady's attack upon him with a broom. Incidentally, it transpired that he could pay for what he wanted. Tom Jones later found no obstacle placed in the way of the gratification of those desires which had been so carefully excited by the lady, who, to quote Fielding's delightful phrase, "could feast heartily at the table of love, without reflecting that some other already had been, or hereafter might be, feasted with the same repast". The standard of comfort varied as it does to-day, and Lord Torrington must, one feels, have been particularly unfortunate in his choice, when he wrote:

"I look upon an inn, as the seat of all roguery, profaneness, and debauchery; and sicken of them every day, by hearing nothing but oaths, and abuse of each other, and brutality to horses."[1]

[1] *The Torrington Diaries*, Vol. I, p. 105. This, however, was before he had become acquainted with his cherished "Haycock" at Wansford.

He certainly seems to have been hard to please, for on another occasion we find him noting:

"The imposition in travelling is abominable; the innkeepers are insolent, the hostlers are sulky, the chambermaids are pert, and the waiters are impertinent; the meat is tough, the wine is foul, the beer is hard, the sheets are wet, the linen is dirty, and the knives are never cleaned."[1]

Still, Torrington had only himself to blame, for he often avoided the best inn, as when he passed over the "Crown" at Blandford for another house.[2]

Another institution which had so far resisted all change was the fair, and much of the business of the country was still transacted at them. Some, however, were already marked by a rowdiness and a licence which in a more polite, or more hypocritical, age was to lead to a curtailment of their number. Such a one was the so-called Horn Fair, held annually at Charlton, in Kent, on St. Luke's Day, the suppression of which was demanded by Defoe on the ground that

"the women are especially impudent for that day; as if it was a day that justified the giving themselves a loose to all manner of indecency and immodesty, without any reproach, or without suffering the censure which such behaviour would deserve at another time".[3]

If tradition is to be believed the origin of the fair rendered such a celebration by no means unfitting. The story goes that one day when King John was hunting from Eltham he lost his way, and stopped at a cottage in Charlton to inquire it. He was so struck by the beauty of the woman who opened the door to him that he persuaded her to grant him the last favours, and was reaping his reward when her husband suddenly appeared. To save his life the King was obliged to reveal his identity, and to make a substantial grant of land to the man he had thus cuckolded. In memory of this event, a fair was started for the sale of horns, and every kind of goods made

[1] *The Torrington Diaries.*, Vol. I, p. 53.
[2] For the inns of the period *cf.* Burke, T.: *The English Inn, passim.*
[3] *A Tour through England and Wales.*

from that material. A riotous mob met at Cuckold's Point, near Deptford, and marched through that town and Greenwich to Charlton with horns of different kinds upon their heads. A sermon was always preached at Charlton Church on the occasion of the fair.

Most of the fairs were, however, for the conduct of more serious business. There was a great fair for poultry at Dorking, which provided employment for the whole district; and there Defoe was struck by the size of the capons he saw, which were anything up to 6 lb. in weight, and sold for between 4s. and 4s. 6d. each. One of the largest fairs in England for lambs was held annually at the same place on Holy Thursday. At Andover there was a great sheep fair, where several hundred thousand sheep were sold on each occasion. At Atherstone there was

"a great cheese fair on September 8th; from whence the great cheese factors carry the vast quantities of cheese they buy to Stourbridge Fair, which begins about the same time, but holds much longer; and here it is sold again for the supply of the counties of Essex, Suffolk, and Norfolk".[1]

It had also been the practice to engage servants at a fair. By the time of George I the custom was beginning to die out, though there were still fairs of this nature so near London as Enfield, Waltham, and Epping. At some of them it was not unusual for those who wished to be hired to hold in their hands the implements of their craft, and carters appeared with a whip, labourers with a spade and woodmen with a bill.

Unfortunately, all the survivals of an earlier England were by no means of so picturesque a nature as the inns and fairs. One of them was Newgate, and the treatment of prisoners there shows the eighteenth century in another light. An Act of Parliament allowed a rent of half a crown on those who were incarcerated, but that hardly saved them from lying on hard boards. Every kind of malpractice was perpetrated upon a prisoner. For twenty guineas he might buy the right of living in the Governor's house, but when he had parted with

1 *Op. cit.*

his money, he found that all he had acquired was the right of walking all day in the fetid press-yard, and of eating in the pot-house rooms connected with it. The Governor defended this practice on the ground that his house consisted of every part in Newgate which was not actually within the prison, and he called the press-yard external, as it suited his pocket to do so. As soon as a prisoner passed through the gates his fellow-victims found out if he had any money; if so, a horde of ruffians at once proceeded to get drunk at his expense. This payment was known as "garnish", and was not abolished until the reign of George IV. After this, the turnkeys proceeded to show the prisoners various sets of fetters, pointing out the weight of some and the lightness of others; the lighter they were the more they cost. If the new-comer proved recalcitrant, he was given a taste of the "Condemned Hold". This salubrious spot was a dungeon in the arch below Newgate, and even at midday it was so dark that a candle merely served to accentuate the blackness.

The amenities of the press-yard were relative. When the new-comer entered it he probably saw but a handful of prisoners at first. Of these one or two might be reading books or newspapers, and others would be playing cards; others again, the most numerous section, were to be found in the drinking boxes, or at the windows on the different floors of the buildings that gave on to the yard. As soon as a new-comer was seen to enter, all these forsook their several occupations, crowded round him, and exacted his "footing", that is to say, a dozen bottles of wine and tobacco in proportion. If he still had any money left he was now able to mix with this company until he was hanged, or met with some other fate. Female companionship was to be had for the asking, or rather for the paying. At ten o'clock the prisoners, male and female, were sent to their respective rooms, but if they were sufficiently generous their doors were left unlocked, and the turnkeys only bolted those at the foot of the various staircases. When these were opened at eight in the morning, the roll was called in the press-yard, and those who had been drunk the previous night were fined a groat: this was at once spent on liquor, consumed

with the turnkeys. Visitors from outside were allowed into
the press-yard, where they had the opportunity of drinking
and smoking, singing and swearing, with the regular inmates.
An Act of 1751 subsequently forbade the sale of spirits in
prisons, but it was generally evaded: in the King's Bench
prison there were at one time no less than thirty gin shops, and,
as late as 1776, 120 gallons of gin were sold weekly, besides
other spirits and eight butts of beer. Seven years later the
Ordinary, i.e. chaplain, of Newgate is found writing to Dr.
Bentham that it was difficult to prevent spirits being smuggled
in because "women who are chiefly the conveyors of them
secrete them in such ways that it would be termed the grossest
insult to search for them".[1] It must, of course, be remembered
that the eighteenth-century prison was not a place of detention
for those who had been convicted, but rather a temporary
abode whence the prisoner who had been found guilty passed
on to the gallows, pillory, stocks, or was fined or transported.

Another institution which recalled a rougher age was
Bridewell, which served as a workhouse and house of correction.
Vagrants and harlots were made to beat hemp there; and a
typical scene in the women's section is depicted in Plate IV
of *The Harlot's Progress*. A contemporary who visited Bridewell says of the women at work there:

"They smelt as frowsily as so many goats in a Welsh gentleman's stable, and looked with as much modesty as so many
Newgate Saints canonized at the Old Bailey."[2]

The whipping of women there was one of the sights of the
town, and there was always a crowd of idlers and visitors. The
women were brought before the Governor and Court, and
what then ensued is best described in the words of the witness
already quoted;

"Another accusation being then delivered by a flat-cap
against a poor wretch, who had no friend to speak on her
behalf, proclamation was made, viz: 'All you who are willing
E——th T——ll should have present punishment, pray
hold up your hands.' This was done accordingly, and then

---

[1] *cf.* George, M. D.: *London Life in the XVIIIth Century*, pp. 300–301, 397.
[2] Ward, E.: *The London Spy*, p. 108.

she was ordered the civility of the house, and was forced to show her tender back to the grave sages of the august assembly, who were moved by her modest mien, together with the whiteness of her skin, to give her but gentle correction."[1]

The whipping went on until the Governor knocked with his hammer, and the wretched victims used to call out, "Oh, good Sir Robert, knock! Pray, good Sir Robert, knock." Many a brawl was started by one woman of the streets using this phrase to another as a reflection upon her reputation, for those engaged in the oldest profession have always resented the suggestion that such is their means of gaining a livelihood.

Was the eighteenth century immoral? Its Victorian successor held hands up in horror at its alleged excesses, but the difference between one age and another in the matter of morals is but one of standpoint. The eighteenth century was bawdy, and it liked its humour broad. It did not snigger in corners, or officially deceive itself that a naked woman on the stage was less likely to put ideas into the heads of the audience if she kept still than if she moved. Customs such as the Horn Fair at Charlton were doubtless obscene, but they never pretended to be anything else. There was also a large amount of rollicking fun connected with them which is missing in the merely suggestive performances of a later generation. For example, every new Parliament there was a mock election of two members to represent the borough of Garret, that is to say, a few straggling cottages near Wandsworth. The qualification of a voter was that he had enjoyed a woman in the open air in that district. Large numbers of people used to come out from London for the occasion, and so much custom resulted to the local publicans that they found it in their interest to contribute largely to the expense of the ceremony. No doubt it was all very shocking, but one wonders whether it was any worse for the morals of those who took part in it than the entertainment attended by pleasure-seekers of a later day. As Mr. Hartmann very truly says of the early years of Louis XIV:

[1] *The London Spy.*, p. 109.

"Though love-intrigues may have been the vogue, society still continued to look askance at the inevitable physical consequences of amorous indiscretions, and, since contraceptives were unknown, morals can never have been quite as loose as the memoirs and romances of the period might lead one to suppose."[1]

The same observation may well be applied to the eighteenth century.

When one turns from the social life of the country to its economic development, it is to be struck with the fact that in 1714 the mass of the people still lived in the south and southwest. Wiltshire and Somerset were the principal centres of the wool industry; and Defoe could write of Frome that it

"is now reckoned to have more people in it, than the city of Bath, and some say, than even Salisbury itself, and if their trade continues to increase for a few years more, as it has done for those past, it is very likely to be one of the greatest and wealthiest inland towns in England".[2]

The iron industry was still vigorous in Sussex. Nevertheless, coming events were already casting their shadows before them. The wool industry was beginning to grow in the West Riding of Yorkshire, and the coal trade was firmly established round Newcastle-on-Tyne. The badness of the roads and the absence of canals compelled manufacturers to avoid, so far as possible, the interior of the country, and to carry on their business by the banks of navigable rivers, or near a port. Next to the merchants of London, those of Bristol still led the way, but Liverpool was coming up fast, and Glasgow was laying the foundation of its reputation. To quote Mr. G. D. H. Cole's Introduction to Defoe's *A Tour through England and Wales:*

"All round the coast—but especially in the south—are studded little ports of vital significance in the national life. For to these ports comes, by road or river, the merchandise of the interior, seeking ever the shortest route to the sea, which affords by far the cheapest and easiest means of

---

[1] *Charles II and Madame*, p. 32.   [2] *Op. cit.*

transport. Many of these little ports have their own commerce with foreign lands; but most of them are chiefly occupied in carrying goods to the great ports of England itself—and above all to London. Coastwise shipping possesses an economic importance which it is hard to appreciate in a railway age."

In the east and south-east the so-called "Domestic System" of manufacture was still in full force—that is to say, the spinning was done by poor people in their own homes; the master clothiers, who mostly lived in the larger centres of population, sent out the wool to them weekly, and at the same time collected the yarn which had been spun and finished. Norwich, for example, was full of operatives working at their looms in the garrets of their homes. In Yorkshire this system was falling into disuse. Many of the operatives there were already small capitalists, employing labour themselves in workshops attached to their houses. Such men had independent access to the market, and they could deal with the merchants on equal terms. Before George III was dead their sons and grandsons had built up the factory system based on steam.

In spite of the extensive decentralization of the national activities, London was pre-eminent to an extent unknown before or since. It was the largest city in Western Europe, and was estimated to contain about 700,000 inhabitants,[1] while the population of the whole country was some 6,500,000.[2] It is true that the proportion of Londoners to the total population has since risen, but the relative importance of the capital has declined. Until the end of the eighteenth century there was no other town of the first rank; York, Bristol, and Winchester were in decline, and Birmingham, Manchester, and Liverpool were still in the early stages of development. Mr. Roscoe estimated that in the seventies and eighties Liverpool had 39,000 inhabitants, Birmingham 30,000, and Manchester no more than 22,000.[3] The predominance of the capital, however, did not rest upon its size alone, but also upon its character. It was, of course, continually being recruited from the country, but it was an entity all the same. The old mediaeval city had been a community of traders, and the London that was to come was to be a mere agglomeration of individuals with no common tie. In the eighteenth century it was of a size that enabled its citizens to have an identity of outlook, even if it were only that from the greatest lord to the meanest beggar they thought themselves infinitely superior to the rest of the inhabitants of the country. "I will venture to say," Dr. Johnson asserted, "there is more learning and science within the circumference of ten miles from where we now sit, than in all the rest of the kingdom." On another occasion he went even further, and declared that "when a man is tired of London, he is tired of life".[1]

Such was the background against which the drama of the eighteenth century was played.

"It was an age of great men. England has known since no orators, no actors, no critics, no satirists, no generals, no admirals, and no heroes of the stature common in those days. . . . It was not an age of regrets; the Augustans saw clear, if not below the surface. They were not afraid of scandal: they lived hard, drank deep, and loved recklessly. They had courage and pride and dignity and no sentiment at all; but whenever a challenge was offered to the integrity of their inheritance they met it with resolute patriotism. They were men, they saved the State."[2]

---

[1] Boswell, J.: *Life of Samuel Johnson.*   [2] Jerrold, D.: *England,* pp. 73 and 75.

CHAPTER II

WHITE ROSE OR WHITE HORSE?

THE first problem which eighteenth-century Britain had to settle was the choice between the White Rose of Stuart and the White Horse of Hanover. Legally, the decision had been taken by the Act of Settlement in 1701, and from the moment Anne died on that August morning at Kensington the King of Great Britain, France, and Ireland was George I, Elector of Hanover. That is to say, if it be admitted that Parliament has the right to determine the succession to the throne. Otherwise, the lawful monarch was James III and VIII. In what proportions public opinion was divided between them it is by no means easy to say. In 1743 Pulteney estimated that two-thirds of the country was still Tory;[1] and thirty-five years later Dr. Johnson horrified Boswell with the remark, "If England were fairly polled, the present King would be sent away to-night, and his adherents hanged to-morrow."[2] The course of events soon proved that there was to be considerable doubt for many years to come where English sympathies lay, but there could be none as to opinion in Ireland. The Catholic majority was for the Stuarts, and the Protestant minority was for Hanover, but the latter had entrenched itself so firmly since it violated the Treaty of Limerick that not a dog barked on the other side of St. George's Channel even when Charles Edward was at Derby. As for Scotland, where the issue was finally decided, the lines of division were by no means so clearly defined as some writers would have us suppose, and it was not a simple affair of Catholic and Episcopalian against Presbyterian. Major Eardley-Simpson, for example, has recently produced fresh evidence from Dr. Blaikie's papers to show that by far the greater part of the clansmen who marched to Derby were not only Protestant, but Presbyterian.[3]

[1] Coxe, W.: *Life of Sir Robert Walpole.*   [2] Boswell, J.: *Life of Samuel Johnson.*
[3] *Derby and the Forty-five,* p. 187.

Although Anne had clearly been failing in health for some weeks, her death was so sudden that it took the Jacobites completely by surprise. Whether Bolingbroke is to be included in their number at that date is a moot point, and the balance of probability is that his immediate aims went no further than getting himself into supreme power so that he could negotiate on equal terms with either candidate.[1] On July 27th he achieved his purpose, but so far from having six weeks, which he wanted, to put those he could trust in all the more influential offices, he did not have six days. "The Earl of Oxford", he wrote to Swift, "was removed on Tuesday, the Queen died on Sunday. What a world is this! And how does fortune banter us!" How much truth is to be attached to the story that Ormonde, Atterbury, and the Earl Marischal[2] at once met to discuss the proclamation of James, and that Atterbury offered to proclaim him at Charing Cross in his lawn sleeves, it is difficult to say. The most popular version of the story is given in Spence's *Anecdotes* on the authority of Dean Lockier, who says that when Ormonde wished to consult the Council, "Damm it, Sir, said Atterbury in a great heat (for he did not value swearing), you very well know that things have not been concerted enough for that yet, and that we have not a moment to lose."[3] This is a little hard on the Bishop, who was not addicted to the use of bad language. Nevertheless, whatever deliberations may have taken place were ineffectual, for George I was duly proclaimed without opposition. Not for the first, or last, time the Whigs struck while their opponents were hesitating.

The weakness of the Jacobites lay neither in their numbers nor in their enthusiasm, but in their leaders. In England these were Bolingbroke, Ormonde, Sir William Wyndham, and Lord Lansdowne, while in Scotland it was Mar—"Bobbing John" as he was by no means inappropriately termed—who put himself at their head.

[1] cf. Hassall, A.: *Life of Viscount Bolingbroke*, pp. 80–97.

[2] The Duke of Ormonde was Commander-in-Chief and Lord Warden of the Cinque Ports; Francis Atterbury was Bishop of Rochester; and the Earl Marischal was Captain of the Scottish Horse Guards.

[3] For a discussion of the whole matter cf. Beeching, H. C.: *Francis Atterbury*, pp. 253–257.

Bolingbroke was at this time thirty-seven years of age, and was at the summit of his career. Neither his brains nor his ability have ever been called in question. He had recently been primarily responsible for the conclusion of the Treaty of Utrecht, which, although violently attacked by contemporary Whigs, has commended itself to posterity.[1] Unfortunately, these advantages were offset by an entire lack of balance. Bolingbroke was a man to whom excess, both in the matter of wine and women, became habitual. Voltaire is responsible for the story that when he first entered the ministry a *demimondaine* was heard to remark to two of her professional sisters, "Seven thousand guineas a year, my girls, and all for us." At the same time, Bolingbroke had the merit of not being a hypocrite, for

> "he himself bragged that in one day he was the happiest man alive, got drunk, harangued the Queen, and at night was put to bed to a beautiful young lady, and was tuck'd up by two of the prettiest young Peers in England, Lord Jersey and Bathurst".[2]

He was equally ready to cater for the requirements of a friend, and he is found writing to Thomas Coke, M.P. for Derbyshire:

> "As to whores, dear friend, I am unable to help thee. I have heard of a certain housemaid that is very handsome; if she can be got ready against your arrival, she shall serve for the first meal."[3]

Nevertheless, Bolingbroke was also an indefatigable worker in his official capacity, and what chiefly militated against his success was not his lack of industry, but the mistrust he inspired. In later life he acquired some reputation as a political philosopher, and it is one of the more curious paradoxes of the century that the man who was disgraced by the first George should have exercised so considerable a posthumous influence over the third monarch of the name.

[1] *cf.* Seeley, Sir John: *The Expansion of England*, pp. 131–132.
[2] Trevelyan, G. M.: *England under Queen Anne*, Vol. III, p. 283.
[3] *H.M.C. Coke MSS.*, p. 61.

The second Duke of Ormonde had not always been a Jacobite. He fought for William at the Boyne, and was twice Lord-Lieutenant of Ireland. When the Tories came into office, and Marlborough was dismissed, Ormonde, in 1712, was appointed Captain-General, and he seems about that time to have transferred his allegiance to James. With Bolingbroke he shared the fatal defect of doing the wrong thing at the critical moment, but whereas the former hesitated (and was lost) because he could not decide which course would the better serve his own interests, Ormonde seems merely to have lost his head. The truth is that he was a greatly overrated figure; his liberality and his genial manner made him popular, and because he was popular it came to be assumed that he must be a leader of men: a common error in English political circles. He was one of that type of politician who is always about to do something, but never does; accordingly, though for some years Tory mobs continued to shout themselves hoarse with cries of "High Church and Ormonde", the Duke himself had no influence upon the course of events. Wyndham was a Somerset squire, who also, as will be seen, was too prone to procrastination when the situation demanded action, but his career subsequently commended itself to Disraeli, who saw, or professed to see, in him the prototype of a Lord George Bentinck.[1] Wyndham was superior to Bolingbroke and Ormonde in that he did not fly the country, but he was equally incompetent when the time came to translate words into deeds.

George Granville, Lord Lansdowne, was better suited to the part of an Opposition leader than any of his colleagues.[2] He had organized Cornwall in the Tory interest very effectively indeed during the latter years of Anne, and he had recently married Lady Mary Thynne, the widow of Viscount Weymouth's heir: this brought him Longleat, and £12,000 a year, so that in addition to Cornwall he was in a position to influence the rest of the West of England. Lansdowne was no more

---

[1] cf. Monypenny, W. F.: Life of Benjamin Disraeli, Earl of Beaconsfield, Vol. I, pp. 218, 219, and 221, also ibid. (Monypenny and Buckle), Vol. III, pp. 100–101.
[2] The best account of his career is Handasyde, E.: Granville the Polite.

strict in his habits than were his friends, and on one occasion he is found writing to Harley:

"We constantly remember you, I can't say in our prayers, for I fear we don't all pray, but in our cups, for we all drink, and when our hearts are most open, your image is most conspicuous."[1]

Had Granville been properly backed, his genius for organization would have been invaluable to the Jacobite cause. Latterly he had come into contact with Mar, who was destined to head the rising in Scotland. Mar had been a Whig at the time of the Union, and a Tory in the last days of Anne: indeed, his Jacobitism would appear to have been due to no higher motive than the conviction that he had nothing to hope from Hanover. When he finally decided to call upon Scotland to rise for James he came direct from George's *levée*, and once he had taken the field he showed himself to be one of the most ineffective insurgents that ever plunged a kingdom into civil strife. It is only too true that on many occasions in history great causes have been led by unworthy men, but it is difficult to resist the conclusion that very rarely has a movement marked by so much that was admirable as was Jacobitism been headed by such unattractive figures as Bolingbroke, Ormonde, Wyndham, and Mar. Granville is the only Jacobite leader at this period for whom it is possible to entertain any other feeling than contempt.

On the other side there were few outstanding personalities save Walpole and Stanhope,[2] but there was all the strength that comes from unity of purpose and the fear of losing cherished, if dubiously acquired, possession. Above all, the Whigs were in control of the machinery of government, for Bolingbroke had been denied his six weeks. Their opponents were divided between ardent legitimists who would have James on any terms, moderate Jacobites who wanted to arrange in advance the terms upon which he was to return, and Tories who had only decided to support him because they saw no hope for themselves under the rule of his rival. The great

[1] *H.M.C. Portland MSS. Harley Papers*, Vol. II, p. 527.
[2] For the latter *cf.* Williams, B.: *Stanhope, passim.*

Revolution families of Cavendish, Russell, and Bentinck unhesitatingly threw their influence into the scale on behalf of that new order which had raised them from country squires to great magnates, and they were supported by the commercial classes which had enriched themselves during the long wars with France. The vested interests were for Hanover to a man, since they had no desire for the return of a system in which the monarchy claimed to regulate them for the sake of the nation as a whole. The Whigs were a minority, but a determined one, and to defend themselves they had never failed to use any weapon that came to hand, from the days of the warming-pan lie. Against them the divided counsels of the Jacobites could not prevail, and they had resources denied to the plain country gentlemen and simple yeomen, who asked for nothing more than to be left alone to live in the old traditional England of their fathers under the House of Stuart. The majority of the clergy were, it is true, for James, but preferment lay in the hands of the Whig bishops.

Whatever differences of opinion there may be as to the justice of the Jacobite and Hanoverian causes, there can be none, in the light of the fuller knowledge of to-day, as to the respective merits of the rival candidates for the throne. The latest biographer of George I describes him as "a man of singularly unattractive manners and unamiable disposition", and continues:

> "The treatment he accorded his mother, the unrelenting cruelty he displayed to his most unfortunate and ill-starred wife, his unworthy and undignified conduct toward his only son, leave a stain on his memory no attempts of laudatory biographers can efface, no consideration of political difficulties can minimize."[1]

His mother confessed that at the age of seventeen he had seduced a member of her household, while he treated his young wife with the extreme of brutality both before and after his separation from her. The nature of a man can often be gauged by the women he keeps, and George's mistresses

[1] Imber-Terry, Sir H. M., Bt.: *A Constitutional King:* George I, p. 384.

were both ugly and unpleasant. If he was not the worst of English monarchs, he was personally the most unattractive, though his successor ran him close in that respect. Even the Whigs made no pretence of liking him, though it was to their interest to keep him on the throne. James III, on the contrary, was above all else a great gentleman. He did not possess the initiative of his son, or the good-humoured cynicism of his uncle, but there runs through all his enormous correspondence a devotion to duty which was lacking in the Guelphs until Victoria, with the exception of George III. No Hanoverian, moreover, would have compensated out of his own pocket the poor Scottish villagers whose homes had been burnt to cover the Royal retreat from Perth in 1716. Until recently the character of "Old Mr. Misfortunate" has been under the cloud of Thackeray's misrepresentation in *Henry Esmond*, but it is now generally realized that in rejecting him for his boorish German relative Great Britain was definitely the loser.[1]

For some months it appeared as if the nation was prepared to accept the change of dynasty without demur. George duly came over from Hanover, and was crowned. To quote Bolingbroke, "There was a perfect calm and universal submission through the whole kingdom."[2] Whether the Tory submission was quite as complete as Bolingbroke, writing his *apologia* three years later, would have us believe, or whether it was due to the failure of the Tory leaders, not least Bolingbroke himself, to act at the critical moment, is another matter. What is clear is that the effect of the stupefaction soon began to wear off, and not the least important reason for this was the avowed determination of the victorious Whigs to ensure that they alone should enjoy the sweets of office under the new monarch. A little more moderation on the part of George and his ministers, and there might have been no Fifteen at all, for the Jacobites would have been deprived even of the poor leaders they had. Bolingbroke was dismissed about a month after the Queen's death, and he spent the autumn and

---

[1] The best short biography of James III and VIII is *The Old Chevalier*, by A. and H. Tayler. Larger works are *James Francis Edward, The Old Chevalier*, by M. Haile, and *The King over the Water*, by A. Shield and A. Lang.

[2] *A Letter to Sir William Wyndham.*

winter in the country, where he has left it upon record that he found the tide of Jacobite feeling steadily rising.[1] Parliament met in March 1715, and when it proceeded to arraign the ministers of the previous reign, the rumblings of the coming storm became audible. To Bolingbroke discretion seemed the better part of valour, and in the same month he fled overseas, disguised by a black wig, and with a theatrical riding-coat buttoned over his chin. One of his first acts was to tell the Duke of Berwick, the son of James II by Arabella Churchill, of the state of feeling in England,[2] and in July he succeeded Sir Thomas Higgons as Secretary of State to James.

Meanwhile, public opinion was rising. Already, in October 1714, there had been a Jacobite riot at Bristol, accompanied by loss of life,[3] and on April 23rd, 1715, the anniversary of Anne's coronation, there were disturbances in London, as also was the case on Restoration Day, May 29th.[4] Oxford was another centre of disorder, and as the new King's birthday was on the 28th the chances of an uproar were increased. The Constitution Club, a Whig organization consisting of both dons and undergraduates, met at the "King's Head" to celebrate George's birthday, which they proposed to do by having a bonfire, and burning in effigy Queen Anne, Ormonde, and Sacheverell. This was asking for trouble, and as it was market day the streets were crowded. The local Jacobites cunningly took a room above that in which their opponents were meeting, and ordered drinks for the crowd below; on this "the mob threw the bonfire about, and guzzled up the drink . . . and many of the scholars now mixed with them".[5] The Proctors then arrived on the scene, and ordered all the members of the University at the "King's Head" back to their colleges. This, however, did not terminate the proceedings, for an Oriel man got into New College, and fired a pistol from one of the windows, though without hurting anyone. Hearne proudly bears witness to the unpopularity of the new dynasty, and says:

[1] A Letter to Sir William Wyndham.
[2] Mémoires du Maréchal de Berwick, Vol. II, p. 201 et seq.
[3] H.M.C. Stuart Papers, Vol. I, p. 335.
[4] The Flying-Post, April 23–26, and May 5–7.
[5] The St. James's Post, May 30–June 1.

"Some of the bells were jambled in Oxford by the care of the Whiggish fanatical crew; but as I did not observe the day in the least myself, so it was little taken notice of (unless by way of ridicule) by other honest people."[1]

The next night, about eleven o'clock, another Oriel undergraduate, this time from his own college, fired at and wounded a Brasenose Jacobite who was returning home; this was a signal for further disturbances in the High, during the course of which the windows of both the colleges concerned were broken.[2]

What is significant about these disturbances is that the authorities took no disciplinary action beyond gating a few of the ringleaders, which would seem to show where their sympathies lay. The London Press, on the other hand, took a serious view of the contempt towards constituted authority displayed by the youth of Oxford, as one extract from *The St. James's Post* will serve to show:

"If such examples as these are given in one of our nurseries of religion and learning, we may quickly expect to find all our endeavours towards promoting piety and virtue will grow vain and useless, and that mobbing, resistance, and impiety will come to be more profitably introduced into education."[3]

Dislike of the new regime, combined with the apathy of the local authorities in its support, caused Jacobite sympathy to spread very rapidly during the ensuing weeks among all classes, and in nearly every part of the country. On June 10th, James's birthday, there were particularly violent demonstrations in West Bromwich, Wolverhampton, Manchester, Warrington, and Leeds, with which the magistrates made little attempt to interfere. In Leeds there was certainly no doubt where the latter's sympathies lay, for the Mayor of that town had previously announced that taking the oath to King George was the bitterest pill that he ever swallowed. At Manchester the Presbyterian meeting-house was pulled down, and a detachment of regular troops sent to restore order was

---

[1] *Reliquiae Hearnianae*, Vol. I, pp. 329 *et seq.*
[2] *The Post Boy*, June 2–4.   [3] May 30–June 1.

thrown back. In the West the same agitation prevailed, and there were disturbances of one sort or another in Somerset, Wiltshire, and Gloucester. In the last-named place there was a Jacobite dinner at the "Swan", and a Whig magistrate who attempted to intervene was very roughly handled. At the next Quarter Sessions at Marlborough, one John Napper, a clothier of Trowbridge, was convicted of having uttered "villainous words highly reflecting on His Sacred Majesty King George", and, after being fined, was compelled to make public recantation in Trowbridge market-place.[1]

That Jacobite feeling was growing in intensity is obvious, but it is by no means so clear how far political differences affected social life. Thirty years later the ordinary Englishman had certainly adopted a live-and-let-live attitude, and it never seems to have occurred to any of the Whig neighbours of Squire Western to take strong exception to his political opinions. Readers of *Tom Jones* will remember that when, at the inn at Upton, Partridge refused to drink to King George with the sergeant, he suffered no ill consequences from his Jacobitism. Such evidence as exists, not least in contemporary newspapers, would seem to show that there was more bitterness in 1715. The groundswell of the troubles of the previous century was still obvious, and the passions aroused by the Popish Plot and similar conspiracies had not yet died down. The severity of the Government increased, rather than diminished, the agitation. The Tory leaders were impeached, and the Riot Act of 1553, which made the wrecking of registered places of worship a capital offence, was renewed. These measures defeated their purpose, for Hoffmann, the Prussian Minister, wrote that the cause of James had made a greater advance in eight months than in the four years of Tory ministry in the previous reign.[2]

During the latter part of June, and the whole of July, it must have appeared to both Whigs and Jacobites that a general rising in favour of the Stuarts was imminent. All over the country magistrates stood aside while mobs cheered for

---

[1] cf. *The Flying-Post*, June 18–21; *ibid.*, *June* 14–16; *The Political State of Great Britain*, Vol. X, p. 416 *et seq.*

[2] cf. Michael, Prof.: *Englische Geschichte im 18 Jahrhundert*, Vol. I, p. 486.

"No Hanover, no Marlborough, but a Stuart and a Berwick: Ormonde and no King George". In particular, there was rioting in Sheffield, Wigan, Stafford, Lichfield, Wolverhampton, Birmingham, Dudley, Newcastle-under-Lyme, Shrewsbury, Bridgnorth, Wem, Wrexham, and Bath. Only East Anglia, traditionally Left in its sympathies, and the Home Counties, overawed by London, were immune. Had the Government's opponents possessed a leader worthy of the name to take advantage of this enthusiasm George would have had to return to Hanover, but in the end the only purpose served by the demonstrations was to put the Whigs on their guard, and to give them time to make their preparations. The responsibility for this state of affairs rests primarily with Ormonde. He had retired to Richmond after his impeachment was voted on June 17th, and from there had been preparing for a rising in the West. His instruments were the Tory officers whom the new administration had retired, and his plan was to obtain possession of Plymouth, Bristol, and Exeter, which were to be the centres of the rising. It was believed that from Richmond he intended to withdraw into Devon, and relays of horses were ready to enable him to do so. When, however, he heard that the Government was sending troops to Richmond to arrest him, Ormonde lost his head, and escaped to France on July 21st without so much as leaving any instructions behind him. Given his character, it would be an exaggeration to say that Ormonde's flight deprived the Jacobites of a leader, but he might have served as a rallying-point; while his action undoubtedly served to cool the ardour of the French Government.[1]

After the departure of Ormonde the lead in the West was taken by Lansdowne, and from his house of Longleat the conspiracy was directed. A Jacobite arsenal was established at Bath, where there were collected three pieces of cannon, with the means of casting more, as well as eleven chests of fire-arms,

[1] Ormonde probably sailed from Shoreham (cf. S.A.C., Vol. XXV, p. 172). Carte, in a Memo of July 1739, says that the night Ormonde left Richmond the Cabinet decided that the Elector should embark for Holland if the Duke set up His Majesty's standard in any part of England, it being their unanimous opinion that the army would not stand by them, or, if it would, it would be too weak to defend them against the vast numbers he would have with him.

and a hogshead full of basket-hilt swords. Further arms had
been ordered from France. The plan of campaign at this
time was for the rising to begin in several places in the West
simultaneously, but for the centre of it to be at Bath. The
risings in the North of England and in Scotland were to be
purely subsidiary, and James himself was to land near Plymouth.
The first step was to be the seizure of Bristol,where the moving
spirit was a merchant of the name of Hart, and of Plymouth,
where Sir John Maclean, Ormonde's secretary, claimed to have
won over the officers of the garrison.[1] This would give the
Jacobites possession of the two great ports of the West, and
thus enable them to communicate with their friends on the
Continent. It was sound strategy, and showed that the
lessons of the Civil War, when the King suffered greatly from
the lack of seaports, had not been forgotten. Meanwhile the
disturbances all over the kingdom continued, and in addition
to those places already mentioned there was rioting at Peterborough, Leek, and Burton-on-Trent. When a Captain
Burrows arrived at Oxford to beat up for dragoons, he and
his men were pelted with stones by Balliol undergraduates, and
compelled to desist from their recruiting activities. This
prompted an Oxonian Whig to write to *The Flying Post:*

"Things are come to that pass here that if any tradesman
speaks a word against such proceedings he is threatened with
ruin, for there's hardly a college servant, such as manciples
and cooks, but are Jacks."[2]

It had not been easy for James, far away in Lorraine,
whither he had been compelled to betake himself on the conclusion of the Treaty of Utrecht in 1713, to discover the state
of feeling in the British Isles, and Allan Cameron, a brother of
Lochiel, who had already been in England in June, was sent
over again to find out the real position. Cameron landed at
Deal, where the news of Ormonde's flight reached him, and

---

[1] *cf. H.M.C. Stuart Papers,* Vol. I, pp. 532–533; *Compleat History of the late Rebellion,*
p. 31; and *Dawks's News-Letter,* Sept. 24. Maclean was, according to Burnet, head of
the clan Maclean, and he fought for James at Sheriffmuir, though he had betrayed the
Scottish plot of 1706 to Nottingham. Was Hort, or Hart, the same as the man of that
name who had been President of the ultra-Royalist Gloucestershire Society in 1700?

[2] August 30–September 1.

where he himself was arrested. However, after being taken to London, he contrived to escape, and got into communication, through one Menzies, with Mar, Arran (Ormonde's brother), Lansdowne, and Wyndham. When these discussions were over, Wyndham sent Cameron to the West, where he embarked at Weymouth. Cameron reported that the advice of the English Jacobites was that James should not lose a day in coming over.[1] On this occasion at any rate it is difficult to resist the conclusion that such optimism was not unjustified, for the tide of Hanoverian unpopularity was rising steadily. What did more than anything else (except the incompetence of the Jacobite leaders) to disappoint these hopes was the death of Louis XIV on September 1st, and Mar's precipitate action in calling the Scottish Jacobites to arms on the 6th.

The Jacobites had delayed so long that the Government had by now got wind of what was afoot, and wisely decided to strike where the danger was greatest, namely, in London and the West. On September 2nd Lieutenant-Colonel Paul, of the First Regiment of Foot Guards,[2] was arrested on the charge of enlisting men in the service of James. Two days later the titular Duke of Powis was taken, and on the 21st the same befell Lords Lansdowne and Duplin, while a warrant was issued for the arrest of the Earl of Jersey. On the 21st, too, Stanhope secured the consent of the House of Commons to the arrest of six of its members, namely, Sir William Wyndham, Sir John Packington, Edward Harvey, Thomas Forster, John Anstis, and Corbet Kynaston, respectively M.P.s for Somerset, Worcester, Clitheroe, Northumberland, Launceston, and Shrewsbury. The consent of the House was given *nem. con.*, and there is no record of the numbers of those who were absent or refused to vote.[3] Forster was captured at Preston, and imprisoned in Newgate, whence he effected his escape to Avignon; Wyndham we shall meet again; but it is not without

---

[1] cf. *H.M.C. Stuart Papers*, Vol. III, p. 557 *et seq.*

[2] This was Marlborough's own regiment. The Duke had contributed £4,000 in all to James's service between April and August.

[3] cf. *Compleat History of the late Rebellion*, p. 26; and *The Political State of Great Britain*, Vol. X, p. 310 *et seq.* There is a reference to Packington in *The Lockhart Papers*, Vol. I, p. 441.

interest to see what happened to the others. Packington was arrested at his house in Worcestershire, and brought to London, where, after having been examined, he was released. Harvey attempted to commit suicide, but without success, and was duly secured. Anstis soon cleared himself, and died thirty years later in the odour of Hanoverian sanctity as Garter King of Arms.[1] It was of him that Pope wrote:

> A man of wealth is dubbed a man of worth.,
> Venus shall give him form, and Anstis birth.[2]

Corbet Kynaston fled overseas.

The Government was only just in time, for Wyndham had already arrived at Bath, where he was greeted with much ringing of church bells, and great demonstrations of loyalty to James. The news of the arrests in London, however, sent a cold shiver down the spines of Wyndham and his friends, and the former hastily withdrew to his seat at Orchard Wyndham, near Minehead. This retreat did not save him, for a day or two later, between four and five in the morning, the emissaries of Stanhope arrived to arrest him. Wyndham promised to come away with them, but on pretext of taking leave of his wife, who was pregnant, he gave them the slip. Disguised as a clergyman, Wyndham made across country to Surrey, where he sent a letter to a friend asking for shelter. The friend was away from home and the letter was opened by his wife. This lady was terrified at the prospect of her husband becoming an accessory to treason, and so gave information to the authorities. Wyndham heard what had happened, and after a visit to his father-in-law, the Duke of Somerset, at Syon House, surrendered to his brother-in-law, Lord Hertford, who was a captain in the Life Guards. He was sent to the Tower, but subsequently released.

After securing the ringleaders of the projected western rising the Government proceeded to move into the disaffected area such forces as might deter their followers from using the arms which had been collected. Lord Berkeley, the Lord-Lieutenant of Gloucestershire, secured Bristol with Stanwick's, Pocock's, and Chudleigh's regiments of foot, and part of

---

[1] There is an account of him in the *D.N.B.*   [2] *Imitation of Horace.*

Lumley's horse, and arrested, among other Jacobites, that
Mr. Hart of whom mention has already been made. Major-
General Wade occupied Bath with Windsor's regiment of
horse and Rich's dragoons, and seized the arsenal which had
been established there, together with about two hundred
horses which were to have mounted the Jacobite cavalry.[1] In
Cornwall, where Hugh Boscawen, later first Viscount Falmouth,
headed the Whig interest, similar precautions were taken; and
on October 8th Sir Richard Vyvyan, one of the leading
Jacobites in that county, was brought up to London under
arrest. That the authorities acted only just in time is further
proved by the fact that James was actually proclaimed at
St. Columb: as the author of *A Compleat History of the late
Rebellion* puts it:

> "The common people in Cornwall were, at this time, so
> ripe for rebellion, that six or seven of them had the insolence
> to proclaim the Pretender at St. Columb; two of them
> were seized; and a reward of £100 each, was offered by the
> Government for apprehending the rest."[2]

The reference to the local Jacobites as "common people" is
peculiarly significant in a Hanoverian writer. In none of the
western counties, however, was there any effective opposition
to the Government's measures, for the Jacobites were everywhere bewildered by the behaviour of their leaders. Had
Ormonde withdrawn to Bath, instead of escaping to France,
the story might well have been very different.

In the South of England there now only remained Oxford,
which was undaunted by what was happening elsewhere.
Ormonde had resigned the Chancellorship of the University
at the time of his flight, and the graduates gave proof of their
Jacobite sentiments by electing his brother, Arran, in his
place by a big majority over the Earl of Pembroke, the Whig
candidate. On September 26th the new Chancellor was
installed, and the event was made the occasion for great
Jacobite demonstrations, while several supporters of the

---

[1] There were several arrests at Bath, and among the Jacobites taken up were Colonel
Lansdon, Captain Doyle, Captain Sinclair, Sir George Brown, Mr. Macartey, Mr. Dun,
and Mr. Macdonnell.   [2] p. 33.

exiled dynasty were given degrees. The political atmosphere of Oxford at the end of September 1715 can well be gauged by a sentence in a letter of an undergraduate to a friend in London:

"I think myself very happy in being settled in this so loyal place, and only want your good company to complete it; for here we fear nothing, but drink James's health every day."[1]

In addition to the Jacobites of the University, there were also in Oxford a number of officers who had been dismissed at George's accession on account of their opinions, notably a Colonel Owen, and these were in touch with the conspirators in Bath and Bristol. Nevertheless, as in those towns, it was the Government which got in its blow first.

So menacing did the situation appear that Major-General Pepper, who was in charge of the operations, did not dare to move on Oxford directly, but ordered his march as if he were making for Bath or Bristol. Meanwhile, he sent a cornet into the city disguised as a countryman to note all the more important strategic points. During the night of October 5th-6th he himself made a forced march with his own regiment of dragoons and a detachment of Tyrell's, and entered the city the moment the gates were opened in the morning. Once inside, he dismounted his men, and secured all the points of vantage that the cornet suggested. This done, General Pepper proceeded to arrest some ten or eleven suspects,[2] but he failed to catch Colonel Owen, who took refuge in Magdalen, which the soldiers made no effort to enter. Possibly their commander remembered what had followed on an attempt to interfere with the privileges of that college a generation before. After issuing a stern warning to the Vice-Chancellor and the Mayor, Pepper withdrew his dragoons towards Abingdon, taking his prisoners with him.

---

[1] *The Political State of Great Britain*, Vol. X, p. 341 *et seq.*
[2] The most important of these were Mr. Gordon, Mr. Ken, Dr. Dorrel, Mr. Wilson, Capt. Halstead, Mr. Spelman (of Norfolk), and one Lloyd, who kept a coffee-house at Charing Cross. *cf. The Political State of Great Britain*, Vol. X, p. 341 *et seq.*

This prompt action deprived the Oxford Jacobites of their leaders, but it only momentarily damped their enthusiasm, and arrangements were made to raise a regiment for the Jacobite service from among the undergraduates. On the night of October 27th James was actually proclaimed at Oxford, but on the next day the Government secured the city with Handasyde's regiment of foot. That the authorities were within their rights in taking the steps they did to secure the submission of Oxford must be admitted, but one wonders what the Whig historians would have said had a Stuart behaved in a similar manner.

It may not be out of place at this point to remark that Jacobitism in Oxford continued at least until the sixth decade of the century, as is proved by an incident in the history of Corpus Christi. In the Registers of Punishments of that college there appears under the date of December 20th, 1754, the following significant entry, "*Nos convictu privati sumus per septimanam, quod effigiem quandam quae Pseudoprincipem Carolum repraesentare credebatur, in Camera Baccalaureorum communi appendi jussimus, unde non leve scandalum Collegio et universae Academiae abortum est. Et ab iisdem admoniti sumus ut Deum timeamus, Regem optimum honoremus.*"[1] College tradition avers that certain pressure, as unpleasant as it is unprintable, was applied to freshmen who failed to do suitable honour to the bust of Prince Charles. Among the five undergraduates who got into trouble on this occasion was John Cooke, who was President of Corpus from 1783 to 1823, and who was elected Vice-Chancellor in 1788. When the Allied Sovereigns visited Oxford after the overthrow of Napoleon, Cooke provided hospitality to the King of Prussia: long before then, however, he had probably forgotten his old loyalties, for on December 3rd, 1803, there was a bet recorded in the Corpus Wager Book "Whether Cardinal York is now Living". Oxford had apparently forgotten the very existence of the last Stuarts.

To return, however, to the Fifteen. While these various events had been taking place elsewhere the authorities had not

---

[1] *cf.* Fowler, T.: *The History of Corpus Christi College*, pp. 286–287.

been idle in the capital. Lords Scarsdale and Duplin were sent to the Tower, and the names of several others who fell under suspicion have also come down to us. A Mr. Crawley, son of Sir Ambrose Crawley, and prominent in the iron trade, was arrested, but was released a few days later. Francis Francia, a Jew, was actually put on his trial, but acquitted.[1] One Ozinda, who kept a chocolate-house near St. James's Palace, was committed to Newgate, as were an undertaker called King, and Joseph Scriven, a militia sergeant. That the fears of the Government were by no means groundless is proved by the fact that on October 12th twelve chests of arms, each of which contained equipment for fifty men, were discovered at the "King's Arms" in Holborn. No risks were run by the authorities, and among those arrested was a Jacobite journalist, George Dormer, who "imposed upon the well-meaning people in the country by his scandalous and false accounts of affairs".[2] Even Divine Providence seemed to the Whigs to be aiding them, for we learn that while three men, who had just served their apprenticeship, were treating their masters at the "Fountain" in Aldersgate Street, one of them began to attack the Government, "using bitter imprecations in his discourses", when "on a sudden some phlegm or choler rising in his throat he dropped down dead from the table. A remarkable judgment of Heaven on such as repine at the happiness they enjoy".[3]

On October 20th there took place at the Old Bailey, before the Lord Chief Justice, the trial of Joseph Sullivan, *alias* Silver, Felix Hara, and Robert Whitby, all of Colonel Paul's company of the Guards, on a charge of high treason. The evidence against the defendants was that they encouraged men to enlist for the service of James in this company, and that Colonel Paul was fully cognizant of what was taking place. Witnesses also stated that Sullivan was active in securing recruits to go to France, where he assured them that an army was being prepared to invade England under the command of

---

[1] cf. State Trials, Vol. XV, pp. 897–994.
[2] The Political State of Great Britain, Vol. X, p. 416 et seq.
[3] ibid.

the Duke of Ormonde. The case against the prisoners seems
to have been pretty clear. Their counsel objected to one of
the Crown witnesses on the ground that he was so drunk on
the material occasion that he had to be carried home, having
lost the half-crown which Sullivan was alleged to have given
him for entering James's service; and to another as a common
whore, who lived in a garret, and lay on a wisp of straw; but it
was all to no purpose. The three men were convicted, and
duly executed on October 28th, Sullivan's head then being
fixed on Temple Bar.

It only remains to add that when there was no longer any
prospect of success Ormonde did make an appearance off the
coast of Cornwall, but on being informed that there was no
chance of a rising, returned to Brittany.[1] At this juncture
James himself arrived at St. Malo, where he soon became
dubious of the political capacity of Ormonde and his associates,
for he wrote to Bolingbroke:

"The Duke of Ormonde had a crowd of people with him
who were inconvenient in all respects; they were continually
whispering notions and jealousies into his ears, and he, I
fear, trusted them too much, everybody knew everything
and would play the minister."[2]

This projected insurrection in the South and West of
England has been discussed at length because it provides the
key to Whig policy, and so to the whole of English history,
until at least the middle of the century. Had the new regime
merely been compelled to deal with the opposition of the
Highlands, and the sparsely populated North of England, it
would have needed to walk warily, but this abortive conspiracy
had shown how unpopular it was in what was then, except for
London, the richest part of the country. Superficially, it
must appear as if the Government exaggerated the peril in
1715. Mar was a far more contemptible commander than
Prince Charles Edward or Lord George Murray, while, on the
other side, Argyll was greatly superior to the luckless Cope.

---

[1] Bolingbroke, Viscount: *A Letter to Sir William Wyndham.*
[2] *H.M.C. Stuart Papers*, Vol. I, pp. 463–464.

Yet, the evidence cited above shows that the Fifteen, although it never came so near to success as the Forty-five, was infinitely better conceived, and therefore more dangerous to the House of Hanover. The responsibility for failure must be laid at the door of the Duke of Ormonde, for his precipitate flight disorganized everything. It is true that Bolingbroke declared that the Duke "did more than his part",[1] but it is difficult to agree with him, unless one rates that part very low. Berwick, one of the greatest generals of the age, was certainly under no illusions but that Ormonde ruined the Jacobite cause, and he censures him for not going to the West where he already had the nucleus of an army.[2]

Propaganda has made the eighteenth century so peculiarly its own that to many it may come as a surprise to find that those very western countries which were alleged to have been alienated from the Stuarts for ever by the cruelties of Kirke and Jeffreys were so ready to rise for the son of their persecutor. It is useless to attempt to explain this away by declaring that Jacobitism drew its recruits only from the upper classes. By no stretch of the imagination can clothiers, coffee-house keepers, and undertakers be classed among the gentry, and the significant admissions of the Whig writers themselves tell the same story. The country was split from top to bottom on the dynastic question, and to ignore the fact is to obtain an entirely false impression of the early eighteenth century. It is not suggested that the problem was always acute, but it continued to exist, and sides were taken quite independent of class considerations. The promptitude shown by the Government, in such marked contrast with the hesitancy of James II in 1688, certainly prevented any further attempt to translate sympathy into action, though had Charles Edward gone on from Derby there might well have been a different tale to tell. The Whigs, especially Walpole, learnt their lesson. The southern English Jacobites were rich, hated George, but had much to lose; if they were aggrieved they would rise, but, if not, the traditional English tendency not to

[1] *A Letter to Sir William Wyndham.*
[2] *Mémoires du Maréchal de Berwick*, Vol. II, p. 257 *et seq.*

go beyond mere grumbling would prevail. The Whigs took care that they should not be aggrieved. In the other parts of the kingdom the situation was very different. There poverty and grievances went hand in hand, and all but a small minority felt that any change must be for the better. So far as Ireland was concerned, one incident of a slightly later date will suffice to show what Whig rule was like in that unhappy country. In 1759 a Catholic girl of considerable fortune was urged by a suitor to change her faith, and to avoid him she fled to the house of a friend. The latter was denounced to the authorities, and at his trial the Chancellor very aptly summed up the existing state of affairs by declaring that the "law does not presume a Papist to exist in the kingdom, nor can they as much as breathe here without the connivance of the Government".[1] A few Irish families undoubtedly grew fat during this period of Protestant ascendancy, but a terrible legacy of hatred was stored up for the generations that were to come. Certainly England was not the gainer, for the flight of the "wild geese" to France and Spain provided the armies of her rivals with some of their best soldiers. Paris, not Dublin, was the real capital of Ireland in the eighteenth century. It is estimated that between 1691 and 1791 no less than 480,000 Irishmen took service under the French flag.[2] At Fontenoy it was the Irish Brigade, with Lally at its head, that snatched victory out of defeat for France by the impetuosity of its charge upon the hitherto unbroken Anglo-Dutch column; and in the War of American Independence the same corps inflicted more than one reverse upon its English adversaries. It was a high price to pay for the predominance of a small clique at Dublin.

In Scotland the situation was more complicated, for not only differences of religion, but those between Highlands and Lowlands, have to be taken into account. The majority of English writers have misunderstood the position in that country by confusing the clan, with the feudal, system,

---

[1] cf. Hayes, R.: *Irish Swordsmen of France*, pp. 175–176.
[2] For further particulars about the Irish Brigade in France, cf. *Royal United Service Institution Journal*, May 1917. The same publication, of May 1918, gives an account of the Irish troops in the Spanish service.

whereas the latter had no hold in the Highlands at all.[1] Indeed, north of the Highland line the rule of the new dynasty was generally regarded as implying the predominance of the Campbells, and no one who has read the history of the two chief risings, as well as the subsequent trial of James Stewart,[2] is likely to dissent from this opinion. In the Lowlands the more extreme Presbyterians clung to George from fear of a revival of the old "killing times", but neither in 1715 nor in 1745 did they give him much active support, save with their tongues in the pulpit. On the former occasion many of the Lowland nobility and gentry rallied to the Jacobite cause, but they did not carry the weight in their own districts which had been the case at the time of the Civil War. The ordinary Scot, who was neither a Campbell nor a Cameronian, could not forget that the Stuarts were his own people, and the slightest sign of a return to Protestantism on their part would have been a signal for the whole country to rally to the White Rose. It is, in effect, impossible to deny that Jacobitism, with its demand for the repeal of the Union, was in Scotland something of a national movement, just as it was in Ireland from 1688 to 1691. Nevertheless, it was always more than that, and the gallantry of the vast mass of the Scottish Jacobites is in honourable contrast with the timidity and hesitation of too many of their English co-religionists.

In the North of England the Stuart cause represented that Catholic and traditionalist protest against the new order which had been made intermittently ever since the days of Henry VIII. Yorkshire, in spite of the earlier rioting at Leeds, did not rise, but the rest of the North was soon in flames for what was to prove the last time. The men who fought with the luckless Derwentwater little thought that a change was coming which was to make their part of England the arbiter of the national destinies. Of all the figures in the Jacobite martyrology, Derwentwater is perhaps the most pathetic as well as the most attractive; and his ready answer, all unprepared, to the call can but provoke comparison with

---

[1] cf. Cunningham, A.: The Loyal Clans, passim.
[2] cf. in particular The Trial of James Stewart, edited by D. N. Mackay.

the flight of Ormonde and the surrender of Wyndham. For
him it was soon over, and he was never again to gaze from
Dilston over the beautiful valley of the Tyne. As he himself
wrote on the eve of his execution:

> Farewell to pleasant Dilston Hall,
>   My father's ancient seat;
> A stranger now must call thee his,
>   Which gars my heart to greet.
> Farewell each friendly well-known face,
>   My heart has held so dear;
> My heart now must leave their lands
>   Or hold their lives in fear.

Instead of hearing "the Lav'roks wake the day" there was
the dread voice of the Lord High Steward, "It is adjudged by
this Court that you, James, Earl of Derwentwater, William,
Lord Widdrington, William, Earl of Nithsdale, Robert, Earl
of Carnwath, William, Viscount Kenmure, and William, Lord
Nairn, and every of you, return to the prison, whence you
came, from thence you must be drawn to the place of execution; when you come there, you must be hanged by the neck,
but not until you be dead; for you must be cut down alive,
then your bowels must be taken out, and burnt before your
faces: then your heads must be severed from your bodies, and
your bodies divided each into four quarters; and these must
be at the King's disposal. And God Almighty be merciful
to your souls!" On February 24th, 1716, Derwentwater was
executed. In his last words he protested his loyalty to James,
his "rightful and lawful Sovereign", and then continued:

"Some means have been proposed to me for saving my life,
which I looked upon as inconsistent with honour and
conscience, and therefore I rejected them; for, with God's
assistance, I shall prefer any death to the doing a base unworthy action. I only wish now, that the laying down my
life might contribute to the service of my King and country,
and the re-establishment of the ancient and fundamental
Constitution of these kingdoms, without which no lasting
peace or true happiness can attend them; then I should
indeed part with my life even with pleasure. As it is, I can

only pray that these blessings may be bestowed upon my dear country; and since I can do no more, I beseech God to accept of my life as a small sacrifice towards it."

That was Jacobitism at its best, and at its best it was one of the finest sentiments Britain has ever known.[1]

The story of the actual campaign of the Fifteen has been told too often to require repetition.[2] It is a record of blunders; for instead of concerted action in the West, the North, and in Scotland, there was no co-ordination, and the movement was crushed piecemeal. In spite of the certainty of failure, however, James came to share the sufferings of those who were fighting for him, an attitude which in these latter days does not always commend itself to illustrious exiles. Nevertheless, the failure of the Fifteen settled nothing. The Jacobites of Scotland, unlike those of England, had not been beaten in the field, but had just dispersed, and the authorities were under no illusion but that they would one day strike another blow. Even in the South loyalty to James served as a rallying-point of opposition, and the Government could never be quite sure that those who were continually toasting the "King over the water" might not one day be persuaded to draw the sword rather than the cork. Eternal vigilance was the price which the Elector of Hanover had to pay for being *de facto* King of Great Britain, France, and Ireland, and it is extremely doubtful whether, to the day of his death he regarded himself as more than a temporary occupant of the English throne. Certainly he never took the trouble to acquaint himself with the language or institutions of his new subjects.

It is a serious, if not uncommon, mistake to suppose that Jacobitism even in England was dead between 1715 and 1745. One scheme after another was concocted for a rising with foreign support. Until the death of Charles XII of Sweden in 1718 much reliance was placed upon Swedish help.[3] When this was realized to be vain, Spain took the place of Sweden,

---

[1] *cf.* Skeet, F. J. A.: *The Life of James, third Earl of Derwentwater, and Charles, fifth Earl of Derwentwater, passim.*

[2] *cf.* the present author's *The Jacobite Movement*, pp. 127–148.

[3] *cf.* Mr. Francis Steuart's article in the *Scottish Historical Review*, Vol. XXIII, No. 90.

and although England did not stir, a handful of Spanish soldiers were in 1719 landed on the west coast of Scotland. They were joined by a few Highlanders, and opposed by some Government troops, mostly Dutch: after a skirmish, the Spaniards were compelled to surrender, and the Nineteen came to an end.[1] The birth of Charles Edward in 1720 greatly encouraged the Jacobites, while the bursting of the South Sea Bubble was a serious blow to the regime. The country gentry had always regarded with the greatest suspicion the connection between the Whigs and the City, and while Anne was still on the throne the following song had been very popular with the supporters of James:

> Let the Whigs that love trade, the South Seas invade,
> And there we will give 'em debentures
> For the money they've lent, till the whole sum be spent,
> And a sponge wipe out all their adventures.
> They shall have for director their German Elector,
> Who certainly will not play booty;[2]
> He's too much in the stock the project to shock,
> Good Princess Sophia, adieu t'ye.

The fact that London was chosen as the scene of Jacobite operations on this occasion tells its own tale, and the South Sea Bubble had ruined many who were consequently ready for any desperate stroke. The ring-leader was a barrister of the Middle Temple, Christopher Layer, and when he came to be tried, in November 1722, one of the counsel for the Crown was a Serjeant Pengelly, who was said to have been a natural son of Richard Cromwell. Layer was certainly prepared to carry matters with a high hand, for the evidence showed that he had been enlisting men at Leytonstone and Romford, and with them he proposed to seize the Tower, St. James's Palace, and the Royal Exchange. George was to be captured, and, to increase the confusion, the Westminster mob was to be roused to riot. Nor was this all, for Layer was intriguing with Mrs Hughes, Charles Edward's nurse, to carry the Prince to

[1] cf. Dickson, W. K.: The Jacobite Attempt of 1719, passim.
[2] i.e. cheating play, where the player purposely avoids winning. According to the Oxford Dictionary the phrase is traceable to Awdelay's The Fraternitye of Vagabonds 1561.

THE MARCH TO FINCHLEY

After the original painting by Hogarth in the Foundling Hospital. The Guards, a disorderly and ragged assembly, are shown as they pass by Finchley Turnpike in their northern march to quell the '45

A PERSPECTIVE VIEW OF THE EXECUTION OF LORD FERRERS AT TYBURN

May 5th, 1760, for the Murder of his Steward. Printed for Robert Wilkinson 58, Cornhill. *Reproduced from the print in the William Salt Library, Stafford, by permission of the Trustees.*

Scotland as soon as the blow had been struck in London. Unfortunately for Layer, his sexual discretion lagged far behind his political zeal, and he was betrayed by a young lady of easy virtue to whom he had talked too freely. Whatever hopes he may have entertained of high legal preferment under James were at an end, and he was executed at Tyburn on May 17th, 1723.[1]

There were more important people than the wretched Layer involved in this plot, though some of them had much greater success in concealing their complicity. The Government, at any rate, was thoroughly alarmed, and the Habeas Corpus Act was suspended for a whole year, which is the longest period for which this has ever been done. That they were, from their own point of view, fully justified in this step is proved by the state of public opinion at the time on the evidence of no less a witness than the Speaker of the House of Commons, Sir Richard Onslow, who wrote:

"If some bold men had taken advantage of the general disorder men's minds were in to provoke them to insurrection, the rage against the Government was such for having, as they thought, drawn them into this ruin (*i.e.* the South Sea Bubble) that I am almost persuaded, the King being at that time abroad, that could the Pretender then have landed at the Tower, he might have rode to St. James's with very few hands held up against him."[2]

One of the first suspects to be arrested was George Kelly, a Non-Juring clergyman who had been born in Roscommon. Kelly was a veritable professional where intrigue was concerned, and in one capacity or another he was mixed up in nearly every Jacobite plot. When he was arrested he kept the messenger at bay with a drawn sword while he burned at a candle such of his correspondence as was incriminating. Nevertheless, he had to spend fourteen years in the Tower before he escaped. Even that did not cure him of his love of adventure, for Kelly was one of "The Seven Men of Moidart" who landed in Scotland with Charles Edward.

---

[1] cf. *State Trials*, Vol. XVI, pp. 93–322.   [2] *H.M.C. Onslow MSS.*, p. 504.

The next prisoners were the Duke of Norfolk, the Earl of Orrery, and Lord North, while Mar, who had by now changed sides again, laid information against Atterbury. This placed Walpole in a dilemma, for he had not enough evidence against the latter to send him to the scaffold, and he had no desire, by exiling him, to provide James with a counsellor of exceptional ability. He therefore determined to see what would be the effect of offering a bribe. Walpole was always prepared to bid high for the man he wanted, and he made no exception of the present occasion. In return for the bishopric of Winchester at the next vacancy, and in the meantime an annual pension of £5,000, together with the Tellership of the Exchequer for his son-in-law, Atterbury was asked to cease his opposition to the Government, and to allow his gout to prevent his attendance at the House of Lords. Such were the normal methods by which the Whig supremacy was maintained, and Walpole must have been pained as well as surprised when his offer was summarily rejected. There was nothing for it but a Bill of Pains and Penalties, which, after a brilliant speech by the Bishop in his defence, passed its third reading in the House of Lords by eighty-three votes to forty-three. Atterbury thereupon left the country. When he reached Calais he heard that Bolingbroke, who had now made his peace with the Government, was in the town on his way to England. "Then," said he, "I am exchanged."[1]

The politics of the Bishop of Rochester were a reflection of those of the great majority of the clergy. Whoever may have gained by the accession of the House of Hanover to the throne, the Church of England lost its soul. If the seventeenth century witnessed its apogee, the eighteenth marked its nadir. *Quieta non movere* was the doctrine of the victorious Whigs, and they applied it to the Church as well as to the State. James II was certainly a difficult master for any Anglican to serve, but had his son been restored the Church of England would have been in a far stronger position than in actual practice it has ever known, for with the memory of his father

[1] *cf.* Beeching, H. C.: *Atterbury*, pp. 263–307; also *R.O.*, MSS., *State Papers, Dom.*, G.I., bundles 38, 51, and 53.

before him he would never have ventured to interfere with its working. As it was, the Church was treated as a mere branch of the Civil Service, with the not unnatural consequence that when a revival of religion took place later in the century it was driven outside the Establishment. The social position of the clergy was incredibly low, as contemporary literature so well testifies. Parson Adams seldom rose above the kitchen during his journey with Joseph Andrews, and Fielding considered a match between Parson Supple and Mrs. Waters a very suitable arrangement for both of them. There can surely be no more eloquent testimony to the depths to which the Church of England had sunk than that a great contemporary novelist should have seen nothing odd in marrying one of its ministers, with whom he had shown considerable sympathy, to a lady who had already granted her favours to more than one of his characters. Had such a thing been exceptional Fielding was far too perfect a master of his craft to have concluded a book on this note.[1]

It was not only in England that the clergy were Jacobite, for the same was the case in America.[2] In South Carolina in particular there was strong support for James, and when his health was drunk by the laity those clergyman who were present rarely displayed any reluctance to honour the toast. The Quakers in Pennsylvania were Jacobite to a man, and during the war Louis XIV had given instructions to the French privateers not to attack their ships on account of their loyalty to James. In New Jersey the leader of the clerical Jacobites was the Rev. John Talbot, Rector of Burlington, who refused to take the oaths to George, or to pray for him by name in the Liturgy. During a visit to England he was actually, though irregularly, consecrated a bishop,[3] and seems to have attempted to found a Non-Juring Church in America. However that may be, it is clear that in his views he was not

---

[1] "Keene, Bishop of Chester, . . . is a man that will not prejudice his fortune by any ill-placed scruples. My father gave him a living of £700 a year to marry one of his natural daughters; he took the living; and my father dying soon after, he dispensed with himself from taking the wife, but he was so generous as to give her very near one year's income of the living" (Horace Walpole to Sir Horace Mann, Dec. 11, 1752).

[2] I am indebted to the Society for the Propagation of the Gospel for information on this point.   [3] cf. Broxap, H.: The Later Non-Jurors, pp. 87-91.

exceptional, for the American clergy were as Jacobite as their English brethren. In Scotland the Episcopal Church had been in open opposition ever since the Revolution, and it was not until the death of Charles Edward in 1788 that its ministers began to pray for the House of Hanover. A Roman Cardinal as King was too much even for their loyal stomachs. In an age when there were relatively few newspapers, when means of communication were bad, and when the mass of the people could neither read nor write, it would be difficult to exaggerate the influence of the pulpit, and that influence was very largely exercised on behalf of James.

No fewer than four hundred beneficed clergymen had refused to take the oaths to William and Mary, on the ground that to do so would be to break the oath which they had previously taken to James II. At their head had been the Archbishop of Canterbury, and the Bishops of Bath and Wells, Chichester, Peterborough, Ely, Gloucester, Worcester, and Norwich. In February 1690 those who would not take the oaths were deprived, and there is nothing finer in English history than the behaviour of those clergymen who walked out of their rectories and vicarages, often to face extreme poverty, for what they believed to be right. The only analogy is the Disruption in Scotland in 1843. There is much that is sordid and mean in the story of Jacobitism, but if the movement sometimes touched the depths it also reached the heights, as this well illustrates. Of course there were many clergymen who openly acknowledged the new order while secretly hoping for a return of the old. When, too, the names of the reigning family were mentioned in the prayers it was by no means unusual for them to be drowned by an outbreak of coughing on the part of the congregation. It was also possible to guess the political opinions of a clergyman from his choice of collect for the King; if he prayed for "thy chosen Servant George" he was a Whig, but if only for "George thy Servant" he was a Jacobite, or at least a Tory.

As for the actual Non-Jurors, they regarded themselves, with some justification, as the true Church of England, and they were careful to preserve the episcopal succession; this they did until 1805, when their last bishop, Charles Booth, died. The Church itself lasted even longer, and it did not come to an end until the death of the last Non-Juror, James Yeowell, in 1875. It always obtained the *congé d'élire* for its bishops from the Stuart monarchs, but in practice it was autocephalous. At one time the Non-Jurors sought to enter into a close association with the Orthodox Church, but the negotiations broke down. Nor was it long before they began to have doctrinal, as well as political, differences with the Establishment. In 1718 a new communion office was introduced. It was derived partly from the primitive liturgies, and partly from the First Prayer Book of Edward VI, and the innovations, or "usages" as they were termed, were four in number, that is to say, the mixed chalice, prayers for the faithful departed, prayer for the descent of the Holy Ghost on the consecrated elements, and what was termed the Oblatory Prayer offering the elements to the Father as symbols of His Son's Body and Blood. This caused a split between Usagers and Non-Usagers which continued until 1731, when it came to an end with the victory of the former.

The Non-Jurors, although limited in numbers, did much to keep alive what enthusiasm there was in matters of religion during the reigns of the first two Georges. One of the earlier acts of the Whig Government, in 1717, was to suppress Convocation, save for the transaction of merely formal business, and it was not revived until 1852. This stifled, as it was meant to do, all discussion, and it is significant that the outstanding religious figure of the period, William Law, should have been a Non-Juror, though not an active Jacobite. The influence of the Non-Jurors upon ecclesiastical history is now held by many authorities to have been considerable, and there is evidence on the doctrinal side that it made itself felt in the early days of the Oxford Movement. The Government regarded them with the gravest suspicion, which was only natural, not least because they were strongest in that citadel of Jacobitism, Manchester.[1] For the rest, the Church of

[1] The chief authorities on this subject are Lothbury, T.: *History of the Non-jurors*; Overton, J. H.: *The Non-jurors*; and Broxap, H.: *The Later Non-jurors*, and *A Biography of Thomas Deacon.*

England, having sold its soul to the Whigs, was reaping a transient material advantage from the transaction. Its old rival of the previous century, Presbyterianism, was dying or dead, for many of the latter's erstwhile supporters had forsaken it for Deism or Unitarianism. The Whigs, too, were more skilful than Cromwell, for they permeated the Church rather than attempt to break it by the sledge-hammer blows of the Lord Protector. Above all, the patronage exercised by Walpole proved a narcotic which few save Atterbury had the strength to resist.

Sometimes, in the case of the lower orders, the zeal of the Jacobites was too much for their manners. For example, in April 1719 the Princess of Wales was being carried in her chair from Leicester Fields to St. James's, when a chairman availed himself of the opportunity to spit in her face three times. He was subsequently whipped from Somerset House to the Haymarket, but it was not until the flesh on his back was in ribbons that he could be prevailed upon to cry "God save King George".[1] The lash was freely employed in defence of the new dispensation. A thousand lashes was not considered at all excessive punishment for a soldier who raised his mug of beer to James's health, and on at least one occasion a servant-girl who said she wished all the hairs on her head were dragoons to fight for the rightful King was publicly whipped; dripping with blood, and disfigured for life, the poor child nevertheless refused to renounce her Jacobitism.

The failure of Layer and his associates was followed by a period during which Jacobite activities were mainly carried on in the House of Commons, where the leader of James's supporters was William Shippen. He came of a Cheshire family of considerable importance, and was the brother-in-law of John Anstis. The Shippens were Quakers, and one of William's uncles was the first Mayor of Philadelphia.[2] William Shippen had sat in the Parliaments of Anne's reign, but it was not until after the accession of the new dynasty, and the disappearance

---

[1] cf. Doran, J.: *London in the Jacobite Times*, Vol. I, p. 329.
[2] The late Rear-Admiral Edward Shippen, M.D., U.S.N., was a direct descendant of the Mayor, and there are several families of the name of Shippen in New York and elsewhere.

of the old Tory leaders, that he began to come to the front. Lord Rosebery placed him high among the Parliamentarians of the day, not far behind Chesterfield and Carteret,[1] while Pope wrote of him:

> I love to pour out all myself, as plain
> As honest Shippen, or downright Montaigne.

When it is remembered that Shippen was a politician all his life Pope's epithet clearly marks him as a man of exceptional qualities.

As a Quaker he refused to be in any way implicated in the Fifteen, and in consequence the rumour began to be circulated that he had betrayed his friends to the Government. Accordingly, on September 28th, 1715, he

> "looking upon it as a reflection on his steady principles, went, betwixt two and three a clock to the Royal Exchange (in full Exchange-time) and fixed the following certificate to one of the pillars, he staying there a considerable time to justify the truth thereof".[2]

The notice ran as follows:

> "Whereas there has been a report industriously spread, that Mr. Shippen has given information at the Secretary's office against several persons said to be concerned in a plot, and an intended invasion from abroad, I do hereby declare that the said report is utterly false, scandalous, and malicious, and an impudent lie and forgery.
>
> "WILLIAM SHIPPEN.
>
> "September 28, 1715."

Shippen was the first Leader of the Opposition in the modern sense of the term. There had in the past been men like Shaftesbury who had attacked the Government of the day in Parliament, but their action there had always been subsidiary to the preparation of a *coup de main*. Shippen fought in the House of Commons alone, and his principles did not allow of him fighting elsewhere. He was subject to

---

[1] *cf.* Rosebery, Lord: *Chatham, His Early Life and Connections*, p. 148.
[2] *The Political State of Great Britain*, Vol. X, p. 416 *et seq.*

handicaps unknown to his successors, for an injudicious speech might, and did, land him in the Tower. Yet the records show that on an important division the Jacobites were generally some fifty strong, to whom were often added Wyndham's followers and some discontented Whigs. Against the Septennial Bill he mustered no less than 160 votes on the second reading, which greatly enhanced his prestige. On another occasion he referred to George as "a stranger to our language and Constitution"; this observation was too much to the point to be made with impunity, and Shippen was sent to the Tower. While there he received several offers of financial assistance, including one, characteristically enough, from the Prince of Wales.[1] On his release he resumed all his old activities and in 1726 he attacked the Treaties of Vienna and Hanover as framed "for the defence of His Majesty's dominions in Germany" contrary to the Act of Succession. How far Shippen took his instructions from his master in Rome it is impossible to say: there are, however, one or two undated and unsigned papers among the Stuart MSS. at Windsor Castle, addressed to James, which gave an account of the Parliamentary debates, and may have been written by Shippen. He died at his house in Norfolk Street in 1743. Had he lived three years longer he might have become the first Prime Minister of a second Restoration.[2]

During the thirties of the century there was a lull in Jacobite activities, and that for several reasons. Walpole took the greatest care not to sponsor any measure, after the Excise Bill, which could possibly provide a lever for the opponents of the dynasty, and in this he was remarkably successful. Then, again, the Jacobites were waiting until Charles Edward grew up, for his father would clearly never again be able to strike a blow for his rights. Nevertheless, there was no growth of affection for the House of Hanover, and there was probably more dissatisfaction with it on the eve of the Forty-five than on any previous occasion. George II was a slight improvement on his father, and his wife, Caroline, did something to raise

---

[1] cf. The Gentleman's Magazine for 1812.
[2] For further information about Shippen cf. the present author's The Jacobite Movement, pp. 161–169.

the tone of the Court; but even on the rare occasions when the
King did the right thing it was in the wrong way, as when he
led the British troops at Dettingen in a Hanoverian uniform.
It would be inaccurate to say that there was great enthusiasm
for the Stuarts, but there was little opposition to them save
from the vested interests. Carlisle put up the feeblest of
resistances, Manchester was captured by a drummer and a
whore, and Charles Edward arrived at Derby without having
fired a shot. It is impossible to disagree with Major Eardley
Simpson that

> "if the army of the White Rose had marched over Swarkeston
> Bridge on the morning of 6th December, 1745, within a
> week James III would have been proclaimed in London,
> while Newcastle and Bedford encouraged an enthusiastic
> populace to welcome Charles not only as the Prince Regent
> of the Kingdom, but as the victorious leader who had
> restored the native House without the aid of a foreign
> bayonet".[1]

Smollett was of the same opinion:

> "Had Charles proceeded in his career with that expedition
> he had hitherto used, he might have made himself master of
> the metropolis, where he would certainly have been joined
> by a considerable number of his well-wishers, who waited
> impatiently for his approach."[2]

Every morning the walls of London were covered with
Jacobite proclamations. The method employed to outwit the
authorities was as follows: towards dusk a porter, with an
enormous bundle on his shoulders, would rest against a wall,
while out of the bundle a small boy would arise and paste up a
notice. The authorities never seem to have detected this
trick.

Even Culloden did not mark the end of Jacobitism, for there
was in 1750 a very definite revival of the movement, which
culminated in the Elibank Plot two years later. The most
active Jacobite at this time was Dr. King, Principal of St.

[1] *Derby and the Forty-five*, p. 213.
[2] *A Complete History of England*, Vol. XI, p. 225.

Mary's Hall at Oxford, whom the Earl Marischal, now after many vicissitudes Prussian representative in Paris, described to Frederick the Great as *"homme d'esprit, vif, agissant"*.[1] In September 1750 Charles Edward himself paid a visit to London, and his appearance was by no means welcome to those of his supporters who had little desire to exchange the drinking of toasts for definite action. His arrival certainly took some of his friends by surprise, not least Lady Primrose. This lady was playing cards at her house in Essex Street, Strand, when the Prince suddenly walked into the room; but she had the presence of mind to continue the game as if she had not recognized him, and so avoided arousing the suspicions of such of her guests as were Whigs. From a note in Charles Edward's own handwriting in the Stuart Papers we know that he remained in London from September 16th to the 22nd, when he went to Paris. There was a meeting at a house in Pall Mall, which is said to have been attended, among others, by the Duke of Beaufort and the Earl of Westmorland, the latter being then Chancellor of Oxford University. That this conference had no result is clear, and its chief interest lies in the fact that it was probably the last occasion on which the English Jacobites formally met together to discuss the restoration of the Stuarts.

At this point a new recruit arrived in the person of Alexander Murray, a brother of the fifth Lord Elibank. Murray had been charged with intimidation and violence at a Westminster election, and he was subsequently imprisoned for refusing to beg the pardon of the House of Commons on his knees. He declared that he only went down on his knees to God, and apparently saw no reason why he should make an exception in the case of Parliament. In November 1751 he fled to France, and openly espoused the Jacobite cause. Then ensued a complicated intrigue of which the principal ingredients were a sudden blow in London and a rising in the Highlands. Many people took a hand in it, among them Frederick the Great, whose policy at the moment it suited to show the British Government how unpleasant he could be if he had a mind.

[1] *Politische Correspondenz Friedrichs des Grossen,* Vol. IX, p. 356.

What is of importance is that even at this late date so shrewd a politician as the King of Prussia should have thought that a Jacobite attempt might succeed, and it was generally taken for granted by all concerned that there would be no rally on the part of the populace to the Guelphs. In the end that mysterious figure, Pickle, betrayed the whole plot to the authorities. James created Alexander Murray Earl of Westminster; and Archibald Cameron, the only one of the conspirators whom the Government was able to catch, was hanged, thus becoming the last Jacobite to suffer death for his opinions. His wife vainly petitioned George II for her husband's life, but all the answer she received was to be imprisoned in her turn as the readiest method of preventing her from worrying that august monarch with her importunities.[1]

Thereafter the Jacobite twilight rapidly deepened into night. Rumour has it that Charles Edward was present at the coronation of George III in 1761, and it seems probable that he did visit England two years later. There are other evidences that Jacobitism was not quite dead. In or about 1771 "The Oyster and Parched Pea Club" was founded at Preston, and at the same time "The Royal Oak Club" came into existence in Edinburgh; both were Jacobite institutions. It was in 1777, too, that Dr. Johnson made the observation, already quoted, to Boswell. In Scotland, one of the last adherents of the Stuarts was Laurence Oliphant, Laird of Gask.[2] So pronounced were his views that when his attainder was removed the Lord Chamberlain hinted to George III that the old Jacobite would never accept such a favour from him as King of England. "Say then," replied George, "that the Elector of Hanover does it." Oliphant was the "well-known Perthshire gentleman" of the preface to *Redgauntlet*. Finally, there is the evidence of Lord Liverpool, quoted by Stapleton in his *Some Official Correspondence of George Canning*, that as late as 1824 there were those who would not acknowledge the title of the House of Hanover to the British throne. The last

---

[1] For a full account of the Elibank Plot *cf. Royal Historical Society Transactions,* Fourth Series, Vol. XIV, pp. 175–196.

[2] *cf.* Oliphant, T. L. K.: *The Jacobite Lairds of Gask, passim.*

time that a Stuart set foot on British soil was in 1798, when the Cardinal Duke of York crossed on a British man-of-war from Naples to Messina, where tradition has it that with the King and Queen of the Two Sicilies, and Sir William and Lady Hamilton, he was a guest at a dinner given by Nelson upon his flagship.

Jacobitism in the British Isles may, during the first five decades of the eighteenth century, be likened to an iceberg: that part of it which is visible often appears of little importance, but as it is impossible to tell how far it extends below the surface, the wise navigator does not omit any precaution. Walpole acted the part of the wise navigator from the Whig standpoint. It is impossible to understand the eighteenth century unless these facts are grasped. There was always the probability, generally the certainty, that any disturbance would be turned to Jacobite ends; at Newcastle-on-Tyne bargees on strike had proclaimed Charles Edward as King Charles III.[1] This meant that the only safe policy for the regime was to stifle all enthusiasm, and it was accordingly adopted. For a time all went well, but the world will not stand still even at the dictation of a Whig oligarchy, and later in the century movements began which could not be drugged, or dragooned, into quiescence. It was then that the evils of Whig rule began to make themselves felt with increasing force. Had the Church not become to all intents and purposes a branch of the Civil Service it is more than probable that Wesley would never have been driven outside it; had the deliberate policy of successive administrations not been to concentrate property in ever fewer hands, and then to make it sacrosanct, the yeomanry would not have disappeared, and in spite of the Industrial Revolution the balance between town and country might have been preserved. As a recent writer has well described it:

"Game Laws and the cruel mishandling of the Enclosure Acts were a sign that Parliament had become the organ of the rich. Property was almost an object of worship, its responsibilities forgotten, its privileges savagely vindicated. The Church, aristocratically controlled, tainted with

[1] *cf.* Bates, C. J.: *History of Northumberland*, p. 266.

flunkeyism . . . lost for itself the allegiance of the poor. The disastrous twist given to our industrial system at its birth set the seal on a long and tragic process, the slow depression in the wages and status of the working man."[1]

These were the results of the victory of the White Horse over the White Rose.

[1] John, E.: *King Charles I*, p. ix.

CHAPTER III

THE AGE OF REASON

ENGLISH society until the death of Anne had been dominated by the Court. The brilliance of the latter in some reigns had rivalled that of France, and even William III, morose as he was by nature, had realized the necessity of making the throne the social as well as the political centre of the national life. With the advent of the House of Hanover this state of affairs came to an abrupt end. Many of those who had been the ornaments of the Court were in declared opposition to the new dynasty, while others withdrew to their estates, and but rarely visited London. Nor was the Court of George I of a nature to attract any save those who were compelled by sheer necessity to attend it. The new monarch had arrived in England with a household of about a hundred persons, including two Turkish pages and one washerwoman. With regard to the apparent inadequacy of the laundry staff, Sir Henry Imbert-Terry is of the opinion that it possesses no historical value

"except in so far as it may bear on the strong objection evinced by the first members of the House of Guelph to washing their dirty linen in public, as shown in their systematic habit of destroying all documents which could throw light on the many unsavoury episodes which stain their domestic records."[1]

The character of George I has been sufficiently indicated in the previous chapter, but as evidence of the type of Court which he maintained it may not be out of place to quote Lord Chesterfield:

"George I was lazy and inactive even in his pleasures, which therefore were lowly sensual. He was coolly intrepid and indolently benevolent. He was diffident of his own parts,

[1] *A Constitutional King: George I*, p. 141.

which made him speak little in public and prefer in his own social, which were his favourite hours, the company of wags and buffoons. Even his mistress, the Duchess of Kendal, with whom he passed most of his time and who held all influence over him, was little better than an idiot. Importunity alone could make him act, and then only to get rid of it. His views and affections were singly confined to the narrow compass of his Electorate. England was too big for him."[1]

Of George's taste in women the same nobleman observes:

"The King loved pleasure, and was not delicate in his choice of it. No woman came amiss to him, if they were very willing and very fat . . . the standard of His Majesty's taste made all those ladies who aspired to his favour, and who were near the statutable size, strain and swell themselves like the frogs in the fable to rival the bulk and diginity of the ox. Some succeeded, and others burst."[2]

It was all very different from Whitehall in the days of the Stuarts.

Two mistresses were the female ornaments of the Court, namely, Baroness Kielmansegg, who was created Countess of Darlington, and Baroness von der Schulenburg, who became Duchess of Kendal. The latter acted as a political intermediary, attached by strong financial ties to Walpole, while the former drove a lucrative trade in vending small Court favours. The woman who should have been Queen of England, Sophia Dorothea of Celle, had been divorced by her husband in 1694 on a charge of adultery with Königsmarck, whom the Jacobites alleged to be the father of George II. Her fate, which recalls that of her great-granddaughter, the unhappy wife of Christian VII of Denmark, was one of the most cruel in modern history. She was still little more than a girl when the tribunal that pronounced sentence of divorce debarred her from ever marrying again, though leaving George at liberty to do so. For the remaining thirty-two

[1] *Characters of Eminent Persons of His Own Time*, Vol. II, p. 432.
[2] *ibid.*, Vol. II, p. 439.

years of her life she was confined to the castle of Ahlden, which is situated in the dreary plains of North Germany, where she was cut off from all society of her own age and rank; she was not allowed to see her children, and when her son, later George II, attempted to gain access to his mother, he was forcibly prevented. The wretched woman died in 1726.[1]

The influence of the King upon the course of English history was negative, but considerable.

"He could speak no English, and was past the age of learning. Our customs and laws were all mysteries to him, which he neither tried to understand, nor was capable of understanding if he endeavoured it."[2]

In these circumstances he was, in his new kingdom, like a man lost in a fog. Not one of his ministers could speak German, and not all of them knew French. The most important of them, Walpole, was ignorant of every living language save his own, and was reduced to conversing with the monarch in dog Latin. As he himself once put it, he "controlled George by bad Latin and good punch". The dispatches of British ambassadors and ministers were ordered to be translated into French, though the Sovereign was considerate enough to add that the French need not be of the best. Until the death of Anne the Kings and Queens of England had frequently been present when ministers met, but George I discontinued the practice, for he could not understand a word that was being said. He preferred to leave his advisers to discuss affairs without him, and to receive reports from one or other of them as to their conclusions. In his absence the leading minister took the chair, and so the office of Prime Minister, although unknown to the Constitution, came into existence. As for George himself, he was generally content to put his signature to documents of the contents of which he knew nothing. In foreign questions, on the other hand, he took a lively interest.

The French ambassador wrote to his master, Louis XV:

---

[1] cf. Wilkins, W. H.: *The Love of an Uncrowned Queen, passim.*
[2] *Letters of Lady Mary Wortley Montagu*, Vol. I, p. 111.

"The King has no predilection for the English nation, and never receives in private any English of either sex, none even of his principal officers are invited to his chamber in the morning to dress him, nor in the evening to undress him. These offices are performed by the Turks who are his *valets de chambre*, and who give him everything he wants in private. He rather considers England as a temporary possession to be made the most of while it lasts, than as a perpetual inheritance for himself and his family."[1]

The King abominated that pageantry which is rightly so dear to the hearts of the English people, and he appeared in public as little as possible. Music was the only art for which he had any liking, but when he did attend the opera he sat at the back of the box; on at least one occasion he went with the two Turks and Nicolini the singer.[2] A Frenchman, Saussure, is evidence for the fact that George could relax occasionally, for when three ladies were presented

"the King kissed them all affectionately on the lips, and I remarked that he seemed to take most pleasure in kissing the prettiest of the three."[3]

It appears, however, that all the ladies did not appreciate the Royal favour, for some merely proffered their cheeks. It is hardly surprising that such a monarch and such a Court should have had no influence upon the social life of the country.

The Prince of Wales, as has already been suggested, was in some ways an improvement on his father, with whom he was always on the worst of terms. His first appearance as King was not impressive. George I had died suddenly in Hanover the year after his wife, and on the afternoon on June 14th, 1727, his son was asleep after dinner at Richmond Lodge, when a man entered his room, and knelt before him in his jack-boots. The Prince asked with the strongest of German accents who had dared to disturb his repose. "I am Sir Robert Walpole," was the reply. "I have the honour to announce to Your

[1] Quoted by Coxe, W.: *The Life of Sir Robert Walpole*.
[2] cf. *H.M.C. Stuart Papers*, Vol. II, p. 141.
[3] *A Foreign View of England in the Reign of George I*, p. 43.

Majesty that Your Royal father, King George I, died at Osnaburg, on Saturday last, the 10th inst." To which the new monarch answered, "Dat is one big lie."[1] Yet on occasions he could be dignified, or rather he did not hesitate to show his disapproval of any affront to his dignity. In 1742, for example, Horace Walpole wrote to Sir Horace Mann:

"There has been a great fracas at Kensington, one of the Mesdames (i.e. the King's daughters) pulled the chair from under Countess Deloraine at cards, who, being provoked that her monarch was diverted with her disgrace, with the malice of a hobby-horse, gave him just such another fall. But alas! the Monarch, like Louis XIV, is mortal in the part that touched the ground, and was so hurt and so angry that the Countess is disgraced, and her German rival (i.e. Lady Yarmouth) remains in the sole and quiet possession of her Royal master's favour."

In any event, a sense of humour was not one of the King's more prominent characteristics. He was at the play on one occasion in his later years, and during the course of it one of the characters, an intriguing chambermaid, said to an old gentleman, "You are villainously old; you are sixty-six; you can't have the impudence to think of living above two years." At this the King was heard to exclaim in a passion, "This is damned stuff."[2]

Within narrow limits he was also more sociable than his father had been, and he was not interested solely in fat women. He sometimes attended the subscription-masquerades, which were so prominent a feature of his reign, and Horace Walpole related how "the King was very well disguised in an old-fashioned English habit, and much pleased with somebody who desired him to hold their cup as they were drinking tea". Costumes varied greatly on these occasions.

"The Duke (i.e. of Cumberland) had a dress of the same kind, but was so immensely corpulent, that he looked like Cacofago, the drunken Captain in *Rule a Wife and Have a*

---

[1] cf. Thackeray, W. M.: *The Four Georges.*
[2] Horace Walpole to Sir Horace Mann, Nov. 22, 1751.

Wife. The Duchess of Richmond was a Lady Mayoress in the time of James I, and Lord Delawarr Queen Elizabeth's porter, from a picture in the guard-chamber at Kensington: they were admirable masks. Lady Rochford, Miss Evelyn, Miss Bishop, Lady Stafford, and Mrs. Pitt, were in vast beauty, particularly the last, who had a red veil, which made her look gloriously handsome. I forgot Lady Kildare. Mr. Conway was the Duke in Don Quixote, and the finest figure I ever saw. Miss Chudleigh was Iphigenia, but so naked that you would have taken her for Andromeda, and Lady Betty Smithson had such a pyramid of baubles upon her head, that she was exactly the Princess of Babylon in Grammont."[1]

This was the particular subscription-masquerade after which Lord Conway's sister died, and so gave rise to the lampoon:

> Poor Jenny Conway
> She drank lemonade,
> At a masquerade,
> So now she's dead and gone away.

If George II did not set his subjects a very good example in many ways,[2] he was an active, if fussy, little man, and always rose at six o'clock in the morning. This was in marked contrast with the habits of the ordinary member of the upper class. Most men got up about nine, and then attended the *levée* of some great nobleman until eleven or twelve, when they were carried in chairs to one of the more fashionable chocolate- or coffee-houses. If it were fine, a stroll in St. James's Park followed. Dinner was usually taken at two, and being the principal business of the day lasted until about six. After that, for those who were still sufficiently sober, there was the play, and, later still, Tom's and Will's coffee-houses, where one could stay till the small hours drinking, playing cards, or talking politics. Those who desired the company of women of their own class had every evening the choice of a score of houses

---

[1] Horace Walpole to Sir Horace Mann, May 3, 1749.

[2] Notably by the suppression of his father's will under the nose of the Archbishop of Canterbury. George I had left Hanover to his cousin, the Duke of Brunswick-Wolfenbütel.

where receptions were being held, while those who were not so particular had no need to go farther afield than Covent Garden or Drury Lane, where the most exacting requirements could be satisfied.[1] As Steele put it:

> "There is near Covent Garden a street known by the name of Drury, which, before the days of Christianity, was purchased by the Queen of Paphos, and is the only part of Great Britain where the tenure of her vassalage is still in being. All that long course of buildings is under particular districts or ladyships, after the manner of lordships in other ports, over which matrons of known abilities preside, and have, for the support of their age and infirmities, certain taxes paid out of the rewards of the amorous labours of the young. This seraglio of Great Britain is disposed into convenient alleys and apartments, and every house, from the cellar to the garret, inhabited by nymphs of different orders, that persons of every rank may be accommodated."[2]

Indeed, for many years a "Drury Lane Vestal" was as apposite a synonym for a prostitute as was a "Fulham Virgin" in the following century.

George II died as suddenly as his father had done.

> "This is Tuesday; on Friday night the King went to bed in perfect health, and rose so at the next morning at his usual hour of six; he called for and drank his chocolate. At seven, for everything with him was exact and periodic, he went into the closet to dismiss his chocolate. Coming from thence, his *valet de chambre* heard a noise; waited a moment, and heard something like a groan. He ran in, and in a small room between the closet and bedchamber he found the King on the floor, who had cut the right side of his face against the edge of a bureau, and who after a gasp expired."[3]

The contempt felt for the whole Royal Family was admirably expressed in the well-known verses written on the death of Frederick, Prince of Wales, in 1751:

[1] *cf.* Chancellor, E. B.: *The Annals of Covent Garden*, pp. 61–66.
[2] *Tatler*, July 26, 1709.
[3] Horace Walpole to Sir Horace Mann, Oct. 28, 1760.

Here lies poor Fred, who was alive and is dead.
Had it been his father, I had much rather;
Had it been his brother, still better than another;
Had it been his sister, nobody would have missed her;
Had it been the whole generation, so much the better for the
nation.
But since it is Fred, who was alive and is dead,
There is no more to be said.

Frederick was loathed by his parents with a hatred which is quite inexplicable by any fact of which we are in possession. He was certainly weak and foolish, and he was capable on occasions of that outrageous behaviour characteristic of the whole Hanoverian dynasty. When his wife was seized with the first pangs of childbirth at Hampton Court he insisted on removing her to St. James's for her confinement, in spite both of her entreaties and of the danger involved. During the last fourteen years of his life the Prince was in open conflict with his father. The King banished him from Court and refused to receive anybody who visited his son. According to Lord Hervey the Queen said of Frederick, "My dear firstborn is the greatest ass, and the greatest liar, and the greatest canaille, and the greatest beast in the whole world, and I most heartily wish he was out of it." Not to be outdone, the Prince, when he received the bulletins announcing his mother's impending demise, observed, "Well, now we shall have some good news; she cannot hold out much longer." The only light that is thrown upon the real cause of this unedifying quarrel is provided by a memorandum of Lord Hardwicke, the Lord Chancellor:

"Sir Robert Walpole informed me of certain passages between the King and himself, and between the King and the Prince, of too high and secret a nature even to be trusted to this narrative; but from thence I found great reason to think that this unhappy difference between the King and Queen and His Royal Highness turned upon some points of a more interesting and important nature than have hitherto appeared."[1]

[1] Harris, G.: *Life of Lord Chancellor Hardwicke*, Vol. I, p. 382.

The Queen, Caroline of Anspach, had been a very capable woman, but she died in 1737. The worst of the family was her younger son, the Duke of Cumberland, whose brutality in Scotland during the campaign against Prince Charles Edward earned him the nickname of the "Butcher".[1] This inhuman monster had allowed the Jacobite wounded to be gathered into a barn and burned to death; he bade Wolfe, the future conqueror of Quebec, pistol a wounded Jacobite, an order which that officer indignantly refused to obey; he had civilians brutally flogged to extract from them information which they did not possess; and at Fort Augustus he ordered a number of young girls to be seized, stripped naked, and compelled to ride races on horseback in that condition for the delectation of the English soldiers.[2] When the Duke was about to return to England from Scotland, he wrote:

"I am sorry to leave this country in the condition it is in; for all the good that we have done has been a little bloodletting, which has only weakened the madness, but not at all cured; and I tremble for fear that this vile spot may still be the ruin of this island and of our family."[3]

Over the whole period was cast the shadow of Sir Robert Walpole. Until 1742 he dominated the scene in person, and for the next eighteen years the evil that he did lived after him. More than one of Anne's ministers had broken the laws of conventional morality, but it was left for this Norfolk squire to debase the whole public life of the country, and it was not until the accession to power of the younger Pitt that any real improvement took place. Walpole worked on the assumption that every politician had his price, and long before he resigned it was true:

"Had he not been a politician it cannot be doubted that he would have been a great merchant or a great financier. . . . His chief pre-occupation was the keeping out of the rival

---

[1] This nickname is said to be due to the fact that when it was proposed to make Cumberland a member of one of the City Companies, a Jacobite who was present suggested that of the Butchers as the most suitable.

[2] *cf.* Forbes, R.: *The Lyon in Mourning, passim.*

[3] *cf.* Coxe, W.: *The Pelham Administration,* Vol. I, p. 303.

house of Stuart, which would not have employed the firm of Walpole and the Whigs to keep their accounts. . . . His merciless crushing of any rivals was simply the big firm crushing competition, a familiar feature of commerce."[1]

Externally, Walpole was a bluff, hearty man, whose habit it was always to talk bawdy at table, so that everybody could join in the conversation. Actually, he was jealous and vindictive; the very type of *un faux bonhomme*.

As a political strategist Walpole has had few equals, and hardly a superior. He knew that in the interests of that Whig oligarchy, whose servant he was, the country must be taught to think in terms of material prosperity alone, and that enthusiasm of any kind must be repressed at all costs. His claim to distinction lies in the thoroughness with which he worked for this end. Walpole was not content merely to avoid measures calculated to excite public opinion, for his passivity was of an active type, if such an expression is permissible. There was no aspect of the national life which he left untouched, one might almost say uncontaminated, and every institution, religious and secular, was carefully lulled to sleep. Whether his policy was right or wrong it was all of a piece. High statesmanship of the type of Bolingbroke and the Pitts was utterly foreign to Walpole, and what he lacked in himself he disliked and mistrusted in others. His task was to let the generation that had been divided by the Revolution die out, and another which only knew the flesh-pots of Whig rule grow up in its place. Unhappily for England, the result of this was a stagnation and an apathy which proved a forcing-ground for abuses which the statesmen of a later age had the greatest difficulty in eradicating. The Englishman is by nature lazy, and glad of an excuse for doing nothing: Walpole made apathy a political virtue.

It would have been difficult for any man holding these views to have attracted disinterested support, and Walpole signally failed.

"He seemed to aim always at getting people to behave like rational human beings, at showing them the folly of running

[1] Rosebery, Earl of: *Chatham; His Early Life and Connections*, pp. 144–145.

after will-o'-the-wisps or flying into a passion. On the other hand, his words rarely touched their imaginations, still more rarely their consciences. He had little to say about such themes as patriotism, prestige or national glory, and was never heard discoursing on the duty of self-sacrifice or the love of humanity. Walpole had probably a clearer understanding of Everyman in his Everyday humour than any statesman who has ever governed England; but he appears to have had little or no perception of those inward passionate feelings, those tremendous hidden forces, which the elder Pitt, and the younger, and Charles James Fox, each in his different way, knew so well how to evoke and inspire."[1]

For this reason Walpole found, towards the end of his career, all the rising young men banded against him. To some extent, too, this was due to his jealousy of ability, for his Cabinets were mediocre in the extreme. In short, Walpole must bear the responsibility for the cynical indifference with which the political system was worked until the younger Pitt took office.

Society in London in the earlier part of the eighteenth century was, subject to the limitations already mentioned, very much like what it has been ever since, except possibly during the Victorian era, and Horace Walpole's letters have a modern ring:

"The ball broke up at three; but Lincoln, Lord Holderness, Lord Robert Sutton, young Churchill, and a dozen more, grew jolly, stayed till seven in the morning, and drank thirty-two bottles."[2]

"The Duchess of Cleveland died last night of what they call a military fever, which is much about: she had not been ill two days. So the poor creature, her Duke, is again to be let: she payed dear for the hopes of being Duchess Dowager."[3]

"Little Brook's little wife is a little with child."[4]

"Young Churchill has got a daughter by the Frasi; Mr.

[1] Oliver, F. S.: *The Endless Adventure*, Vol. I, pp. 15–16.
[2] Dec. 3, 1741.   [3] April 15, 1742.   [4] Nov. 1, 1742.

Winnington calls it the *opera-comique;* the mother is an opera-girl; the grandmother was Mrs. Oldfield."[1]

There are, however, other allusions which would not ring so true to-day:

"The Duchess of Richmond takes care that house shall not be extinguished: she again lies in, after having been with child seven-and-twenty times: but even this is not so extraordinary as the Duke's fondness for her, or as the vigour of her beauty: her complexion is as fair and blooming as when she was a bride."[2]

"The world is still mad about the Gunnings: the Duchess of Hamilton was presented on Friday; the crowd was so great, that even the noble mob in the drawing-room clambered upon chairs and tables to look at her."[3]

It was, too, one of the few periods in English history when satire was in vogue, and the following verses give some idea of the type of wit that appealed to the London of George II:

A RECEIPT TO MAKE A LORD

OCCASIONED BY A LATE REPORT OF A PROMOTION

Take a man, who by nature's a true son of earth,
By rapine enrich'd, though a beggar by birth;
In genius the lowest, illbred and obscene;
In morals most wicked, most nasty in mien;
By none ever trusted, yet ever employ'd;
In blunders quite fertile, of merit quite void;
A scold in the Senate, abroad a buffoon,
The scorn and the jest of all courts but his own:
A slave to that wealth that ne'er made him a friend,
And proud of that cunning that ne'er gain'd an end;
A dupe in each treaty, a Swiss in each vote;
In manners and form a complete Hottentot.
Such an one could you find, of all men you'd commend him;
But be sure let the curse of each Briton attend him.
Thus fully prepared, add the grace of the throne,
The folly of monarchs and screen of a crown—

[1] July 22, 1744. "Young Churchill" was the illegitimate son of General Charles Churchill, and afterwards married Mary, natural daughter of Sir Robert Walpole.
[2] Feb. 15, 1750.   [3] March 23, 1752.

Take a prince for his purpose, without ears or eyes,
And a long parchment roll stuff'd brim-full of lies:
These mingled together, a fiat shall pass,
And the thing be a Peer, that before was an ass.

This was inspired by the rumour that it was proposed to make Sir Robert Walpole's brother a peer.

LES COURS DE L'EUROPE

L'Allemagne craint tout;
L'Autriche risque tout;
La Baviere espère tout;
La Prusse entreprend tout;
La Mayence vend tout;
Le Portugal regarde tout;
L'Angleterre veut faire tout;
L'Espagne embrouille tout;
La Savoye se défie de tout;
Le Mercure se mêle de tout;
La France achète tout;
Les Jesuites se trouvent par tout;
Rome bénit tout;
Si Dieu ne pourvoye à tout.
Le Diable emportera tout.

The reigns of the first two Georges constituted a period when the members of the great Revolution families had achieved social and political power, but had not yet become gentlemen: still, there were limits to what would be tolerated, and Philip, Duke of Wharton, overstepped them. This nobleman came of a family which had long been noted for its Whig tendencies, and he himself was raised by George I to ducal rank at a very early age, though rather on account of his dead father's merits than of his own. Possessed of very considerable genius, but utterly unstable, he was Hanoverian and Jacobite by turns, until, before he was thirty, he had exhausted even the enormous fortune that had been left him, and yet still owed some £70,000. It was not, however, Wharton's political tergiversations or his extravagance that marked him out among his contemporaries, but his unbridled debauchery. He was President of one of the earlier Hell Fire Clubs, which emulated the excesses of the Mohocks of the previous generation. They were more nuisance to the public, if somewhat less blasphemous, than their successors later in the century, for their members found their chief amusement in beating the watch, slitting the noses of men, and rolling women in barrels down Snow Hill. A contemporary said of them: "They attempt all females of their own species promiscuously—grandmothers and mothers as well as daughters; even their own sisters fear their violence and fly their privacies. Blind and bold love is their motto." Much of this was probably exaggeration, but an Act of Parliament had finally to be passed for their suppression. As for Wharton himself, he went into exile, and died in the Spanish service in his early thirties, having received the Garter from both James and George.[1] Pope called Wharton "the scorn and wonder of our days", and summed up his character admirably.

Another eccentric nobleman of this period was Lord Ferrers. Having for some years kept a mistress, by whom he had two or three children, he suddenly married a sister of Sir William Meredith, a Cheshire baronet. From the beginning he treated his wife, a very pretty woman, atrociously. He accused her of having beguiled him into marriage in that she met him drunk at an assembly in the country, and kept him so until the marriage ceremony was over; but, as Horace Walpole observed, "As he always kept himself so afterwards, one need not impute it to her." He beat his wife regularly, and always took pistols to bed with him, threatening to kill her before morning.[2] Finally, Lady Ferrers obtained a separation by Act of Parliament, and receivers were appointed for her husband's estate to ensure that she received her allowance. Lord Ferrers secured the nomination of his steward, a man named Johnson, as one of them, and when he heard that the latter had paid Lady Ferrers a sum of fifty pounds without his knowledge, murdered him in the most barbarous manner. He shot the wretched Johnson at three in the afternoon, and, hours later, when there

[1] The riband of the order was changed from light blue to dark blue on the accession of the House of Hanover.

[2] Before his marriage he is said to have beaten a groom so severely that the man died of the injuries he had received.

appeared to be some hope of his recovery, tried to tear off the bandages. When he heard his victim was dead, he said he gloried in having killed him. What gave to contemporaries an added interest in the tragedy was the fact that the aunt of Lord Ferrers was no less a person than the Countess of Huntingdon, the "Saint Teresa of the Methodists", as Horace Walpole described her.

In due course Ferrers was tried by his peers, unanimously found guilty, and sentenced to be hanged, though the legend that he was allowed a silken rope as the privilege of his rank appears to have no foundation in fact. He asked to see his mistress, a Mrs. Clifford, before he died, but this request was refused on the advice of Lady Huntingdon, who declared that "it would be letting him die in adultery". The procession from the Tower to Tyburn was one of the most remarkable that London has ever seen. There were thousands of people waiting when it commenced at nine o'clock in the morning of May 5th, 1760. First went a string of constables; then one of the sheriffs in a coach and six, with the horses decorated with ribbons; after that came Lord Ferrers, in his own coach and six, with his coachman on the box, and dragoons riding on either side; the procession was terminated by two more coaches and a detachment of Household Cavalry. Ferrers displayed the utmost unconcern, and showed himself freely to the crowds that lined the route, for, as he put it to the sheriff who was in the carriage with him, "they never saw a lord hanged, and perhaps will never see another". The scaffold was hung with black, and under the gallows instead of the usual cart, was a platform, which was to be struck from under the condemned man. Unfortunately for Ferrers, this contrivance did not work properly, since his toes touched it; however, the executioners got hold of his legs as they were dangling, and by pulling on them put him out of his misery in a few minutes. After that the sheriffs started eating and drinking on the scaffold while the corpse was hanging over their heads, and even helped one of their friends up to join them. When they had finished, the procession re-formed, and the body was taken to Surgeons' Hall to be dissected, while at Tyburn there was a free fight for souvenirs in the shape of the rope and the black cloth.[1]

If authority allowed the poor to gloat over the execution of a nobleman, it could be hard enough on them at other times. One night in July 1742 a party of drunken constables took it into their heads to put into execution the law against disorderly persons, and proceeded to arrest every woman they met, until they had collected between twenty and thirty. They then put them into St. Martin's round-house, where they remained for the night with both doors and windows closed. The women had neither air to breathe nor room to move, and even their cries for water went unheard. Many of them, too, were not disorderly persons at all, but either beggars or working-women. When the door was opened in the morning four of them were found suffocated, two died soon afterwards, and a dozen more were in a serious condition. One of the dead was a washerwoman, who was pregnant, and when arrested had been returning home late from washing. The keeper of the round-house was charged with wilful murder, but acquitted. To quote Horace Walpole once more: "The greatest criminals in this town are the officers of justice; there is no tyranny they do not exercise, no villainy of which they do not partake." Money alone could buy immunity from injustice, for the same night that this outrage was perpetrated a bagnio in Covent Garden was raided, and Lord George Graham and the Hon. John Spencer were only saved from the round-house by the length of their purses.

When one passed east from the fashionable world of St. James's, it was to find a society that was endeavouring to adjust itself to an old system in decay, namely, that of apprenticeship.[2] The dead hand of a bygone age had a later generation in its grasp. The Tudors and Stuarts had, quite understandably, endeavoured to restrict the growth of the capital by prohibiting the erection of new buildings, but the main result of their efforts had been overcrowding in those that did

---

[1] Lady Ferrers afterwards married Lord Frederick Campbell, and was unfortunately burned to death.

[2] For those who would understand the life of working-class London in the eighteenth century, *London Life in the XVIIIth Century* by M. D. George is indispensable.

exist, with the most disastrous consequences from a social, moral, and economic point of view. The jurisdiction of the City remained limited to the square mile, and the outlying districts were administered on a parish basis as if they were still sparsely populated rural communities. The normal method of learning a trade was apprenticeship. This has much to recommend it in the abstract, but in practice, for lack of effective supervision, it worked badly in the eighteenth century. Parish children, and the offspring of poor parents, were apprenticed to trades where there was no hope of advancement, and where they were little better than slaves. One example, though of a slightly later date, will suffice. Ann Barnard, a child of twelve, was bound apprentice to a woman who sold old clothes in the streets, while her husband was employed at a pot-house in Lambeth. The family lived in a garret in Bell Yard, Westminster, where the child was left to look after a baby. It was only when she was criminally assaulted by another inmate of the house that these facts came to light.[1] In such circumstances apprenticeship was a hollow mockery. A child was taken for the ready money, and then treated worse than a slave in the plantations. To quote Blake:

> When my mother died I was very young,
> And my father sold me while yet my tongue
> Could scarcely cry "'weep, 'weep, 'weep".
> So your chimneys I sweep and in soot I sleep.

In the City the situation was definitely better, but industry was fast leaving it even at the beginning of the eighteenth century, and the freedom of the City was chiefly sought by those who wished to open shops there. Outside its boundaries apprenticeship usually began before the age of fourteen, and lasted until twenty-four.

"Any person, master or journeyman, man or woman, housekeeper or lodger, who would undertake to provide food, lodging, and instruction, sometimes also clothes, medicines, and washing, could take an apprentice, all the

[1] cf. Old Bailey Sessions Papers, Feb. 1784 (Rape Trial).

earnings of the apprentice, whether for the master or a third person, being the property of the master."[1]

In effect, apprenticeship had become merely a means of ensuring a regular supply of cheap labour. Even in the heyday of the system the apprentices had been riotous and disorderly, and in its decline they furnished many a recruit to the criminal classes. The Newgate Calendar contains innumerable instances of apprentices robbing or murdering their employers: in 1735 a little girl of nine was sentenced to death for stealing twenty-seven guineas from her mistress.[2] Ill-treatment of apprentices was also frequent, and the famous case of Mrs. Brownrigg was by no means unique. On the one side was despair, and on the other cruelty, so it is hardly surprising that the system in its decay should have been marked by the most flagrant abuses.

The general level of civilization was still further lowered by an orgy of spirit-drinking, chiefly gin, which reached its peak between 1720 and 1751, and was deliberately encouraged by Parliament. Defoe put the matter quite bluntly:

"In times of plenty and a moderate price of corn, the distilling of corn is one of the most essential things to support the landed interest that any branch of trade can help us to, and therefore especially to be preserved and tenderly used."[3]

In the days of Charles I the monarchy had tried to hold the balance by granting a charter of incorporation to the distillers of London, but since the Revolution the landed interest had become supreme, and the charter was ignored. Anyone was free to distil on giving notice to the Commissioners of Excise and paying a very low duty, while no licence from the justices was required to retail spirits. The result may be seen in Hogarth's *Gin Lane*. By 1750 it was computed that in the City one house in every twenty-five was a gin-shop, in

---

[1] George, M. D.: *London Life in the XVIIIth Century*, p. 226.
[2] *Old Bailey Sessions Papers*, July 1735.
[3] Quoted by George, M. D.: *op. cit.*, p. 29.

Westminster one in every eight, and in Holborn one in every five and a quarter.

"What must become of an infant who is conceived in gin, with the poisonous distillations of which it is nourished, both in the womb and at the breast?"[1]

The gin-sodden populace was prone to commit the most unnatural crimes, of which one instance will suffice. A woman fetched her two-year-old child from the workhouse, where it had just been newly clothed, on the pretext of spending the afternoon with it. She then strangled the infant, left its body in a ditch in Bethnal Green, and sold the clothes for one and fourpence, which she spent on gin.[2] An examination of the life of working-class London at this time can but lead to agreement with the sentiments expressed by the Rev. James Townley in 1751:

> Gin, cursed fiend, with fury fraught,
> Makes human race a prey,
> It enters by a deadly draught,
> And steals our life away.

Not that the reverend gentleman was a prohibitionist, for he continues:

> Beer, happy produce of our isle,
> Can sinewy strength impart,
> And wearied with fatigue and toil,
> Can cheer each manly heart.

It is impossible to resist the conclusion that in the reigns of the first two Georges the mass of the population in London was more depraved and debased than at any other period of English history. They were brutalized to an inconceivable degree, and religion had no longer the slightest hold over them. This was in some measure the inevitable consequence of a system which openly worked for the enrichment of the wealthy and the impoverishment of the poor, and it was noticeable, though to nothing like the same extent, in the provincial

[1] Fielding, H.: *An Enquiry into the Reasons of the late Increase of Robbers*, p. 19.
[2] *Old Bailey Sessions Papers*, Feb. 1734.

towns and in the countryside. Graft in high places, deliberately encouraged by the statesmen of the day, notably Sir Robert Walpole, was matched by the degradation of the masses, and there was a decided set-back in every aspect of life in comparison with the century before.[1] The country

"after the prolonged occupation with the business of pulling down one King and setting up another, had imbibed a dangerous contempt of all authority whatsoever. . . . In all classes the same lawlessness was to be found; showing itself among the higher by a fashionable indifference to all that had once been honoured as virtue, an equally fashionable indulgence towards debauchery, and an irresistible tendency to decide every dispute by immediate and indiscriminate force. Among the lower classes, despite the most sanguinary penal code in Europe, brutal crime, not of violence only, was dangerously rife. No man who was worth robbing could consider himself safe in London, whether in the streets or in his own house. Patrols of Horse and Foot Guards failed to ensure the security of the road between Piccadilly and Kensington; and further afield the footpad and the highwayman reigned almost undisturbed".[2]

Where, however, London had the advantage over the rest of the country was that after about 1760 conditions began to improve, both economically and socially, while elsewhere they grew steadily worse. By the death of George IV the position of the ordinary working-class Londoner may have been far from ideal, yet it was a great deal better, not only than that of his grandfather, but also than that of the contemporary factory-hand or farm-labourer. In the early part of the eighteenth century the mob of the capital, composed of beings so degraded as scarcely to deserve the appellation of human, was a real menace, but after the Gordon Riots in 1780 it began to change its character, and by 1830 the cynical, good-humoured Londoner of to-day was already recognizable. He

[1] Those who may be inclined to question this are advised to read Mr. Arthur Bryant's *The England of Charles II*, and to compare the situation depicted there with life in early Georgian England.

[2] Fortescue, Hon. Sir J. W.: *History of the British Army*, Vol. II, pp. 14–15.

is very different from the sadistic beast who hung about Tyburn, went to see women whipped at Bridewell, and whose chief amusement was to watch weaker animals being torn to pieces by stronger ones.

In spite of its relative size, the London of those days would be strangely unfamiliar to the present generation. If one arrived at what is now Marble Arch, close to where the Tyburn gallows stood, and drove along Oxford Street there were few streets yet in existence on the left; farther on, in Great Russell Street, stood Montague House, a white building, long and low, with a courtyard. Behind were its gardens, from where there was a view across Lamb's Conduit Fields to the green heights of Highgate. The Foundling Hospital, established in 1741, had not a house near it. London, it is true, was creeping outwards, but along existing roads and lanes. Bethnal Green was still a hamlet, and from the London Hospital at the end of Whitechapel Street the high road ran east through the villages of Mile End, New Town, and Old Town. The middle of the century witnessed the construction of several new roads, and this had the effect of opening up fresh districts. The most important of these thoroughfares was the New Road from Paddington to Islington, which was made across fields in 1756-1757, and of which different portions are now known as Marylebone Road, Euston Road, and Pentonville Road. In the west, the road from Hyde Park Corner through Knightsbridge to Kensington was still better than a country lane, and it was decidedly unsafe at night owing to the activities of footpads, not a few of whom were privates in the Guards, whose task it was supposed to be to patrol it.

The growth of the capital was, in the main, already haphazard to a degree.

"The dominant fact in the development of London from the time of Elizabeth has been the cleavage between the East and West, accentuated by the position of the City between the two. Many factors have combined to produce this, and the process once started has been cumulative; as poor people flocked into a district the well-to-do withdrew. While West London was developed largely by the laying out of streets and squares on long leases, regulated by private and local Acts, East London grew obscurely, its development apparently influenced by the customs (confirmed by statute) of the great liberty of the manors of Stepney and Hackney, by which the copyholders were empowered to grant leases of thirty-one years without fine to the lord of the manor, under penalty of forfeiture of the copyhold if a longer lease was granted."[1]

The ordinary Londoner rarely went farther afield than the villages in the immediate neighbourhood of the capital, such as Knightsbridge, Kensington, Hampstead, and Hoxton.

"A rich citizen of London has perhaps some very valuable relatives or friends in the West; he thinks no more of visiting them than of travelling the deserts of Nubia, which might as well be in the moon, or in Limbo Patrum, considering them as a sort of separate being."[2]

Yet, in view of the state of the roads it is surprising how much, not how little, traffic there was on them, at any rate in the vicinity of London. From the "George" and "Blue Boar" in Holborn no less than eighty-four coaches left every day: four days a week a coach went to Oxford, and twice a week to Bristol. The journey to York took thirty hours, and cost £3 6s. 3d.[3] The first stage-coach, from London to Coventry, had commenced running as long ago as 1659, but it was not until the reign of George III that there was much improvement in this method of conveyance, and those who could afford to do so either rode on horseback or travelled in their own carriages. In 1784 the coaches began to carry the mails, and five years later they were provided with springs, of which they had previously been innocent. The next step was the introduction of lighter vehicles; and by the end of the century it was possible, thanks also to the improvement in the roads, to get from London to Brighton in eight hours at the cost of some fifteen shillings for a single fare. Before George IV was

---

[1] George, M. D.: *London Life in the XVIIIth Century*, p. 65.
[2] *The Gentleman's Magazine*, Vol. XXII, p. 553.
[3] *cf.* Roscoe, E. S.: *The English Scene in the Eighteenth Century*, pp. 14–15.

dead, over three hundred coaches used to pass Hyde Park daily. The gradual change in the speed of travelling, even by coach, can be gauged from the fact that in 1750 it took three days to go from London to Bath. In 1776 Johnson started at 11.0 a.m., and arrived the next day at 7.0 p.m. In 1827 Dickens makes his hero leave at 7.0 a.m., and arrive at 7.30 p.m. The difficulties of travelling explain to no inconsiderable extent the indifference of the ordinary townsman to the wilder beauties of nature, and the monuments of the past were still regarded in the light of quarries. The formal garden was much admired, and the influence of Holland and Versailles reigned supreme in matters horticultural. Nor is this remarkable when it is remembered that those places where nature was to be seen at its wildest were precisely those that were most unsafe. Even the beauty of a sunset over the sea is liable to be marred by the possible arrival of a landing-party from a hostile ship, and it is not easy to wax enthusiastic about a Highland glen when at any moment a wild clansman with a claymore may rise from the heather. The Englishman only became sentimental when he could be so with safety. The polite world of the first two Georges still regarded Gothic as a synonym for barbaric, and it was, curiously enough, left for that man of his age, Horace Walpole, to initiate a reaction with the building of his house at Strawberry Hill. As Miss Stuart has reminded us:

> "People tired of parterres and pediments before they tired of the heroic couplet; and landscape gardeners were making trees hang over somewhat poetical . . . before the colourless and rigid conventions of the Pope-Boileau school in England had been touched by the genius of Gray and by the talent—to call it nothing higher—of Macpherson, Chatterton, and the two Wartons."[1]

In these circumstances it is hardly surprising that to the ordinary Englishman of that time Scotland was as unknown as is Abyssinia to his descendant of to-day. Communication between London and Edinburgh was very restricted, and on at

---

[1] Stuart, D. M.: *Horace Walpole*, pp. 102–103.

least one occasion the mail from the English capital contained
but a single letter. The Highlands were terrifying even to the
Lowlanders, and Scott assuredly did not exaggerate in his
account of the fears of Bailie Nicol Jarvie in the mountains of
the North. Yet from time to time an Englishman did cross
the Highland line, and such a one was Edward Burt, who has
left a description of a dinner with Lord Lovat at a place which
has been identified as Castle Dounie:[1]

"Our entertainment consisted of a great number of
dishes, at a long table, all brought in under covers, but
almost cold. What the greatest part of them were, I could
not tell, nor did I enquire, for they were disguised after the
French manner; but there was placed next to me a dish
which I guessed to be boiled beef. I say that was my
conjecture, for it was covered all over with stewed cabbage,
like a smothered rabbit, and over all a deluge of bad butter.
... We had very good wine, but did not drink much of it;
but one thing, I should have told you, was intolerable, viz.
the number of Highlanders that attended at table, whose
feet and foul linen, or woollen, I don't know which, were
more than a match for the odour of the dishes."[2]

Simon Fraser, eleventh Lord Lovat, is typical of eighteenth-
century politics at their worst. He had been everything by
turns, but nothing long. One of his earlier escapades was to
proclaim James VIII at Inverness when Dutch William died,
but he soon afterwards changed sides, and betrayed the
Jacobite secrets to the British Government. He then had the
temerity to visit Queen Mary of Modena in her exile at St.
Germain-en-Laye, but his duplicity was discovered, and
Louis XIV sent him to cool his heels for three years in prison,
first at Angoulême and later in the Bastille. During the
Fifteen he espoused the cause of Hanover, but his loyalty was
always for sale. In private life Lovat was equally unscrupulous.
His predecessor in the title had left an only daughter, whom he
determined to marry in order to obtain the estates, of which

---

[1] cf. Burton, J. H.: *Lives of Simon Lord Lovat, and Duncan Forbes of Culloden*, p. 175.
[2] Burt, E.: *Letters from a Gentleman in the North of Scotland*, Vol. I, p. 158.

the disposal was in doubt. In this project he was unsuccessful, so he transferred his attentions to the young lady's mother. With the aid of a number of his clansmen he seized the unwilling bride in her own house, in spite of the fact that she was the sister of the Marquess of Atholl, the most powerful nobleman in Scotland. Lovat then compelled a priest to read the marriage service between them, after which he cut the laces of his victim's stays with his dirk, and forced her to bed; the marriage was thereupon consummated in the presence of Lovat's retainers, while the bagpipes played in the next room to drown the screams of the victim.[1] In the Forty-five he sent his clan to the aid of Charles Edward with his son at its head, while he himself remained at home. This characteristic behaviour, however, did not save him, and in due course Lovat was beheaded on Tower Hill.

The behaviour of Simon Fraser was in no way representative of his fellow-countrymen. If Scotland, in his person, furnished the century with one of its most disreputable characters, it also supplied one of the noblest in Flora MacDonald, and it was to her, rather than to Lovat, that the vast majority of the Scottish people approximated. When it is remembered that for months Charles Edward was in hiding after his defeat at Culloden with a price of £30,000 on his head, and that many people knew where he was, no further testimony to the Scottish character is required, and the treachery of a Lovat or a Murray of Broughton is seen but to be the exception that proves the rule. Indeed, it is probably not going too far to suggest that in no other part of the British Isles would the fugitive Prince's secret have been so safe as among the poor Highlanders to whom he entrusted himself.

If the early eighteenth century travelled little, there was one place to which it did resort, and that was Bath. Royalty had occasionally visited the town for more than a hundred years; Anne of Denmark, Charles II, and Queen Anne had all been there, but it was only after the accession of the House of Hanover that Bath really came into its own. In a way it was

---

[1] Jesse, J. H.: *Memoirs of the Pretenders and Their Adherents*, pp. 77–90.

unique, for it was a meeting-place of town and country. Thither went the men and women of fashion in London, as well as the country squire and his wife; some of those who came to Bath did so because their health required that they should take the waters, but many, possibly the majority, had no other motive than social intercourse. Parents brought their daughters in the hope of finding suitable husbands, and adventurers of either sex frequented the town in order to enrich themselves in one of a hundred ways.

"A man has daily opportunities of seeing the most remarkable characters of the community. He sees them in their natural attitudes and true colours, descended from their pedestals, and divested of their formal draperies, undisguised by art and affectation. Here we have ministers of state, judges, generals, bishops, projectors, philosophers, wits, poets, players, chemists, fiddlers, and buffoons. . . . Another entertainment peculiar to Bath arises from the general mixture of all degrees, assembled in our public rooms without distinction of rank or fortune."[1]

Bath, in effect, was the Riviera of the eighteenth century. The city owed its importance to Beau Nash, who for many years governed with a rod of iron the very mixed company which gathered there. He was born at Swansea in 1674, and, after having been sent down from Oxford, led a riotous life in the Temple as a student of law; about 1704 he contrived to get himself appointed master of ceremonies at Bath, which was henceforth to be associated with his name. Many stories are told of his despotic sway. One day, having forbidden ladies to appear at assemblies in white aprons, he saw the Duchess of Queensberry wearing one; Nash tore it off with the remark that "such articles are suitable only for abigails", and the Duchess promptly begged his pardon. He was equally severe on country squires who appeared in high boots and spurs, and he wrote a lampoon which ended with the words:

> For why shouldn't we
> In dress be as free,
> As Hog's Norton Squire in boots.[2]

[1] Smollett, T. G.: *Humphrey Clinker*.   [2] Goldsmith, O.: *Life of Nash*, p. 60.

It is not surprising that Nash regarded Wesley as a nuisance when the latter began to preach at Bath in 1739. He appeared on the scene in person, and asked Wesley by what authority he did these things.

"I replied, 'By the authority of Jesus Christ, conveyed to me by the (now) Archbishop of Canterbury, when he laid his hands upon me and said, "Take thou authority to preach the Gospel.'" He said, 'This is contrary to Act of Parliament. This is a Conventicle.' I answered, 'Sir, the Conventicles mentioned in the Act (as the preamble shows) are seditious meetings, but this is not such. Here is no shadow of sedition. Therefore it is not contrary to the Act.' He replied, 'I say it is. But, besides, your preaching frightens people out of their wits.' 'Sir, did you ever hear me preach?' 'No.' 'How then can you judge of what you never heard?' 'Sir, by common report.' 'Common report is not enough. Give me leave, sir, to ask—is not your name Nash.' 'My name is Nash.' 'Sir, I dare not judge of you by common report. I believe it is not enough to judge by.' Here he paused a while, and, having recovered himself, asked: 'I desire to know what these people come here for?' On which one replied, 'Sir, leave him to me. Let an old woman answer him. You, Mr. Nash, take care of your body. We take care of our souls, and for the good of our souls we come here.' "[1]

The art of doing nothing without being bored was carried to perfection at Bath. The tone, in many instances one might almost say the pace, was set by the ladies. In the morning they were carried in closed chairs, with nothing on but their underclothing, to the Cross-Bath, where the music played them into the water. Each bather was provided with a little wooden dish, which floated beside her, and in which she put her handkerchief, nosegay, snuffbox, and some patches, though the heat of the water is said to have rendered it no easy task to get these last to stick. Men and women were supposed to keep to their respective sides of the bath, but they

---

[1] Wesley's *Journal*, June 5, 1739.

by no means always did so, and the morning passed in discourse and flirtation. After an hour or two spent in this way, chairs were called, and the ladies returned to their lodgings. In the afternoon there was generally a play, and on at least two evenings a week there was a ball. The rest of the time was spent in walking about, or in playing cards.[1]

Although Bath became fashionable in the early part of the eighteenth century, it was not until the reign of George III that its rebuilding was seriously taken in hand. The houses of the old city were ancient, dilapidated, and dirty, and the transformation was due to the two Woods, father and son.

"The peculiar merit of the Woods in proposing and accomplishing this task was that they were architects and not mere builders; that they had the beauty of the city they were transforming always before their eyes; that they conceived and carried out a harmonious whole."[2]

Furthermore, the houses they built were comfortable as well as handsome. Queen's Square, the Circus, the parades, and the Lower Rooms were the work of the elder Wood, while the Royal Crescent was both designed and completed by his son. Pulteney Bridge was built in 1769, but Pulteney Street and Laura Place came later. As the century grew older Bath became more staid, and therefore more dull, than it had been in the days of the first two Georges, for pleasure-seekers were beginning to discover, in a more settled age, the attractions of the seaside. Yet it was still much frequented, and it was from Bath that the younger Pitt set out in 1806 on what was to prove his last journey.

Bath was the latest of the watering-places, but it had many predecessors, some of which continued to attract visitors, if in diminishing numbers, throughout the century. Difficulties of communication had at first rendered popular those springs which were near the capital, and among them Tunbridge Wells was pre-eminent. It had been a favourite resort of Charles II, and one of the few churches dedicated to the Royal

[1] The waters of Bath were reputed to be most efficacious in procuring conception, and a visit to the city enabled many ladies to present their husbands with a son and heir.
[2] Barbeau, A.: *Life and Letters at Bath in the 18th Century*, p. 285.

Martyr is still to be found there. Defoe described Tunbridge
Wells as a place that

"wants nothing that can add to the felicities of life, or that
can make a man or woman completely happy, always
provided they have money".[1]

If the nobility and gentry in the reign of George I went to
Tunbridge Wells, the merchants and richer citizens patronized
Epsom, while the lower classes flocked to Dulwich and
Streatham. On a Sunday, or holiday, in summer these last
were crowded with Londoners who had walked out, and very
unruly they became on occasion. One of the attractions of
Epsom was the races on Banstead Downs. During the summer
it was by no means unusual for the City men of the time to
move their families down to Epsom, while they themselves
rode each day to and from their places of business in London.
Less innocent were the motives of those who resorted on
Sunday afternoons to Box Hill, which for a few years enjoyed
an unsavoury reputation. On the top of the hill there was a
large beech tree, and at its foot was a vault which had been
converted into a place of entertainment. Local residents
objected to the debauchery of which this underground
restaurant became the scene, and when appeals to the magistrates to interfere proved fruitless, they took the law into their
own hands, and blew the place up with gunpowder.

Not only in the watering-places, but also in the country-
towns, the centre of social life was the assembly-rooms.
Defoe, always *bourgeois* in his outlook, viewed them with the
gravest suspicion as potential, if not actual sinks of iniquity.
He does, indeed, defend the ladies of Bury St. Edmunds from
the aspersions cast upon their virtue by a previous writer, but
he is obviously surprised that they should emerge from the
local assembly-rooms with their purity unsullied.

"I do not at all doubt, but that the scandalous liberty some
take at those assemblies, will in time bring them out of
credit with the virtuous part of the sex here, as it has
already done in Kent and other places; and that those

[1] *A Tour through England and Wales.*

ladies who most value their reputation, will be seen less there than they have been; for though the institution of them has been innocent and virtuous, the ill use of them, and the scandalous behaviour of some people at them, will in time arm virtue against them, and they will be laid down as they have been set up, without much satisfaction."

At Winchester he found the "new fashioned way of conversing by assemblies" already established, and piously hoped that the city would "escape the ill consequences". Lyme Regis, on the other hand, to the great satisfaction of Defoe had so far escaped infection, because "the Dorsetshire ladies are equal in beauty, and may be superior in reputation". Defoe was sadly out in his prognostications, for as with so many social institutions, the assembly-rooms soon became boring rather than vicious, and those who frequented them found their intelligence, not their morals, offended.[1]

It cannot really be claimed for the reigns of the first two Georges that they represent anything more than a period of stagnation in the national life, which compares very unfavourably with what had gone before as well as with what was to follow. Perhaps it is in the arts that this difference is most marked. Fielding, Smollett, and Richardson in prose, and Pope and Gay in verse, alone redeem the era from sterility; Bolingbroke's writings were more important for the influence they came to exercise over George III than for any special merit of their own; while the other men of letters whose fame has stood the test of time were mostly either survivors from the seventeenth century, or had not attained maturity by 1760. The stage was to some extent an exception. Not only could it boast one of the greatest actors of all time in David Garrick, but there was James Quin among the men, and Anne Oldfield, Lavinia Fenton, and Mrs. Woffington among the women. At the same time there can be no doubt that the theatre still suffered in the eyes of many under the reputation for licence which it had acquired in the days of the Restoration, and a contemporary writer of moderate views could say:

[1] cf. The Torrington Diaries, Vol. I, p. 87 et seq.

"Although of plays it is said that they teach morality, and of the stage that it is the mirror of human life, these assertions are mere declamation . . . on the contrary, a play-house and the regions about it, are the very hotbeds of vice: how else comes it to pass that no sooner is a play-house opened in any part of the kingdom, than it at once becomes surrounded by a halo of brothels?"[1]

It was not a little unfortunate that the stage should have been in such bad repute at the very moment a religious revival was being inaugurated by Wesley, for it originated on the part of a section of the population that hatred for the theatre and everything connected with it which was to become one of the most unpleasing characteristics of the nineteenth century. The intolerance which seemed to have been buried with the Commonwealth was given a new lease of life.

It must be admitted, too, that the lives of some of the leading actresses were by no means exemplary. Lavinia Fenton, the original Polly Peachum of *The Beggar's Opera*, was first the mistress, and later the wife, of the Duke of Bolton; they had three sons before they were married and on her death Horace Walpole wrote to Mann:

"The famous Polly, Duchess of Bolton, is dead, having, after a life of merit, relapsed into her Pollyhood. Two years ago, ill at Tunbridge, she picked up an Irish surgeon. When she was dying, this fellow sent for a lawyer to make her will, but the man, finding who was to be her heir, instead of her children, refused to draw it. The Court of Chancery did furnish one other, not quite so scrupulous, and her three sons have but a thousand pounds apiece; the surgeon about nine thousand."[2]

Anne Oldfield, who made her name as Lady Betty Modish in Cibber's comedy of *The Careless Husband*, lived first with Arthur Maynwaring, a minor politician, and then with General Churchill, by whom she became the mother of the boy who later married Horace Walpole's half-sister. She was, however, a great favourite of Queen Caroline, and on her death

---

[1] Hawkins, Sir J.: *Life of Johnson*, pp. 75–76.   [2] Feb. 3, 1760.

in 1730 she was buried at the foot of Congreve's monument in Westminster Abbey. As for Mrs. Woffington, perhaps the only one of the three still remembered, the elder Sheridan described her to Windham as "a most willing bitch, artful, dissembling, lewd and malicious. A very captivating woman, and never failed to get a great influence over all men that lived with her." She once said to him of her sister in the latter's presence that

"there were two things she should never become, by her advice—a whore, and an actress, for she had sufficiently experienced the inconveniences of those ways of life herself."[1]

One of her numerous lovers was Domenico Angelo Malevolti Tremamondo, the famous *maître d'armes*. In Paris he once held a public assault-at-arms with a bouquet given by his mistress on his breast, and it is said that not a leaf of it was disturbed by any opponent.

[1] Ketton-Cremer, R. W.: *The Early Life and Diaries of William Windham*, pp. 79–80.

CHAPTER IV

FARMER GEORGE

ON October 28th, 1760, Horace Walpole wrote to Mann of the new monarch that he

"has behaved with the greatest propriety, dignity, and decency. He read his speech to the Council with much grace, and dismissed the guards on himself to wait on his grandfather's body. It is intimated, that he means to employ the same ministers, but with reserve to himself of more authority than has lately been in fashion."

For many years to come propriety, decency, and authority were to be the order of the day, even if dignity was sometimes lacking. The deaths of kings are always hailed as ushering in a new era, for man is by nature so dissatisfied an animal that he must always be acclaiming something that he fondly believes to be new. Nevertheless the accession of George III really did mark the beginning of a change more remarkable than any which had taken place since the reign of Henry VIII. The final triumph of the principles of the Revolution at Culloden began to make itself felt in every aspect of the national life, and before long the transformation of the latter on its material side was accelerated by a series of inventions. The lifetime of George III witnessed those changes that mark the difference between the England of Charles II and that of Victoria.

Froude, writing of the England of the Middle Ages, says:

"And now it is all gone—like an unsubstantial pageant faded; and between us and the old English there lies a gulf of mystery which the prose of the historian will never adequately bridge. They cannot come to us, and our imagination can but feebly penetrate to them. Only among the aisles of the cathedral, only as we gaze upon their silent figures sleeping on their tombs, some faint conceptions float before us of what these men were when they were alive and perhaps in the sound of church bells, that peculiar creation of mediaeval age, which falls upon the ear like the echo of a vanished world."[1]

This passage might much more aptly have been written about the difference between the England of George II and that of George IV, for there was a far greater resemblance between the country before and after the Reformation than is commonly supposed. The real dividing-line is the Industrial Revolution, and the reign of the third George saw not only its arrival, but also its final victory. Before 1760 England was agricultural, while after 1820 her wealth was mainly derived from her manufactures. Besides this fact the loss of America, and even the struggle against Napoleon, seem relatively unimportant.

The third George was a marked advance upon both his immediate predecessors. First of all, his private life was exemplary, and if, like his grand-daughter, he laid himself open to a charge of prudery, it was venial, because it was high time that the Court set society an example of decency. That he was narrow-minded and obstinate is undeniable, and he was very often a veritable thorn in the side of his ministers; but not a little of his strength lay in the fact that his prejudices were those of the vast majority of his subjects. In marked contrast with many contemporary politicians he displayed a great devotion to duty, and that was something, even if his ideas of duty were narrow. It is true that George III could only think of one thing at a time, but, as that is also one of the most prominent characteristics of the English people, what might have proved a source of weakness served as an additional bond of union between them and him. Above all, he was not a foreigner, and the country was sick to death of alien monarchs whom the Whig magnates had imposed upon it, and, in moments of crisis, kept on the throne by the bayonets of alien mercenaries.[2] He spoke English, French, and German fluently,

---

[1] *History of England*, Ch. 1.

[2] The Nineteen had been suppressed by Dutch troops, and in 1746 the British Government hired no less than six battalions of Hessians, who were commanded by Prince Frederick of Hesse-Cassel. Unlike his brother-in-law, the Duke of Cumberland, the Prince made war like a gentleman, *cf.* Duke, W.: *Lord George Murray and the Forty-five*, pp. 171–174.

though his orthography left much to be desired. In short, George III had much to recommend him to that new middle-class England that was coming into existence, and he was certainly the best of the Hanoverians until Victoria.

As a politician he was remarkably astute, and in spite of the limitations imposed upon him both by nature and the Constitution he remained the central figure on the political stage until the accession to power of the younger Pitt. The King was not always too scrupulous or too dignified in his methods. Shelburne, no novice in intrigue himself, said of George that

"by the familiarity of his intercourse he obtained your confidence, procured from you your opinion of different public characters, and then availed himself of this knowledge to sow dissension."[1]

During the General Election of 1780 he did not hesitate to do all in his power to get Admiral Keppel beaten at Windsor. On one occasion he went into a draper's shop in that town, and said in his peremptory way, "The Queen wants a gown, wants a gown. No Keppel. No Keppel."[2] Windsor duly obeyed the Royal behest. He was also a shrewd judge of the right moment to go to the country. In 1780 he secured a fresh lease of life for the tottering North administration by dissolving before the terror produced by the Gordon Riots was forgotten, and twenty-seven years later he secured the support of the electorate for the dismissal of a ministry which had a majority in the House of Commons. He was certainly curt towards those whom he did not like, as may be seen in his note to Lord North when Fox's India Bill was beaten in the House of Lords:

"Lord North is by this required to send me the Seals of his Department, and to acquaint Mr. Fox to send those of the Foreign Department. Mr. Frazer or Mr. Nepean will be the proper channel of delivering them to me this night; I choose this method as audiences on such occasions must be unpleasant.[3]

[1] Nicholls, J.: *Recollections and Reflections during the Reign of George III*, Vol. I, p. 389.
[2] cf. Rose, J. H.: *The Life of William Pitt*, Vol. I, p. 74.
[3] *The Correspondence of King George the Third from 1760 to December, 1783*, edited by the Hon. Sir John Fortescue, Vol. VI, p. 476.

So ended the hated Fox-North Coalition.

When Horace Walpole wrote that the new King proposed to reserve to himself "more authority than has lately been in fashion" he proved for once to be a true prophet. George had been brought up on the writings of Bolingbroke, and in particular upon *The Ideal of a Patriot King*, which was published in 1749. To many who would otherwise have agreed with him the author of this work had become obnoxious on account of his Deistic theories, which had been given to the world after his death. To Dr. Johnson, stout Tory as he was, Bolingbroke was anathema.

"Sir, he was a scoundrel, and a coward: a scoundrel for charging a blunderbuss against religion and morality; a coward, because he had not resolution to fire it off himself, but left half a crown to a beggarly Scotchman, to draw the trigger after his death."[1]

George knew nothing of Bolingbroke's religious views, and probably little of his private life, for he would assuredly have disapproved of both, but his political doctrines he determined to put into practice. It was in no way surprising that such should have been his attitude, for his father, Frederick, had been closely associated with Bolingbroke, and was in fact the latter's chief weapon against the dominant Whig oligarchs. In the King's youth there had been many complaints that those responsible for his education were little better than Jacobites.[2]

So far as Bolingbroke personally was concerned it is to be noted that it was not until he had most signally failed as a statesman that he began to acquire a reputation as a political philosopher,[3] and had he been able to make up his mind during the last few weeks of Anne's reign he could have presented the country with a Patriot King in the person of James III, instead of merely with a volume on the need for one. Nevertheless, in this book, which is far more quoted than read at the present time, Bolingbroke showed a thorough grasp of the true

[1] Boswell, J.: *Life of Samuel Johnson.*
[2] *cf.* Horace Walpole's letter to Sir Horace Mann, Dec. 11, 1752.
[3] In this respect he was by no means unique in the history of this country.

principle of monarchy as the embodiment of the national idea, with the occupant of the throne standing above the *guerres de pots de chambre* of the parties. He wrote, it is true, with the immediate purpose of providing Frederick, Prince of Wales, with a stick with which to belabour his father's ministers, but, with all his faults, Bolingbroke was too great a genius to produce an argument that should merely serve so transient an end. He stated the case for monarchy, and what he wrote holds for all time. What neither he nor George III realized was the difficulty of any but a legitimate dynasty providing a Patriot King. The Hanoverians were usurpers, and in the last resort they were dependent upon the minority whose fortunes were linked with theirs; for both in 1715 and 1745 the English people had shown in no uncertain fashion that it was not prepared to lift a finger to keep them on the throne. Those who thought with Bolingbroke wanted neither George II nor Frederick, Prince of Wales, but James III. Yet the power of the Crown under the Constitution was still very great, and it was no wonder that Bolingbroke did not see the flaw in his scheme. Whether, even had the Jacobites proved victorious, the revival of the old national monarchy at that time was still possible is open to doubt, for James would have owed his restoration far more to the efforts of a party than his uncle had done in 1660. Be that as it may, the Stuarts alone could have reigned as Bolingbroke wished the monarchs of England to reign, for their title in no way depended upon Parliamentary sanction. To quote Dr. Johnson:

"Sir, this Hanoverian family is *isolée* here. They have no friends. Now the Stuarts had friends who stuck by them so late as 1745. When the right of the King is not reverenced, there will not be reverence for those appointed by the King."[1]

When George III began to put Bolingbroke's theories into practice, he found, in spite of this fundamental weakness, that he was in an exceptionally strong position. He was, with all his limitations, a man who always knew his own mind, and

[1] Boswell, J.: *Life of Samuel Johnson.*

that is so rare in English political circles as to give an enormous advantage to one so happily placed. Then the decay of Jacobitism had rallied to him those stalwart monarchists in countless manor-houses and rectories who had hitherto looked across the water for inspiration. The Whigs, too, were not what they were, for, as their position became more secure, they had split into factions, divided from one another rather by personalities than by policy, and the country was getting very tired of being governed by a few rich men and their dependants. Furthermore, the Whigs had been dominant for so long that their leaders barely took the trouble to be civil to the King, and the following letter from George to the then Lord Chancellor, Lord Northington, shows the sort of treatment to which the monarch was subjected:

"So very extraordinary an affair has happened this day that I cannot help troubling you with it. The Duke of Bedford came to ask leave to go for some time to Woburn, and then began a harangue complaining that though I supported him and his colleagues, yet that I appeared not to like them, consequently that he and they were resolved when he came again to Town to resign if they did not meet with a kind reception, and those they thought their enemies were not frowned upon.

"You will, my dear Lord, easily conceive what indignation I felt at so very offensive a declaration, yet I mastered my temper, and we parted with cool civility. Can anyone in their senses think this mode of acting the way to obtain favour? No, but his Grace has not much of that ingredient in his composition. I beg you will send me a line in answer, whether any part of this was known to you.

"Richmond Lodge.
"June 12th, 1765."[1]

When the King came to the throne the administration was a Whig coalition, and the leading men in the ministry were the Duke of Newcastle and William Pitt the elder. George determined that his first step should be to break up the

[1] *The Correspondence of King George the Third from 1760 to December, 1783*, edited by the Hon. Sir John Fortescue, Vol. I, pp. 116–117.

Government, and he insisted upon adding a sentence of his own to the speech with which he opened Parliament. The new clause began, "Born and educated in this country, I glory in the name of Britain", and went on to express the Royal confidence in the loyalty of the people, and the monarch's desire to promote their welfare. The phrasing was unexceptionable, but the speech was, as everyone knew, the ministers' and not the King's. The word "Britain", however, had an ominously Scottish ring, and its insertion was generally believed to be due to the Earl of Bute. This nobleman was the chosen instrument of George III in his efforts to revive the direct influence of the Crown. He had been the friend and adviser of the King's father, and after Frederick's death inculcated his son with the ideas of Bolingbroke. From 1760 to 1765 he exercised, in one capacity or another, very great influence indeed, but became in the process one of the most unpopular men in the country, not least on the score of his nationality, for Dr. Johnson was by no means alone in his dislike of the Scots. Bute was attacked in the street, and on one occasion his coach was destroyed. Nor was this all, for the most scandalous accusations were made in respect of his relations with the King's mother, and a skirt and a jack-boot were continually being burnt together in public.

It was an age of little men, for the great leaders of the next generation were still in the nursery, but there was one giant, William Pitt, later Earl of Chatham. He had not hesitated to stoop to intrigue when all the efforts of the Opposition had been concentrated upon compassing the fall of Walpole, but once he was in power he proved himself one of the greatest statesmen this country has ever known.

"The situation which Pitt occupied at the close of the reign of George II was the most enviable ever occupied by any public man in English history. He had conciliated the King; he domineered over the House of Commons; he was adored by the people; he was admired by all Europe. He was the first Englishman of his time; and he had made England the first country in the world."[1]

[1] Macaulay, Lord: *William Pitt, Earl of Chatham.*

It was he who guided the country to victory in the Seven Years War, and so impressed his personality upon Parliament that he obtained without any serious opposition those subsidies for Britain's foreign allies which had previously only been extracted with the greatest difficulty.

> No more they made a fiddle-faddle
> About a Hessian horse or saddle.
> No more of continental measures;
> No more of wasting British treasures.
> Ten millions, and a vote of credit,
> 'Tis right. He can't be wrong who did it.

Pitt had in the past been as opposed to the policy of subsidies as anyone.

"The troops of Hanover, whom we are now expected to pay, marched into the Low Countries, where they still remain. They marched to the place most distant from the enemy, least in danger of an attack, and most strongly fortified had an attack been designed. They have, therefore, no other claim to be paid than that they left their own country for a place of greater security. I shall not, therefore, be surprised, after such another glorious campaign . . . to be told that the money of this nation cannot be more properly employed than in hiring Hanoverians to eat and sleep."[1]

Nevertheless, Pitt was not so inconsistent as may appear, for his objection was to hiring Hanoverians who took British money, and did nothing in return for it. In the Seven Years War he gave the subsidies to Frederick the Great, whose hard-fighting Prussians justified Pitt's contention that he had won America on the plains of Germany.

George and the great minister soon came to loggerheads. The former was obstinate, and the latter imperious. The King wished to intimidate or bribe Parliament into submission, and Pitt would neither be intimidated nor bribed. "The Great Commoner", as he was called, also began to fail in health about this time, and his temper, never of the best, rendered

[1] *History of the Parliamentary Debates*, Vol. XII, p. 1033.

him an extremely difficult colleague. All this made George's task easier, for Pitt was the main obstacle in his path. The new King had not been a year on the throne before the minister resigned, and there then ensued a series of bewildering ministerial changes, inexplicable on any ground other than the Royal search for a pliable Premier. The figures of Newcastle, Bute, Grenville, and Rockingham all flit, somewhat unsubstantially, across the stage, to be followed by Chatham and Grafton, and lastly there appeared Lord North, who was Prime Minister from 1770 to 1782, and lost the American colonies.

"Lord North's abilities," wrote the Duke of Grafton, "though great, did not mark him as a character suited to the management and direction of great military operations. His lordship was formed for the enjoyment of domestic comforts, and to shine in the most elegant societies; his knowledge, however, was very extensive, as was his wit; but he became confused when he was agitated by the great scenes of active life."[1]

A modern historian is not so kind.

"Lord North was a coarse and heavy man, with a wide mouth, thick lips, and puffy cheeks, which seemed typical of his policy. He resembled Walpole in his knowledge of men's foibles and contempt of humanity. True, he excelled him in affability; but he signally fell behind him in the sterner qualities which master men and beat down obstacles."[2]

In him George found a more satisfactory instrument than Bute for putting Bolingbroke's theories into practice.

If North was a pliable instrument for the King, the political system of the day was admirably adapted to the latter's purpose. The deliberate corruption of Parliament had been begun by the Whigs in the reign of Charles II, and Walpole had completed it. George now proposed to employ in his own interest the machinery of patronage which had hitherto been

---

[1] Quoted by Mumby, F. A.: *George III and the American Revolution*, p. 289.
[2] Rose, J. H.: *The Life of William Pitt*, Vol. I, p. 78.

used by the Whigs in the name of the Crown, but really for
their own ends. The cause "for which Hampden died in the
field and Sidney perished on the scaffold" had become synony-
mous with the narrowest oligarchical rule. The movements of
population had not been reflected in Parliamentary representation. Manchester, Leeds, Sheffield, and Birmingham
were unrepresented, and Scotland had 45 members returned
by only 4,000 voters, while 19 small Cornish boroughs
returned 38 members. Out of the 513 members for England
and Wales, 254 sat for constituencies which, taken together,
numbered only 11,500 voters, and 56 boroughs had each less
than 40 voters. It was estimated that 71 peers, together with
the Lords of the Treasury, could absolutely nominate 90
members of the House of Commons, and could procure the
return of 77 more; that 91 commoners could nominate 82
members, and procure the return of 57; so that 162 people
could, together with the Treasury, nominate 306 members, or
a substantial majority of the House of Commons.

To understand the success of the King in re-establishing to
a very considerable extent the personal power of the throne,
it is necessary to realize that no secret was made of this state of
affairs.

"A pretence of ignorance was, indeed, idle when seats were
openly advertised for sale in the newspapers; when £5,000
had been left by will for the purchase of a seat in Parliament;
when a seat had been reckoned amongst the saleable assets
of a bankrupt, and when a defaulting debtor had paid the
market price for a seat in order that, under the protection of
Parliamentary privilege, he might evade his creditors by
escaping from England without arrest."[1]

In many instances a seat in Parliament was as much in the gift
of a patron as was a living. In 1766 the Corporation of Oxford,
which was in debt, offered to secure the return of the sitting
members in exchange for a loan of £4,000 free of interest.
This was cheap, for the price of seats was steadily rising. In
the thirties £2,000 seems to have been regarded as the normal

---

[1] Veitch, G. S.: *The Genesis of Parliamentary Reform*, pp. 3-4.

price of a seat.[1] By 1784 the electors of Wallingford were able to sell the election to the members for £6,000, while in 1812 the Duke of Bedford sold his "property in the borough of Camelford" for £32,000.[2] How many years', or rather elections', purchase this represented is a matter for conjecture. In the same year, 1812, Canning wrote to Bootle Wilbraham in connection with his candidature for Liverpool:

> "Now Mr. Gladstone says that £10,000 will be wanted. They cannot start with less. About £2,000 is subscribed. He thinks by the end of this week the subscriptions may amount to £6,000 or £7,000 in Liverpool. The remainder they must have in London."[3]

The counties each returned two members, irrespective of their size, and they were by no means so easy to influence as the majority of the boroughs. The latter were alike in that they mostly elected two representatives, but there the resemblance ceased. There was no sort of uniformity about either their constitution or the franchise of their electors. There were the scot and lot, and pot-walloper, boroughs where every adult male was an elector if he had control of a separate doorway to his dwelling, if he could provide his own sustenance, and if he had a fire-place at which to cook his meals. The *Oxford Dictionary*, it is interesting to note, defines "potwalloper" as one of the popular alterations of "potwaller", literally the boiler of a pot: "The term applied in some English boroughs, before the Reform Act of 1832, to a man qualified for a Parliamentary vote as a householder (i.e. tenant of a house or distinct part of one) as distinguished from one who was merely a member or inmate of a householder's family; the test of which was having a separate fire-place, on which his own pot was boiled or food cooked for himself and his family." The *Oxford Dictionary* goes on to say it was alleged that, to qualify them as voters, people who were not

---

[1] Rosebery, Earl of: *Chatham: His Early Life and Connections*, pp. 75–76.

[2] *cf.* Oldfield, T. H. B.: *The Representative History of Great Britain and Ireland*, Vol. II, pp. 88–90, and 236.

[3] *cf.* Petrie, Sir Charles: *The Life of George Canning*, p. 100.

householders used to boil pots in the open on improvised fire-places in the presence of witnesses.

Then there were the boroughs where the franchise was confined to the freemen, and all the Lancashire boroughs except Preston were of this type. The freedom could be acquired by right in various ways, such as inheritance, serving an apprenticeship, or marriage with a freeman's daughter, but it was always open to the Corporation to elect to the freedom of the borough an unlimited number of people, who were not necessarily resident within the municipal boundaries. In this way, if an election appeared likely to go against the candidates favoured by the Corporation it was possible to turn a minority into a majority at the last moment by a judicious creation of freemen.

"At the General Election of 1741, Mr. Gibbon (i.e. the father of the historian) and Mr. Delmé stood an expensive and successful contest at Southampton, against Mr. Dummer and Mr. Henley, afterwards Lord Chancellor and Earl of Northington. The Whig candidates had a majority of the resident voters; but the Corporation was firm in the Tory interest; a sudden creation of one hundred and seventy new freemen turned the scale; and a supply was readily obtained of respectable volunteers, who flocked from all parts of England to support the cause of their political friends."[1]

Some constituencies were called burgage-boroughs, for the franchise was attached to a certain holding or burgage. Residence was not essential, or, in many cases, possible. At Downton, in Wiltshire, one of the burgages was in the middle of a stream; at Droitwich the burgages were shares in a disused chalk-pit; while in one Sussex constituency six or eight of them were represented by black stones in the wall round a nobleman's park.[2] In another class were the boroughs where a close Corporation elected the members. The result of all this was ludicrous. Some of the boroughs hardly existed, save in name. The classic instance was Old Sarum, an area of about forty acres of ploughed land on which had once stood the old city of

[1] Gibbon, E.: *Autobiography.*
[2] *cf.* Veitch, G. S.: *The Genesis of Parliamentary Reform*, p. 6.

Salisbury, and which James I had wished to disfranchise. In 1776 it consisted of but a single house, whose occupants sold refreshments to visitors; sixteen years later even this had gone, and at election-time it was necessary to put up a tent to shelter the returning officer while he counted the votes of the seven burgage-holders. Thomas Mozley relates how in later years he met "a bright-looking old fellow, with a full rubicund face and a profusion of white hair", who had once been an elector of Old Sarum. He said he

"had returned two representatives to Parliament for forty years, all honest men and gentlemen, not the sort of men they were sending to Parliament in these days."[1]

Dunwich was largely under the sea; Bossiney, in the parish of Tintagel, had but a single voter after the disfranchisement of revenue officers; while Launceston had twenty electors, Hastings twenty-two, and Lyme Regis thirty-one.

A few of the notes made by that master of electoral strategy, John Robinson, will give an excellent idea how matters stood on the eve of the General Election of 1784, one of the most hotly contested of the century:

"*Middlesex*   . *Perhaps* the same gentleman. Mr. Byng certainly *against*. Mr. Wilkes's support of any government is very uncertain, because the safety of his situation depends on his watching as he calls it all administrations and having no apparent connection with any, but taking the side of all popular questions. Therefore he is classed as doubtful.

"*Oxfordshire*   . Most likely the same members. Lord Charles Spencer is now *con* as in office, but on a change would be *for*. Lord Wenman it is thought would also be favourable but as uncertain is classed doubtful.

"*Shoreham*   . This place is now very open, but yet government with management have considerable weight there notwithstanding it being so laid open. The two gentlemen who now represent this place are well inclined and rather attached to government:

[1] Mozley, T.: *Reminiscences*, Vol. II, p. 13.

with civility they may be made steady and with fairness may be classed very hopeful in either event.

"*Winchelsea*   . The Speaker and Mr. Nesbit. This borough is now, it is feared, in a bad state indeed, and scarce any good voters in it. It was on a compromise between government and Nesbit, and the Speaker was brought in at a very trifling expense and some annual payments. The revenue officers having been struck off leaves scarce a good voter, and besides that, this borough has been so much neglected for near two years past that it is scarce known in what situation it stands until it is again examined. However, as Nesbit is somewhat hampered and wishes to be with administration, it is thought with attention it may be got right again and made *pro*, though probably with some bustle and expense.

"*St. Mawes*   . This borough belongs to the two present members, who probably will represent it again, and Mr. Boscawen may be made steady.

"*Northallerton*   . Mr. Lascelles's and Mr. Pears's borough. Same members. Mr. Lascelles, it is thought, is hopeful now but in case of a change would steadily support.

"*Castle Rising*   . Lord Orford and Miss Howard, married to Mr. Bagot, now Mr. Howard. Is receiver general for London and Middlesex, and might be talked to."[1]

It is difficult to know which to admire the more, the wide political knowledge of Robinson or the felicity of his diction. In such a context phrases like "with civility they may be made steady", "good voters", "is hopeful", and "might be talked to" have a wealth of meaning.

Many years were still to elapse before there was any widespread demand for a change. Walpole had done his work only too well, and as Sir Samuel Romilly wrote to a friend, "The nation seems fallen into a deep sleep."[2] Even the news of

---

[1] *Parliamentary Papers of John Robinson, 1774–1784*, pp. 68–87.
[2] *Memoirs of Sir Samuel Romilly*, Vol. I, p. 141.

the surrender at Yorktown, which virtually ended the War of American Independence, hardly caused a ripple. Political stagnation was everywhere apparent, in the counties as well as in the boroughs. In Yorkshire there was not a single contested election from 1760 to 1800. In the seven general elections between the accession of George III and the end of the century, in which the fifty-two counties of England and Wales chose in the aggregate 644 members of the House of Commons, there were in all only fifty-seven unsuccessful candidates in these constituencies—that is to say, fewer than one in eleven of the members who sat for the counties of England and Wales in those years met with even nominal opposition.[1]

The anomalies of the electoral system in the eighteenth century should not be allowed to obscure the fact that it had certain compensating advantages, not least of which was that the rotten boroughs enabled young men of genius to make their way more rapidly than has been the case since the Reform Act of 1832. The two Pitts and Canning all began their Parliamentary career in this manner. The letters written by the younger Pitt and George Canning in identical circumstances throw light upon the position of many a young M.P. in those days:

"LINCOLN'S INN,
"Thursday Night, Nov. 1780.

"MY DEAR MOTHER,—I can now inform you that I have seen Sir James Lowther, who has repeated to me the offer he had before made, and in the handsomest manner. Judging from my father's principles he concludes that mine would be agreeable to his own, and on that ground—to me of all others the most agreeable—to bring me in. No kind of condition was mentioned, but that if ever our lines of conduct should become opposite, I should give him an opportunity of choosing another person. On such liberal terms I could certainly not hesitate to accept the proposal, than which nothing could be in any respect more agreeable.

[1] cf. Prof. Laprade in his Introduction to the *Parliamentary Papers of John Robinson*, *1774–1784*, p. x.

Appleby is the place I am to represent, and the election will be made (probably in a week or ten days) without my having any trouble, or even visiting my constituents. I shall be in time to be spectator and auditor *at least* of the important scene after the holidays. I would not defer confirming to you this intelligence, which I believe you will not be sorry to hear.

"I am, my dear Mother, etc.,
"W. PITT,"[1]

In July 1793 Canning wrote to a friend of his election for Newtown, Isle of Wight:

"The seat does not cost me one farthing nor put me under the smallest obligation to any one man, woman, or child, Mr. Pitt only excepted."[2]

Then, again, the House of Commons did manage to interpret the views of those who controlled the destinies of the country: its constituents may have been few in number, but then so was the governing class. Moreover, there were limits beyond which even the strongest of Prime Ministers dared not venture, and they were limits which no administration of more recent times would require to consider for a moment. Party allegiance sat lightly on the ordinary M.P., and votes had mostly to be obtained by cajolery or a bribe. Had Parliament sat for more than a fraction of the year, government in such circumstances would have been impossible, but autumn sessions were unknown. With all its faults, the system worked none too badly, and at least England avoided the fate of France.

George III strove hard to adapt it to his own ends, and with no inconsiderable success. By dint of an economy at court which amounted to definite parsimony he formed a Parliamentary group known as "the King's friends", and by 1780 the Whigs were so alarmed that they tabled a motion in the House of Commons to the effect that "the influence of the Crown has increased, is increasing, and ought to be diminished"; it was

---

[1] *cf.* Petrie, Sir Charles: *William Pitt*, pp. 17–18.
[2] *cf.* Petrie, Sir Charles: *The Life of George Canning*, p. 12.

carried, but only by eighteen votes, and within two months the Gordon Riots had made the position of the King stronger than ever. Nor is there the slightest evidence that the war against the American colonies was unpopular; there were some protests in high places, possibly for purposes of advertisement, but the ordinary citizen was in favour of hostilities. What really ruined the Royal scheme was the incompetent ministers by whom George surrounded himself. The King liked mediocrities, and it is not a little significant that the Prime Minister with whom he got on best was Addington, the most insignificant of those who held that office during his reign. The two Pitts, Canning, Fox, and a dozen other statesmen of genius could never be certain of their Royal master, who wanted clerks rather than ministers.

The personal characteristics of Lord North have been sufficiently indicated, but some account of his financial policy is necessary to explain his influence over contemporary politicians. He financed the American War by means of loans, which had the effect of putting considerable sums into the pockets of the bankers, but from which the nation derived little benefit. His custom was to arrange the price of issue with a few friends in the City, and then to allot the scrip well below that figure to his political supporters, who were thus able to sell at a handsome profit. In these circumstances it is not surprising that when he left office the National Debt amounted to £245,466,855, and if this figure should appear a mere trifle to a reader living in a democratic age, the latter must remember that it was only with the greatest difficulty the country could raise £25,000,000 in revenue, a figure below that raised by the Irish Free State to-day. This debt had to no inconsiderable extent been incurred by North's attempt to keep money cheap, but by 1781 the state of public credit was such that the Government had to allot £150 of stock in the three per cents, and £25 in the four per cents, for every £100 actually borrowed. Thus, a loan of £12,000,000 cost the nation £21,000,000, and interest had to be paid on £9,000,000 which had never been received.[1]

[1] cf. Petrie, Sir Charles: *William Pitt*, pp. 39–41.

For more than six of the most critical years of the War of American Independence the Secretary of State for the Colonies was Lord George Germain, who, as Lord George Sackville, had been found in the previous reign by a court martial "unfit to serve His Majesty in any military capacity whatever" for his behaviour at Minden. In 1777 Lord George showed that a change of name had made no difference to his capacity. The plan of campaign in America that year was for Burgoyne and Howe to join forces on the Hudson River, but the latter never received his instructions from England in the proper form, and so Burgoyne was compelled to lay down his arms at Saratoga. Howe would have received the instructions had Germain seen fit to forego a week-end at Knole in order to issue them personally.[1] His colleague at the Admiralty was the Earl of Sandwich, who was a curious combination of rake, hypocrite, and stickler for trifles. He had been one of the most prominent members of the second Hell Fire Club:

"he was the very man to whom Wilkes had thought fit to confide the bawdiest morsels of his *Essay on Woman*, the very man who had signalized his horror of that performance by having it filched from Wilkes's rooms and read aloud to the House of Lords, an action by which he had earned the nickname of Jemmy Twitcher."[2]

This last arose from the fact that *The Beggar's Opera* was being played at Covent Garden at the time, and the audience received with delight Macheath's words, "That Jemmy Twitcher should peach me I own surprised me." The incompetence of Sandwich as a minister was disclosed when he let the Toulon fleet across the Atlantic without informing the British admiral in American waters, and then neglected to ascertain the strength of the fleet at Brest. His next step was to attempt to place the blame on Keppel, but the latter's acquittal of the charges brought against him was received with an enthusiasm unequalled since that of the Seven Bishops. The mob, led by Fox and Lord Derby, beset the Admiralty,

[1] *cf.* Fitzmaurice, Lord Edmond: *Life of the Earl of Shelburne*, Vol. I, pp. 358–359.
[2] Hobhouse, C.: *Fox*, p. 111.

forced the gates, and broke the windows, while the First Lord
and his mistress, Miss Ray, escaped by the back to the Horse
Guards. This lady, who was young enough to be her lover's
daughter, had been an assistant in a milliner's shop in Tavistock
Street. Sandwich had her educated, and then took her to
Hinchingbrooke, where he compelled his wife to submit to her
presence. Two months later Miss Ray was shot dead at
Covent Garden Theatre by a clergyman whose advances she
had rejected, and at the ensuing trial the full story of her
relations with Sandwich was given to a curious world. Nevertheless, it saved the latter from a vote of censure on his
conduct at the Admiralty which the House of Commons,
always reluctant to hit a man when he is down, refused to pass.

Whatever may have been the merits or demerits of the
system by which it was recruited, and of some of the men by
whom it was worked, there can be no question but that the
reign of George III constituted the golden age of Parliament.
It may have been controlled for a time from above, but George
always endeavoured to achieve his ends through it rather
than against it, and only on very rare occasions was it subject
to pressure from below. No longer were its members fearful
of an uprising which should bring back the Stuarts, and so
reduce their importance, while the day was still distant when
the electorate began to regard an M.P. as a delegate to vote as
his constituents wished. Yet from time to time men or
situations arose foreshadowing the changes that were to come.
Chatham looked beyond Parliament to the country, and his
son's speeches in the House of Commons reached a far wider
public than that which heard them delivered; even so, it was
only on the occasion of an election, and that in a mere handful
of constituencies, that a statesman spoke outside Parliament.
Yet before George IV was dead Canning had inaugurated the
custom of addressing public meetings, and Westminster lost its
monopoly.

If it was relatively easy for a young man of promise to get
into the House of Commons, it was for many years very
difficult for him to attain high office once he had been elected.
The elder Pitt was thirty-eight when he first obtained office,

and it was not until ten years later that he entered the Cabinet. These facts, when compared with the meteoric rise to power of his son, attest at once the genius of the latter and the changes that were taking place as the century drew to its close.

"Now, if a man be a bold and popular speaker, both in Parliament and on the platform, but more especially on the platform, he leaps into the Cabinet at once; he disdains anything else. . . . But in the middle of the eighteenth century there was nothing of this. There was no such thing as platform speaking outside the religious movement. A man made himself prominent and formidable in Parliament, but that was a small part of the necessary qualifications for office. The Sovereign then exercised a control, not indeed absolute, but efficacious and material, on the selection of ministers. The great posts were mainly given to peers; while a peerage is now as regards office in the nature of an impediment, if not a disqualification. In those days an industrious duke, or even one like Grafton who was not industrious, could have almost what he chose. But most of the great potentates preferred to brood over affairs in company with hangers-on who brought them the news, or with their feudal members of parliament. Still they formed a vital element in the governments of that time. Pelham's administration at this very time contained five dukes: he himself was the only commoner in it, and he was a duke's brother. It was necessary to have a Chancellor of the Exchequer in the House of Commons, but all the other high offices could be held preferably by peers. The two Secretaries of State were both dukes. A brilliant commoner without family connection or great fortune was an efficient gladiator to be employed in the service of these princes, but he was not allowed to rise beyond a fixed line. The peers lived, as it were, in the steward's room, and the commoners in the servants' hall; in some parlour, high above all, sate the King."[1]

---

[1] Rosebery, Earl of: *Chatham: His Early Life and Connections*, pp. 263–264.

Had it not been for a few outstanding figures Parliament might well have become atrophied, and foremost among those who refused to allow it to go to sleep was Wilkes. He was one of those engaging rogues (there have been several in our own time) whom the British public takes to its heart, and for whom it never loses its affection in spite of their patent rascality. In early life he was a member of the Hell Fire Club. As has been seen, there was more than one organization of this name early in the century, but that which flourished in the fifties and sixties is probably the most notorious. It met at Medmenham Abbey, which belonged to Sir Francis Dashwood, who was for a time Chancellor of the Exchequer, and, in a repentant old age, built West Wycombe Church. The "Franciscans", as they called themselves, were twelve in number, with Dashwood as their Superior, and each bore the name of an apostle. Among the members, in addition to those already mentioned, were Churchill the poet and Bubb Dodington, a minor politician. The licence that prevailed at the meetings of the Hell Fire Club has doubtless been exaggerated, and the proceedings were probably marked by no more than ordinary obscenity, blasphemy, and inebriety. *Omne ignotum pro magnifico*, and these particular rakes, like their fellows down the ages, were by no means loath to give the outside world the impression that they were very depraved indeed. In any event, the subsequent careers of most of them were not particularly vicious. It was at Medmenham that Wilkes quarrelled with Sandwich, it is said, because the former introduced an ape at a stage of the proceedings when the latter was incapable of distinguishing it from the Devil, and so mistook it for His Satanic Majesty.[1] In revenge, Sandwich exposed Wilkes in the House of Lords. However that may be, Wilkes turned the tables with the most stinging repartee in history. Upon Sandwich on one occasion remarking to him so that others might hear, "'Pon my soul, Wilkes, I don't know whether you'll die upon the gallows or of the pox," Wilkes replied, "That depends, my lord, whether I first embrace your lordship's principles or your lordship's

---

[1] *cf.* Johnstone, C.: *Chrysal, or the Adventures of a Guinea,* for a contemporary account of this debauched fraternity; also Chancellor, E. B.: *Lives of the Rakes,* Vol. IV.

mistresses." Wilkes was one of the greatest wits in a witty age.
When George III was recovering from his insanity in 1788 the
Lord Chancellor Thurlow deserted once more to what he
believed to be the winning side, and spoke of the favours he had
received from the King: "When I forget them," he exclaimed,
"may God forget me." "Forget you," remarked Wilkes; "He
will see you damned first."

Nations, or circumstances, makes strange heroes, and there
have been few stranger than Wilkes. Neither his character
nor his parts entitled him to lead the country, and yet for
some years "Wilkes and Liberty" was a most popular cry. The
explanation is that ministers, working through the majority
they had obtained in Parliament, were endeavouring to
stifle all opposition to themselves. They relied upon the
backing of the Crown and the apathy of the country. Unfortunately for them there were still enough politically
minded people who were determined that the powers of the
old monarchy should not be exercised by the Cabinet, even if
it had the support of the new dynasty. The blunders of
ministers made Wilkes the unworthy symbol of this natural
resentment. In his paper *The North Briton* he, in 1763, made
a violent attack on the Government, and during the course of it
he mentioned the names of his opponents in full, instead of
merely using initials, as was the custom of the day. Proceedings
were thereupon taken against him by a general warrant (that
is to say, a warrant in which no individual names are mentioned), but the courts held that he was exempted from arrest
by his privilege as an M.P. Then ensued the episode of
Sandwich's attack on the *Essay on Woman,* which had never
been published, in the House of Lords, while the Commons
voted No. 45 of *The North Briton* to be a seditious libel, and
ordered it to be burnt by the common hangman. Wilkes
found it safer to withdraw to France; when he returned he was
elected for Middlesex, but the House of Commons would not
allow him to take his seat, and declared his defeated opponent
elected in his place. In the end the victory of Parliament
proved to be but Pyrrhic, for the nation showed clearly that it
agreed with Chatham:

"Tyranny is detestable in every shape; but in none so formidable as when it is assumed and exercised by a number of tyrants"[1]

Wilkes had one asset in that age of time-serving, his opposition was at least open, as Byron testified:

> A merry, cock-eyed, curious-looking sprite
>   Upon the instant started from the throng,
> Dress'd in a fashion now forgotten quite;
>   For all the fashions of the flesh stick long
> By people in the next world; where unite
>   All the costumes since Adam's, right or wrong,
> From Eve's fig-leaf down to the petticoat,
> Almost as scanty, of days less remote.

> The spirit look'd around upon the crowds
>   Assembled, and exclaim'd, "My friends of all
> The spheres, we shall catch cold amongst these clouds;
>   So let's to business: why this general call?
> If those are freeholders I see in shrouds,
>   And 'tis for an election that they bawl,
> Behold a candidate with unturn'd coat!
> Saint Peter, may I count upon your vote?"

> "Sir, replied Michael, "you mistake; these things
>   Are of a former life, and what we do
> Above is more august; to judge of kings
>   Is the tribunal met: so now you know."
> "Then I presume those gentlemen with wings,"
>   Said Wilkes, "are cherubs; and that soul below
> Looks much like George the Third, but to my mind
> A good deal older—Bless me: is he blind?"

> "He is what you behold him, and his doom
>   Depends upon his deeds," the Angel said;
> "If you have aught to arraign in him, the tomb
>   Gives licence to the humblest beggar's head
> To lift itself against the loftiest."—"Some,"
>   Said Wilkes, "don't wait to see them laid in lead,
> For such a liberty—and I, for one,
> Have told them what I thought beneath the sun."[2]

The preoccupation of George III with political matters, and

---

[1] cf. Green, W. D.: *William Pitt, Earl of Chatham*, pp. 312–318.
[2] *The Vision of Judgment.*

the economies imposed upon him as a result, had a disastrous effect on the Royal Family, and not least on the Prince of Wales. After a brief, but ardent, passion for Lady Sarah Lennox the King had married Charlotte of Mecklenburg-Strelitz, who, according to Burke, had one virtue, decorum, and one vice, avarice. George, the eldest son, was born at St. James's Palace in 1762.

"The Prince immediately experienced all the disadvantages of his station. Cut off from companions of his own age, he was subjected to a board of instructors and governors, of whom he adored Lord Holderness. The Queen had favoured to be among the number Dr. Dodd, who must have been proficient in handwriting at least, for he was afterwards hung for forgery. All that was possible to human programme was done. The erudite Dr. Markham and the scientific Cyril Jackson gave him that knowledge of Latin and Greek, without which no Georgian gentleman could consider himself complete. . . . So successful were their efforts considered by the Crown that Markham was made Archbishop of York and Jackson Dean of Christ Church."[1]

Such an education anticipated that of the future King Edward VII. The whole family was subjected to the strictest discipline of body as well as of mind, and the Duke of Sussex was actually flogged for asthma.

The King might, for a time, control his sons, but he had more difficulty with his brothers. For two generations the Guelphs had been content to marry German princesses, and even to import German mistresses, but, to quote Mr. Shane Leslie,

"with the brothers and sons of the third George there came a welcome change in taste. The Royal Dukes looked upon the daughters of Albion and beheld that they were fair".[2]

The Duke of Cumberland debauched the wife of Lord

---

[1] cf. Leslie, S.: *George the Fourth*, pp 18–19.   [2] *Op. cit.*, p. 29.

Grosvenor, and as a result had to pay that nobleman the sum
of £10,000 for criminal conversation. He then married Anne,
daughter of Lord Irnham, and widow of one Andrew Horton,
a lady as amorous as she was beautiful. The Duke of Gloucester
also took a widow for a bride in Lady Waldegrave, a bastard
daughter of Horace Walpole's brother.

"She has not a fault in her face and person, and the detail is
charming. A warm complexion tending to brown, fine
eyes, brown hair, fine teeth, and infinite wit and vivacity."[1]

However, the charms of these ladies made no impression upon
George, and the outcome of his brothers' marriages was the
Royal Marriage Act of 1772, by which no descendant of
George II under the age of twenty-six can enter into a valid
marriage without the Sovereign's consent; nor above that age,
should the monarch's consent be withheld, except by giving a
year's notice to the Privy Council. This had the effect of
making the Royal Family a class apart, and so strengthened
those foreign tendencies at Court which had been introduced
nearly sixty years before. The Royal Marriage Act brought
the King little peace. He ultimately became reconciled to the
Duke of Gloucester, but he refused to receive the Duchess,
and there was never a reconciliation with Cumberland and
his wife. As if this were not enough, his sister, Caroline, who
had married Christian VII of Denmark, was accused of
adultery with the Danish minister, Struensee, and imprisoned. In 1792, the sixth son of George III, the Duke of
Sussex, married Lady Augusta Murray, first in Rome, and
then, when the lady found herself pregnant, at St. George's,.
Hanover Square. As soon as the King discovered what had
taken place he had the marriage annulled by the Court of
Arches, and Sussex bowed to his father's will by giving up
Lady Augusta. In this way the morganatic union was
introduced into Great Britain, and the members of the Royal
Family officially allowed to have a different standard of morals
from the rest of the population.[2]

---

[1] Horace Walpole to Sir Horace Mann, April 11, 1759.
[2] cf. MacDonagh, M.: *The English King*, pp. 119-125.

Nevertheless, the King's other embarrassments were as nothing to the liability of the Prince of Wales. When the latter was sixteen he became acquainted with the beautiful and ardent Mary Robinson, better known as "Perdita" for her performance in *The Winter's Tale*, and for several years he enjoyed her expensive favours. As soon as he was eighteen, and had an establishment of his own, he set her up in Berkeley Square. Eventually she proved too costly even for him, and was paid off with a bond of £20,000 to be redeemed when he came of age. After that she passed into the keeping of Fox, and Lady Sarah Lennox is found writing,

"I hear Charles saunters about the streets, and brags that he has not taken a pen in hand since he was out of place. *Pour se désennuyer*, he lives with Mrs. Robinson, goes to Sadler's Wells with her, and is all day figuring away with her. I long to tell him he does it to show that he is superior to Alcibiades, for *his* courtesan forsook him when he was unfortunate, and Mrs. Robinson takes *him* up."[1]

When Selwyn heard of the liaison between Fox and Perdita, he observed, "Well, whom should the 'man of the people' live with but the woman of the people." Selwyn did not like Fox. Once when a malefactor called Charles Fox was hanged at Tyburn, someone asked Selwyn, who took a morbid delight in witnessing public executions, if he had been present. "No," was the reply. "I never attend rehearsals." It was not, however, the Prince's morals, but his extravagance, that constituted the real difficulty, and as the King himself was frugal to a degree, he found his son's weakness the less venial. George drank lemonade and played a quiet game of backgammon in the evening, and he had no sort of sympathy for a young man whose debts amounted to £160,000 by the time he was twenty-three. On more than one occasion Parliament had to come to the rescue, and the situation was not made any easier by the fact that the Prince patronized those who were opposed to his father's ministers.

The early years of the new King began, as has been said, an

---

[1] *cf.* Hobhouse, C.: *Fox*, pp. 153-154.

era of change. There can be little doubt that for the London poor conditions of life improved considerably in the reign of George III:

> ". . . The status of the poorer sort was improving. The average working man was becoming better educated, more self-respecting, and more respected. He is no longer supposed to belong to 'the vile and brutish part of mankind."[1]

In the country circumstances were very different, and as the century drew to its close the decay of rural England became the more marked. As Goldsmith wrote:

> Those healthfull sports that grac'd the peaceful scene,
> Lived in each look, and brighten'd all the green;
> These far departing seek a kinder shire,
> And rural mirth and manners are no more.

Or again:

> Ye friends to truth, ye statesmen who survey
> The rich man's wealth increase, the poor's decay;
> 'Tis yours to judge how wide the limits stand,
> Betwixt a splendid, and a happy land.

It was no poetic licence that prompted the poet to say this, but sober fact. Torrington had a wide knowledge of conditions in all parts of the country, and he was under no illusions as to what was taking place.

> "I shudder at the sight of the (noble as they are called) new county infirmaries, and parish work-houses, built with a grandeur, and loftiness, exceeding most other edifices. . . . Time was, when an abundant yeomanry, with cottage rights well maintained, could support the numerous poor; and, keeping up a true pride, did not suffer them to be physicked, fed, etc., at the parish charge; but, now, debauched, impoverished, and oppressed, they think only of the present day; and rather behold these parish edifices as an honourable, and comfortable retreat, than as places of shame, and mortification."[2]

[1] cf. George, M. D.: London Life in the XVIIIth Century, p. 318.
[2] The Torrington Diaries, Vol. I, p. 263.

A visit to Burford in 1785 prompted Torrington to deplore the decay of the midsummer eve revels in that town, when a painted dragon and a painted giant were carried through the streets to commemorate a Saxon victory in the neighbourhood.

"All such exhibitions are lost in the poverty and distress of the lower people; and a fair is now no more than a larger market. . . . The upper kind of people (even the young farmers) go to London to enjoy the play and the dance; nor will the latter condescend to the old merriment of the malt-house; their wish is to furnish harlotry for the London markets, which they regularly send off with the rest of their cattle."[1]

This decay of the countryside was the direct result of the policy of enclosures, which had been one of the consequences of the fall of the old popular monarchy.

"This process was tragically mismanaged, with the cruellest injustice to the poor. It was conducted by the larger landowners, with their hired lawyers, whose chances of future employment rested on the reputation they could win among landowning gentry. Some of the land came under more productive control, some was laid out in game preserves, and in ornamental parks whose beauty almost justifies the theft. The process was bitterly resisted by the Crown. Not till Charles had been twenty years in his grave did Parliament pass a General Enclosure Act, facilitating the passing of private bills. Not till the final collapse of monarchy under George III did the thing acquire its final swiftness and momentum. . . . The estates of the gentry were nicely 'rounded off'. Yeomen became tenant farmers, liable to rack-renting and eviction."[2]

Between 1760 and 1797 there were no less than 1,539 private Enclosure Acts. In many cases the commons were enclosed without adequate compensation to those who had the right of pasturage on them, and so were deprived of the means of keeping a cow or goose, or of cutting turf for fuel. Some

[1] *The Torrington Diaries*, Vol. I, p. 217.   [2] John, E.: *King Charles I*, pp. 68–69.

received no allotment because they could not prove their claims, while others sold their allotments, and so became mere tenants, to be turned out at the whim of their landlord.

"Nor could the small farmer either keep his place. . . . If his holding was unaffected by enclosure, the loss of domestic industries rendered him less able to pay his rent; if it was to be enclosed, he found himself with a diminished income at the very time when he most needed money; if he managed to keep his land for a while, he was ruined by some violent fluctuation in the price of corn. Sooner or later he sank into the labouring class."[1]

This was exactly what was intended. Well might that strong Tory, Lord Henry Bentinck, write a century and a half later,

"Our modern progress is in reality nothing but a process of recapture by the people of what was once their own."[2]

During the latter part of the eighteenth century there was a rapid increase in the population, though it is impossible to arrive at any exact figures. In 1760 the population of England and Wales was estimated at 6,479,700, while five years earlier that of Scotland was about 1,265,300. By 1800 the estimate for England and Wales was 9,187,176, and for Scotland 1,599,000. Agricultural wages in 1769–1770 varied from 8s. to 10s. a week in Surrey, to 5s. to 6s. in Wiltshire, and to 4s. 11d. in some districts of Lancashire. Bread made from rye or barley was still eaten in some parts of the country, but there was an increasing demand for that made from wheat. In 1769 it cost 2d. a pound near London, and 1½d. farther away from the capital. Meat was about 3d. or 4d. a pound at the same date. The difference between the rate of wages and the cost of living was met by the rights of commonage, and by domestic industries.

At first the poor resisted the encroachments of the rich, and Defoe cites an instance of this at Tring:

"There was an eminent contest here between Mr. Guy and the poor of the parish, about his enclosing part of the

1 *The Political History of England*, Vol. X, p. 275.   2 *Tory Democracy*, p. 5.

common to make him a park; Mr. Guy presuming upon his power, set up his poles, and took in a large parcel of open land, called Wiggington Common; the cottagers and farmers opposed it by their complaints a great while; but finding he went on with his work, and resolved to do it, they rose upon him, pulled down his banks, and forced up his poles, and carried away the wood, or set it on a heap and burnt it; and this they did several times, till he was obliged to desist; after some time he began again, offering to treat with the people, and to give them any equivalent for it; but that not being satisfactory, they mobbed him again. How they accommodated it at last, I know not; but I see that Mr. Gore (Guy's successor in the property) has a park, and a very good one but not large: I mention this as an instance of the popular claim in England; which we call right of commonage, which the poor take to be as much their property, as a rich man's land is his own."[1]

Guy was a prominent Whig, and had entertained William of Orange at Tring. Most unfortunately for the wretched people concerned, the enclosures were coincident with the decay not only of domestic spinning, but also of the other industries which had been carried on in the villages from time immemorial, for with the growth of the big estate came the practice of having farming implements, harness, and household utensils both made and mended in the towns rather than by local labour. In this way the peasantry, deprived at the same time of their ancient rights of commonage and of the possibility of adding to their incomes by carrying on some industry at home, became entirely dependent on agricultural wages at the very time when the latter were not sufficient to provide a livelihood. Consequently, they were either forced into the factories in the towns, or came on the rates. The England divided into two nations, described by Disraeli in *Sybil*, was *in posse* before George III had been long on the throne, and *in esse* before he died.

The distress caused by the Enclosure Acts was widespread. The villages of Wiston and Foston, in Leicestershire, before

[1] *A Tour Through England and Wales.*

enclosure each contained about thirty-five houses; in the former every house disappeared except that of the squire, while the latter was reduced to the parsonage and two herdsmen's cottages.[1] All over the country to-day, not least in the south-west, are to be witnessed the traces of this tragic revolution in shrunken hamlets and desolate lanes once bordered by the cottages of a proud and independent peasantry. The Rev. Richard Warner gives valuable evidence of this as a result of a walking-tour which he took in 1799. Near Cheddar he got into conversation with a friendly labourer.

" 'Ah, Sir,' said my new acquaintance, 'time was when these commons enabled the poor man to support his family, and bring up his children. Here he could turn out his cow and pony, feed his flock of geese, and keep his pig. But the enclosures have deprived him of these advantages. The labourer now has only his 14*d*. per day to depend upon, and that, Sir (God knows) is little enough to keep himself, his wife, and perhaps five or six children, when bread is 3*d*. per pound, and wheat 13*s*. per bushel. The consequence is, the parish must now assist him. Poor-rates increase to a terrible height. The farmer grumbles, and grows hard-hearted. The labourer, knowing that others must maintain his family, become careless, or idle, or a spendthrift, whilst his wife and children are obliged to struggle with want, or to apply to a surly overseer for a scanty allowance.' "

Mr. Warner gives it as his own opinion that the enclosures were a benefit to the landlord, the large farmer, and the clergy,

"but these advantages are purchased by so large a proportion of individual evil, that it becomes a question of morals as well as policy, a question as difficult as it is important, whether that system ought to be generally adopted".[2]

In November 1830 the wretched and starving labourers began to riot for a daily wage of half a crown, but in the course of the disturbances which ensued not a single person was killed

---

[1] *cf*. Howlett, J.: *Enquiry into the Influence which Enclosure has had on Population*, p. 10.
[2] Warner, R.: *A Walk Through some of the Western Counties of England*, pp. 49-52

by the rioters, or even seriously injured. The Whigs were by
then in office, and their vengeance was terrible. Nine men and
boys were hanged, of whom two were executed in the enforced
presence of a number of their friends, 400 were imprisoned,
and 457 were transported to Australia.[1] Meanwhile Macaulay
was searching the dictionary for epithets to describe the Whig
horror at the enormities of Jefferys. It is not suggested that
Whigs were the only landowners who enclosed the common
land, but it was the system established by them that made
enclosures so profitable to the rich. They were but one aspect
of that concentration of property in ever fewer hands which
had been the consequence of the victory of oligarchy over
monarchy.

[1] cf. Trevelyan, G. M.: *Lord Grey of the Reform Bill*, pp. 252–255

CHAPTER V

THE LULL BEFORE THE STORM

THE year 1784 definitely ushered in a new era which fore-shadowed the nineteenth century, and represented a break with the England of Tudor and Stuart times. As we have seen, a silent revolution had been at work for several decades, but it was only now that its effects were beginning to make themselves felt in every department of the national life. As so often in English history the change became personified in an individual, William Pitt, the greatest Prime Minister in the country's annals. Before, however, considering his career, and that of his rival, Charles James Fox, it is necessary to go back a little, and see what had been happening to bring the administration of North and the "King's friends" crashing to the ground.

The position of the ministry had been temporarily re-trieved by the skill of the monarch in turning the Gordon Riots to electoral advantage. This outbreak throws a strong light upon contemporary London, and upon the success that still attended any appeal to religious prejudice. It is also proof of the debased nature of very many of the inhabitants of the capital. The laws against Roman Catholics were still very stringent; as recently as 1767 a priest had been condemned to imprisonment for life, and actually served four years of his sentence, for exercising his office. The hatred felt by the ordinary Englishman towards Catholics was quite unreasoning and was largely the result of Whig propaganda against the Stuarts. Defoe bore testimony to this when he wrote that there were in London ten thousand stout fellows that would spend the last drop of their blood against Popery that do not know whether it be a man or a horse.[1] Nevertheless, a more tolerant attitude was beginning to be adopted, and in 1778

[1] *The Behaviour of Servants.*

Bill was introduced to enable Catholics who abjured the temporal jurisdiction of the Pope to purchase and inherit land, and to free priests from liability to imprisonment. This measure, which only affected England, was passed without a division. It was then proposed to extend the relief to Scotland, but there was such strong opposition in Edinburgh and Glasgow that the idea was abandoned. This encouraged the more extreme English Protestants to agitate for the repeal of the obnoxious measure, and an association was formed for the purpose, with the half-mad Lord George Gordon at his head.

The Gordon Riots may be said to have begun on June 2nd, 1780, when the scum of the capital, about 60,000 strong, led by Lord George, marched to Westminster to present to Parliament a petition for repeal. The House of Commons refused to give it immediate consideration, and so disorderly did the mob become that North called out the Life Guards to protect members, for there were no police worth the name at that time; a fact which should never be forgotten in any consideration of eighteenth-century politics. This proved effective so far as Parliament was concerned, but Lord Hillsborough, one of the Secretaries of State, wrote to the King in the early hours of the following morning that "returning home he observed a fire in Warwick Street, which proved to be made with the furniture of Count Haslang's (i.e. the Bavarian Minister's) chapel".[1] This was Warwick Street, Golden Square. The same fate attended the chapel of the Sardinian Legation, in Duke Street, Lincoln's Inn Fields. The next day was quieter, but on the 4th the criminal elements took the matter into their own hands, and an orgy of looting began. The notes received every few hours by the King from Lord Stormont, another Secretary of State, tell their own story:

"The information I have received gives me strong reason to believe that the same turbulent spirit still continues, and that further outrages may be attempted." "I remained at the office till near two this morning." "The passage to the Houses of Parliament is free, but outrages are begun in the

[1] *The Correspondence of King George the Third from 1760 to December, 1783*, edited by the Hon. Sir John Fortescue, Vol. V, pp. 69–70.

West End of the Town. They have recently attacked Lord Petre's house, to the protection of which a body of Guards is gone." "The outrages continue; the house of Mr. Hyde, a Justice of the Peace who has acted with steadiness in the discharge of his duty, is demolished."[1]

The King's views were not in doubt, for on the 6th he wrote to the Prime Minister,

"Lord North cannot be much surprised at my not thinking the House of Commons have this day advanced so far in the present business as the exigency of the times required; the allowing Lord George Gordon, the avowed head of the tumult, to be at large certainly encourages the continuation of it, to which is to be added the great supineness of the civil magistrates; and I fear without more vigour that this will not subside; indeed unless exemplary punishment is procured it will remain a lasting disgrace, and will be a precedent for future commotions."[2]

It was not long before it became obvious that it was useless to do nothing more than send detachments of the Guards to protect the houses of individuals. The magistrates were too terrified to act, and the other local authorities were quite incompetent. Wilkes was an honourable exception, and displayed both firmness and courage. Meanwhile the mob proceeded from one excess to another, and London to the east of Charing Cross was at its mercy. Lord Mansfield's house at Ken Wood was only saved by the presence of a squadron of Light Horse (his London residence in Bloomsbury Square was sacked), while Newgate was partly burnt, and the prison broken open. By the night of the 7th there were no less than thirty-six fires burning in different parts of the capital. The King's Bench and Fleet prisons, the new Bridewell, and the lower end of Holborn were in flames, and two distilleries were in process of being sacked: the liquor obtained from the latter further infuriated the crowd, a great many of whom

---

[1] *The Correspondence of King George the Third from 1760 to December, 1783*, edited by the Hon. Sir John Fortesque, Vol. V, pp. 70-72.
[2] *ibid.*, edited by W. B. Donne, Vol. II, p. 324.

English Liberty freed from the Fear of General Warrants
and the Seizure of Papers, by the Magnanimity of
ONE MAN.

John Wilkes Esq.r drawn from the Life by W.H.

JOHN WILKES, AS SEEN BY HIS FRIENDS AND BY HIS ENEMIES

The portrait on the left is from a broadsheet entitled "English Liberty Established", printed in London in 1768. That on the right is by Hogarth, whom Wilkes had lampooned in the *North Briton*.

CHARLES JAMES FOX AS A YOUTH, WITH LADY SARAH
BUNBURY AND LADY SUSAN FOX-STRANGEWAYS

After the original by Reynolds in Holland House. Lady Susan Fox-
Strangeways, the figure holding a bird, was Fox's cousin, and subsequently
made a notorious *mésalliance* with an actor named O'Brien. Lady Susan
Bunbury (*née* Lennox) was Fox's aunt.

were, in a state of complete inebriety, killed in the flames or by the falling buildings. The only success obtained by the forces of law and order was at the Bank and the Pay Office, where the rioters were repulsed with heavy loss by the soldiers on guard. The Cabinet did nothing to suppress the disturbances, and its incapacity is revealed by the following minute sent to the King:

> "The disorders increasing to such a degree, and the outrages committed are of such a nature that it is the humble but unanimous opinion of Your Majesty's servants underwritten that where the civil magistrate declines to direct the soldiery to act with effect, other methods must be taken to preserve the peace, and protect the lives and properties of Your Majesty's subjects.
>
> "It is also humbly submitted to Your Majesty that in this dangerous crisis it appears to us absolutely necessary that during the continuance of these disorders the whole military force should be under one command. The manner of doing this is submitted to Your Majesty's wisdom, but our humble opinion is that the appointment should be made immediately.

> Geo. Germain.   Bathurst P.
> North.   Stormont.   Dartmouth C.P.S.
> Amherst.   Hillsborough."[1]

The ministers were as helpless before Lord George Gordon as before George Washington.

This memorandum convinced the King that he must act, and to his credit he did not shirk his duty. As Charles II had intervened personally to save London from the worst effects of the Great Fire,[2] so George III took action to suppress the Gordon Riots. He summoned a special meeting of the Privy Council on the morning of June 7th; when he found that its members hesitated to recommend the employment of troops, he said that if they would not give him advice he would act

---

[1] *The Correspondence of King George the Third from 1760 to December, 1783*, edited by the Hon. Sir John Fortescue, Vol. V, p. 74.
[2] *cf.* Bryant, A.: *King Charles II*, p. 184.

without it, and that he could answer for one magistrate who would do his duty. He then asked the Attorney-General, Wedderburn, later Lord Loughborough, to state the law in the matter. Wedderburn replied that the King in council could order soldiers to suppress a riot without the authority of a magistrate. George thereupon instructed the military to act, and within forty-eight hours the riots were at an end. Seventy-two houses and four jails had been destroyed, while the lowest estimate of the casualties was 285 rioters killed and 173 wounded. At the trials which followed in due course 139 prisoners appeared, of whom 59 were condemned to death, but only 21 were actually executed. Lord George Gordon himself was acquitted, but seven years later he was imprisoned for a libel, and died in Newgate after having become a Jew.

It is not easy to distinguish between the various factors that produced the outbreak.

"Though the excesses of the Gordon Riots are to be explained by the effects of drink and a swamping of the forces of order by the inhabitants of the dangerous districts in London who were always ready to pillage, a strong anti-Catholic spirit undoubtedly played its part. Was this partly due to that prejudice against the Irish of which there are so many indications?"[1]

In other words, was the aggressive Protestantism merely the excuse, and economic competition the real cause, of the disturbances? There had been anti-Irish outbreaks earlier in the century. There was a violent outburst in Spitalfields in 1736, on the ground that the Irish were working at specially low rates; in 1740 an attack was made by the Irish on the butchers of Clare Market, because one of the latter had burnt a "Paddy" in effigy on St. Patrick's Day; and in 1763 there was a pitched battle between a party of sailors and a number of chairmen in Covent Garden. The chairmen had always been an unruly element in the population of London, and once at least there had been a proposal to use them for political ends. Philip Thicknesse writes in his *Memoirs:*

[1] George, M. D.: *London Life in the XVIIIth Century*, pp. 118–119.

THE LULL BEFORE THE STORM

"Mr. Segrave, an Irish officer with only one arm, formerly well known at the Café de Condé, at Paris, assured me that he had been with the Prince (i.e. Charles Edward) in England between the years 1745 and 1756, and that they had laid a plan of seizing the person of the King, as he returned from the play, by a body of Irish chairmen, who were to knock the servants from behind his coach, extinguish the lights, and create a confusion while a party carried the King to the water-side, and hurried him away to France. . . . He also told me that they had more than fifteen hundred chairmen, or that class of people, who were to assemble opposite the Duke of Newcastle's house in Lincoln's Inn Fields the instant they heard any particular news relative to the Pretender."[1]

The Gordon Riots rallied to the side of the Government all who had anything to lose, and, as has been shown, the King's perspicacity in going to the country at once won for the ministers a majority at the ensuing general election. Had the Cabinet displayed even ordinary competence in the conduct of the war against the United States it might have remained in office indefinitely, for popular apathy was unbroken, but that was hardly to be expected from a ministry which contained Germain and Sandwich. In the last week of November 1781 the news arrived of the capitulation of Lord Cornwallis at Yorktown, and the Opposition redoubled its attack. Fox and Burke threatened the impeachment of Germain and Sandwich, while Pitt demanded a clear statement of the Government's policy in face of this disaster, and declared himself in favour of an immediate termination of hostilities. By this time, too, Great Britain was at war not only with the United States, but also with France, Spain, and Holland, and it was only the blunders of her enemies that had prevented actual invasion. For a few weeks the ministry, in spite of falling majorities, struggled on, but in the middle of March 1782 North resigned.

To contemporaries it appeared as if the monarch could not fail to be himself humiliated by the fall of a minister who was

---

[1] cf. Petrie, Sir Charles: *The Jacobite Movement*, p. 240.

so essentially his own creature, but those who took this view overlooked the shrewdness of George III where political tactics were concerned. After long negotiations an administration was formed of men with so little in common as the Marquess of Rockingham, who led the armies of the declining Whig oligarchy, Lord Shelburne, the old comrade-in-arms of Chatham, and Charles James Fox. This meant that the differences between ministers were so considerable that the King was able to play one member of the Cabinet off against another. The Government only lasted four months, for it broke up on the death of the Prime Minister in July, but in the interval it gave Home Rule to Ireland and abolished a number of sinecures at home. The Whigs would have liked to see the Duke of Portland succeed Rockingham, but the King would not hear of it: so Shelburne became Prime Minister, with Pitt, aged twenty-three, as Chancellor of the Exchequer.

For the next two decades Pitt and Fox faced one another across the Parliamentary stage, and their greatness is shown by the fact that Burke, Sheridan, and Windham, who would have been in the first flight in any other age, were definitely on a lower plane when compared with them. The Englishman has a rooted dislike of principles in the abstract, and it is only when they become personified in an individual that he grows enthusiastic about them. The long duel between Pitt and Fox in the eighteenth century, like that between Disraeli and Gladstone in its successor, raised the prestige of Parliament by letting the country see that the problems in which it was interested were being discussed at Westminster. In the days of Walpole such had not been the case, for the division in all classes on the dynastic question was certainly not reflected in the Houses of Parliament with their overwhelming Hanoverian majorities. Furthermore, the protagonists fought as if they meant it, and not as if the fight were prearranged. In character as well as in policy, the two men were as the poles asunder, and the twenty years of their rivalry marked the apogee of Parliament in Great Britain: for the first, and possibly the last, time it was the mirror of that part of the nation which was articulate.

William Pitt was the second son of the great Chatham, and had been born in 1759, that *annus mirabilis* in which Canada was won, and Hawke destroyed the French fleet in Quiberon Bay. His mother was a Grenville, and it was from that side of the family he inherited the aloofness upon which contemporaries placed such stress. From the beginning he was his father's favourite, and Chatham described the boy as "the hope and comfort of my life". That his son should enter public life at the earliest possible moment was Chatham's aim, and young William was brought up with that end in view. The father had been at Eton, but he would not send his son there, for he had

> "scarce observed a boy who was not cowed for life at Eton; a public school might suit a boy of a turbulent, forward disposition, but would not do where there was any gentleness".[1]

Pitt's earlier years were spent at Hayes, in Kent, where he had been born, and at Burton Pynsent, near Taunton, where Chatham had a property which had been given to him by an admirer. In due course he went up to Pembroke Hall (now College), Cambridge. One weakness of Chatham's system was that although his son proved everything that a fond parent could wish, he was brought on too quickly. Ill-health, also, prevented him from mixing with his fellows, and all this, added to a naturally reserved nature, proved a great handicap to him in the leadership of men. In 1778 the young undergraduate was a prominent figure in one of the most dramatic scenes in English history. On April 6th of that year the Duke of Richmond tabled a motion for the recognition of American independence, and Chatham made what was to be his last appearance in the House of Lords. He looked what he was, a dying man. He was dressed in black, his body was swathed in flannel, and he leant upon crutches, while his sons William and James guided him to his place. His words were as memorable as the occasion:

> "I rejoice that the grave has not closed upon me; that I

---

[1] Fitzmaurice, Lord E.: *Life of the Earl of Shelburne*, Vol. I, p. 72.

am still alive to lift up my voice against the dismemberment of this ancient and most noble monarchy. . . . My Lords, His Majesty succeeded to an empire as great in extent as its reputation was unsullied. Shall we tarnish the lustre of this nation by an ignominious surrender of its rights and fairest possessions? Shall this great kingdom now fall prostrate before the House of Bourbon? Surely, my Lords, this nation is no longer what it was! Shall a people that fifteen years ago was the terror of the world now stoop so low as to tell its ancient inveterate enemy, Take all we have, only give us peace? It is impossible.

"In God's name, if it is absolutely necessary to declare either for peace or war, and the former cannot be preserved with honour, why is not the latter commenced without hesitation? I am not, I confess, well informed of the resources of this kingdom; but I trust it has still sufficient to maintain its just rights though I know them not. But, my Lords, any state is better than despair. Let us at least make an effort; and if we must fall, let us fall like men."

When Chatham began to speak the Peers had some difficulty in catching his words, but his voice soon regained its old resonant tone. The effort, however, was too much for him, for when, after a brief reply by the Duke of Richmond, he rose again, it was to fall in a faint. Five weeks later he was dead, and it is recorded that during these last days he bade his son read to him from the *Iliad* the verses describing the burial of Hector and the sorrow of Troy.[1] He was buried in Westminster Abbey, and William was the chief mourner in the absence of his elder brother, the new Earl of Chatham, on active service. George III, head of the dynasty which the dead man had served so faithfully and so long, was unrepresented at the funeral.

Chatham's death left Pitt a poor man, with an income of but £250 a year, and he took chambers in Lincoln's Inn with the intention of practising at the Bar. He was there during the Gordon Riots, and at an entertainment to the officers of the battalion that had been quartered in the Inn for its defence

---

[1] *cf.* Green, W. D.; *William Pitt, Earl of Chatham*, pp. 364–365.

he crossed swords with Edward Gibbon. The latter was a brilliant talker, but expected to be treated with a great deal of deference.

"Judge then of his astonishment, when, after one of his best anecdotes, which touched on 'the fashionable levities of political doctrine then prevalent', a deep but clear voice was heard from the far end of the table calmly but civilly impugning the correctness of the story and the propriety of its political connexion. The applause ceased at once, and Gibbon turned his gaze petulantly on the slim youth who had dared to challenge his unquestioned supremacy, and sat there quietly eating grapes. As the interruption had been hailed with too much approval to be ignored or dismissed with a frown, he endeavoured to crush the youth by heavy artillery. A spirited fire came in return, and a sharp duel of wits began, which the company followed with the keenest interest. Finally the skill and vigour of the attack drove the historian from one position after another and left him defenceless; whereupon he left the room in high dudgeon."[1]

Gibbon, for all his erudition, was a good deal of an old maid. He suffered for years from an enormous hydrocele, which, given the tight breeches of the period, must have been obvious to all his friends: yet he is found writing to Lord Sheffield:

"Have you never observed, through my inexpressibles, a large prominency *circa genitalia*, which, as it was not very painful and very little troublesome, I had strangely neglected for many years."[2]

It is not surprising that such a man should resent the attitude of the youthful Pitt. When one or two of those present endeavoured to persuade Gibbon to return, the historian replied:

"By no means: that young gentleman is, I have no doubt, extremely ingenious and agreeable, but I must acknowledge

[1] Rose, J. H.: *The Life of William Pitt*, Vol. I, pp. 72–73.
[2] *cf.* MacLaurin, C.: *De Mortuis*, pp. 180–190.

that his style of conversation is not exactly what I am accustomed to, so you must positively excuse me."[1]

Gibbon was himself in Parliament from 1774 to 1783, and voted obediently as directed by Lord North.

"I took my seat at the beginning of the memorable contest between Great Britain and America, and supported with many a sincere and silent vote, the rights, though not, perhaps, the interest, of the mother country."[2]

In 1778, however, he gave his vote against the Government on a motion by Fox against sending any more regular troops to America, and declared that the Prime Minister, whom he had hitherto consistently supported, was undeserving of "pardon for the past, applause for the present, or confidence for the future". This act of rebellion gave him, as was the intention, a price, and he was brought to heel once more by being appointed a Lord Commissioner of Trade and Plantations at a salary of £800 a year.

"It must be allowed that our duty was not intolerably severe, and that I enjoyed many days and weeks of repose, without being called away from my library to the office. My acceptance of a place provoked some of the leaders of the Opposition, with whom I had lived in habits of intimacy."[3]

As Fox put it:

> King George, in a fright
> Lest Gibbon should write
>   The story of Britain's disgrace,
> Thought no way so sure
> His pen to secure
>   As to give the historian a place.

Indeed, it is difficult to regard Gibbon's political career with any sympathy. He was as timid a politician as he had been a lover, when his father forbade his marriage to Mlle. Curchod, later Mme. Necker.

---

[1] *Bland Burges Papers*, pp. 60–61.   [2] *Autobiography*.   [3] *ibid.*

"After a painful struggle I yielded to my fate: I sighed as a lover, I obeyed as a son."[1]

The nature and education of Fox were very different from those of his opponent. If the upright character of Pitt caused most men to respect him, the personal charm of his rival made them love him. Fox did and was everything of which the English middle-class, then rapidly growing in power, disapproved. It was said of him:

"Fox had three passions: women, play, and politics. Yet he never formed a creditable connection with a woman; he squandered all his means at the gaming-table; and, except for eleven months, he was invariably in opposition."[2]

He was the son of Henry Fox, created Lord Holland, who made more money out of politics than any of his contemporaries, which was no mean feat. While Chatham was instilling virtue into his son, Holland was doing the opposite, and at the age of fourteen young Fox was taken to Spa, where he was given five guineas a night to initiate him as a gamester. The lesson was not lost upon him, and in later life he is known to have lost £12,000 at one sitting, followed by further sums of £12,000 and £11,000 when he tried to win it back. He was perpetually being dunned by bailiffs and moneylenders, and he was sold up, but he never ceased to retain his hold upon the affections of the House of Commons, or upon the votes of the electorate of Westminster. The Abbé de Lageard once expressed surprise to Pitt that a country where there was such a parade of virtue as in England should tolerate a statesman of the private life of Fox:

"Ah!" was the reply, "you have not been under the wand of the magician."[3]

Burke on one occasion advised Fox, "Lay your foundations deep in public opinion," but that was precisely what the latter was quite incapable of doing. He was always prepared to sacrifice strategy to tactics, with the result that for a fleeting

---

[1] *Autobiography.*   [2] Quoted by Hobhouse, C.: *Fox*, pp. 185–186.
[3] *Life of William Wilberforce* (by his sons), Vol. I, p. 38.

victory in the House of Commons he would risk his position in the country. The classic instance was when he coalesced with North, whom he had attacked most vehemently over a period of years; this disregard for the ordinary conventions of party warfare was too much for the electorate, and Fox was, save for a few months, out of office for the rest of his life. Although he was ten years older than Pitt, the latter was his senior in political wisdom. Fox never looked beyond the walls of the House of Commons or the Subscription Room at Brooks's, demagogue though he was on occasion. He was essentially a House of Commons man, as Johnson once testified:

> "Fox never talks in private company; not from any deter-
> mination not to talk, but because he has not the first motion.
> A man who is used to the applause of the House of Commons,
> has no wish for that of a private company. A man accus-
> tomed to throw for a thousand pounds, if set down to
> throw for sixpence, would not be at the pains to count his
> dice. Burke's talk is the ebullition of his mind; he does not
> talk from a desire of distinction, but because his mind is
> full."[1]

Pitt had no weakness save a taste for port, and he always kept his eyes fixed on the middle-class. When he had made his maiden speech Fox rushed up to congratulate him, and an old member observed that he hoped to live to see them fighting one another as their fathers had done. "I have no doubt," said Pitt, "you hope to attain the age of Methuselah." On the nomination of Fox he was elected to Brooks's, but the old member had not long to wait all the same.

The first task of the Shelburne administration was to make peace, even though that necessitated the recognition of the independence of the United States. Britain had been very badly beaten, and her finances were in the utmost confusion: only the fact that she did not appreciate the seriousness of her position concealed it from the foreigner, and so enabled her to negotiate for terms far more favourable than those which had been granted to defeated France twenty years before. Still,

---

[1] Boswell, J.: *Life of Samuel Johnson.*

Pitt realized that the ministry required strengthening, and he obtained the none too enthusiastic consent of the King and Shelburne to approach Fox. The interview was memorable, for it marked the parting of the ways. Fox asked if it was proposed that Shelburne should remain Prime Minister, and, on receiving a reply in the affirmative, remarked that it was impossible for him to come into any Cabinet in these circumstances. On this Pitt broke off the conversation with the words, "Then we need discuss the matter no further. I did not come here to betray Lord Shelburne." As Mr. Hobhouse very truly observes:

"It was the first recorded occasion on which Fox was snubbed."[1]

At this point the Whig leader made the great mistake of his career. Instead of joining Pitt, with whom he had no differences of any importance, he formed a coalition with North. It proved to be an act of political suicide. The ostensible cause of the alliance was dissatisfaction with the proposed terms of peace, but it was soon discovered that the new administration was unable to obtain any better terms than Shelburne. There have been few British governments more loathed than this one, and when Disraeli declared that the idea of a coalition was repugnant to the nation it was of the Fox-North combination he was thinking. Even the apathy of the late eighteenth-century electorate was to no inconsiderable extent dispelled by this union of lifelong enemies for the sake of office, and the King showed his disapproval by refusing to confer any honours: an attitude which was a greater source of weakness to ministers than the hostility of the electors. Indeed, George recovered most of his lost popularity when it became known that he was in opposition. Pitt sought to shame the administration by bringing forward a motion for Parliamentary Reform, with which many of the ministers had previously been in agreement, but he was beaten by a large majority. Never before or since has such a government of avowed place-hunters held office in this country, and what

---

[1] *Fox*, p. 155; *cf.* also Russell, Lord John (later Earl): *Memorials and Correspondence of C. J. Fox*, Vol. II, p. 33.

brought it down in the end was the attempt to perpetrate a piece of jobbery which would have been unparalleled even in French and American annals, namely, the measure known as Fox's India Bill.

It would be difficult to exaggerate the importance of India in British history during the past two centuries, but it is only on very rare occasions that the man-in-the-street has taken any interest in Indian matters. It was generally agreed that the East India Company stood in need of reform. Ten years before, in 1773, a Regulating Act had been passed which admitted the right of the British Government to supervise the Company's actions, but it settled nothing, and the financial position had become desperate. The commercial revenue of the Company was quite unequal to the administration of a continent, and the maintenance of a standing army of 60,000 men. Every kind of extortion was accordingly practised in order to raise the necessary funds, but the Company continued to stagger along on the verge of bankruptcy while its servants were becoming millionaires. The Company's stock was worth nothing as a security, but it had enormous value as a passport to a job. Burke might well ask what the nominal dividend mattered to a man whose son, before he had been two months in Bengal, could sell the grant of a single contract for £40,000. A post with a salary of £300 a year was worth anything up to £50,000 annually. Yet it would be unfair to place all the blame at the doors of the Company's servants. In 1773 Warren Hastings wrote to the Directors:

"Whatever may have been the conduct of individuals or even of the collective members of your former administrations, the blame is not so much imputable to them as to the want of a principle of government adequate to its substance, and a coercive power to enforce it."[1]

The men who took up positions in India at that time found themselves exposed to the greatest temptation. The younger of them had gone out there to get rich in the shortest possible time, while the elder,

[1] Gleig, G. R.: *Memoirs of the Life of the Right Hon. Warren Hastings*, Vol. I, p. 368.

"gentlemen, who in the ordinary course of nature would have been content to retire as successful traders and end their days in respectable obscurity, were tempted to sell their souls for gain, and so condemned to leave for the scorn of posterity names tarnished by the stain of ignoble greed. The temptation was great, and we must not be surprised that it was too much for the virtue of most of the persons exposed to its snares."[1]

There was no public opinion in India to check abuses, while the native administrations with which the officials of the Company came into contact were corrupt in the extreme. Treachery and murder were the normal instruments of policy:

"Everybody and everything was on sale. Those disagreeable facts must be realized before judgments of unrelenting severity are passed on the failings of the foreigners who had to work in such an atmosphere, and to deal with authorities who never actually were what they professed to be."[2]

When they returned home they were in derision called "nabobs", and were not regarded with any great affection by the mass of their fellow-countrymen. They were the *nouveaux riches* of the late eighteenth century, thus forming the link between those who had filled their pockets on the fall of the old monarchy, and those who were about to do so out of the Industrial Revolution.

Fox and North endeavoured to put the affairs of India in order by taking the government of that country entirely out of the hands of the Company, which in future was to confine its activities to commerce alone. There was a good deal to be said for reform along these lines, but the Bill further provided for seven commissioners in London in whom all Indian patronage, amounting to about £300,000 a year, was to be vested; when the names of these seven were announced it was found that they were all violent partisans of the ministry. This set the seal upon the unpopularity of the Government. James Sayer published a cartoon entitled "Carlo Khan's

[1] Smith, V. A.: *The Oxford History of India*, p. 497.   [2] *ibid.*, p. 498.

Triumphal Entry into Leadenhall Street", representing Fox, in Oriental dress, seated on an elephant with the face of North, and arriving at India House; beside him walks Burke as his trumpeter, while overhead is a crow, the symbol of approaching doom. This cartoon focused public opinion on the weak spot in the Bill.[1] The proposals justified Johnson's observation:

> "Fox is a most extraordinary man; here is a man who has divided the kingdom with Caesar; so that it was a doubt whether the nation should be ruled by the sceptre of George the Third, or the tongue of Fox."[2]

The King had no doubt by whom it should be ruled, and although he could not prevent the passage of the India Bill through the Commons he had sufficient influence to secure its rejection by the Lords. He then dismissed the ministry in the letter already quoted, and on December 19th, 1783, Pitt, not yet twenty-five, became Prime Minister.

The new administration was in a minority in the House of Commons, but Pitt refused to dissolve until he could take the tide of public opinion, which was strongly in his favour, at the flood. The consequence was an interval of as bitter party strife as the country has ever known, though of course only a limited number of people were affected. One day the Prime Minister was returning from a banquet in the City, and as his carriage was going up St. James's Street escorted by an enthusiastic crowd it was attacked outside Brooks's by a party of club servants and chairmen. Pitt escaped into White's, but much damage was done to the carriage. Fox was accused of having planned the outrage, but he had an alibi: "I was in bed with Mrs. Armistead, who is ready to substantiate the fact on oath." Pitt, to his credit, did not even resign from Brooks's. It was in this spirit of violence that the general election was fought in the spring, and the supporters of Fox and North were routed. The most strenuous contest was in Westminster, where Fox was one of the candidates. Admiral Lord Hood was

---

[1] cf. Wright, T.: *England under the House of Hanover*, Vol. II, p. 83.
[2] Boswell, J.: *Life of Samuel Johnson*.

certain of the first seat, and the real fight was between the Whig leader and one Sir Cecil Wray for the second. The poll was open for six weeks, and at the end of a fortnight Wray was 300 votes ahead. At this point the Duchess of Devonshire entered the arena. She dressed herself from head to foot in Fox's colours, buff and blue, and wore a hat covered with foxes' tails.

"Where arguments failed she descended to entreaties: where entreaties failed she resorted to osculation."[1]

Finally Fox won by a majority of 235, but there was a scrutiny before he could take his seat. The Prince of Wales showed his sense of the responsibilities of his position by giving a party at Carlton House to celebrate the event at the very hour, and in full view of the Royal procession down the Mall at the opening of Parliament.

The general election of 1784, and the victory of Pitt, meant more than the defeat of the Fox-North combination, for it marked the end of the King's attempt to apply the theories of Bolingbroke, and of the chaos which had resulted from this attempt. Henceforth, George was ready to support his Prime Minister, so long as the latter did not go too fast in the matter of reform, while the era of the subordination of the national interests to the caprices of Whig magnates was ended. The Prime Minister might be little more than a boy, and most of his colleagues unknown, but they represented a break with all that had gone before, and that in itself was a recommendation to the middle-class. Fox might commend himself to the electors of Westminster, but on both public and private grounds he was anathema in the provinces. The Victorian era was in sight. Pitt was reaping the reward of his own cultivation of, and his rival's contempt for, public opinion. Just before the election he had given proof of the new spirit which was to animate his seventeen years' administration. The Clerkship of the Pells, a sinecure worth £3,000 a year, fell vacant, and Pitt persuaded Colonel Barré, a prominent Whig, to accept it in place of the annual pension of £3,200 which a

---

[1] Hobhouse, C.: *Fox*, p. 194.

previous ministry had conferred upon him. The Prime
Minister was a poor man, and it would only have been in
accordance with precedent had he taken the money for himself, but he preferred to save the country the amount of
Barré's pension. That a minister should act in this way, and
that the country should applaud him for so doing, were
significant signs that times had changed.

The long Premiership of Pitt, and the remarkable manner in
which he impressed his personality both upon contemporaries
and posterity, must not be allowed to obscure the fact that he
was very far from being a dictator, or even from exercising the
power of a twentieth-century Prime Minister. He had no
party machine working for him in the constituencies, and no
whips to enforce obedience in the House of Commons. As late
as 1788 his own personal supporters were said not to number
more than 52, though there voted with them some 185 other
members who could be relied on to follow any minister who
was favourably regarded by the King. Fox had some 150 votes
at his regular command in the House of Commons, but the
rest of the members were independent of Government and
Opposition alike, though many of them had to take their orders
from the borough-owners. In these circumstances it was out
of the question to make every important vote one of confidence,
and measures were introduced by private members which
would now emanate from the Treasury Bench alone. The
executive was dependent upon the legislative in fact as well as
in theory. On the other hand, ministers could be defeated
without their resignation being expected. Pitt had to face a
hostile majority more than once in the Parliament that had
been elected to support him, but that meant nothing more
than a warning not to go fast. Furthermore, members of the
same Cabinet often took opposite sides on issues upon which
agreement would now be considered essential. Catholic
Emancipation, for example, was almost to the end regarded as
an "open" question, and Canning and Eldon could be respectively Foreign Secretary and Lord Chancellor although
they voted against one another in any division on the subject
If the House of Commons was less regimented than in more

recent times it was also much less well-behaved. Members were in the habit of cracking nuts, eating oranges, lying on the benches, and going up into the galleries for a doze. On one occasion Lord North, when Prime Minister, was taxed by a particularly dull speaker with being asleep, and replied that he wished to heaven he was. Once when Burke rose to speak with a packet of papers in his hand, a member exclaimed:

"I do hope the honourable gentleman does not mean to read that large bundle of papers, and bore us with a long speech into the bargain."[1]

Nor was this boredom remarkable when one remembers the length at which members spoke. At the same time emotions were more easily roused then than now, and the ordinary M.P. was not ashamed to weep in the House; indeed, the shedding of tears in public continued until a much later date.[2] Anger, as well as tears, went unrestrained, and in 1778 Burke is found flinging a volume of estimates at the Treasury Bench.[3] The dramatic, too, was by no means eschewed. When Burke was endeavouring to rouse the House against the French Revolution he took with him to Westminster a dagger as a sample of an order which France was alleged to have placed in Birmingham. At what he judged to be the pyschological moment in the speech he was making on the registration of aliens, he produced it from under his coat, and threw it on the floor. This, however, was considered to be going a little too far.

Pitt had another problem to face, namely, that caused by the peculiarities, even eccentricities, of the Royal Family in general, and of the Prince of Wales in particular. Not only was the latter wildly extravagant at a time when the most severe economy was necessary to save the country from bankruptcy, but in 1785 he committed the supreme folly of secretly marrying a Roman Catholic widow, Mrs. Fitzherbert. It was contrary to the Royal Marriage Act for him to marry at all without the King's consent, while marriage with a Catholic was also a violation of the Act of Settlement upon which the

[1] cf. A. A. B.: *Burke: The Founder of Conservatism*, pp. 14–15.
[2] cf. Sichel, W.: *Life of Sheridan*, Vol. I, p. 132.
[3] cf. Newman, B.: *Edmund Burke*, p. 75.

Hanoverian title to the throne depended; if that Act was no longer to mean anything, then the King of England was not George III at Windsor, but Charles III, the erstwhile Bonnie Prince Charlie, in Florence. To do the Prince of Wales justice, he probably never thought of marriage in the first place, but the lady made it the price of possession. Fox urged the Prince strongly against matrimony:

"If there was no marriage I conclude your intercourse would be carried on as it ought, in so private a way as to make it wholly inconsistent with decency or propriety for anyone in public to hazard such a suggestion . . . if I were Mrs. Fitzherbert's father or brother I would advise her not by any means to agree to it, and to prefer any other species of connection with you to one leading to such misery and mischief."[1]

Mrs. Fitzherbert thought otherwise.

Meanwhile the Prince's extravagance continued unabated, and Carlton House "exhibited a perpetual scene of excess, unrestrained by any wise superintendence".[2] The total expenditure of the Prince for the years 1784–1786 was £369,977, and there were also arrears unpaid. No less than £54,000 was spent on Mrs. Fitzherbert.[3] The not unnatural consequence was another appeal to Parliament for money, and during the course of the ensuing discussion allusion was made to the rumour that the Prince was married. Fox denied it, and when further pressed said he spoke with direct authority. What had happened was that "Prinny" had lied to get himself out of a fix, without caring in the least for the reputation or feelings of Mrs. Fitzherbert. That lady at once became the butt of the caricaturists. Gillray depicted her as "Dido Forsaken", seated upon a pyre crucifix in hand, and with her zone of chastity torn, while ministers blew the coronet and Prince of Wales' feathers from her head, and her lover escaped with Fox in a boat named "Honour" sailed by Burke disguised as a Jesuit. It only remains to add that the lie served its

---

[1] Quoted by Leslie, S.: *George the Fourth*, p. 36.
[2] Wraxall, Sir N. W.: *Memoirs*, Vol. IV, p. 306.
[3] *cf.* Wilkins, W. H.: *Mrs. Fitzherbert and George IV*, Vol. I, p. 161.

CARLTON HOUSE: THE SOUTH FRONT

THE GRAND STAIRCASE, CARLTON HOUSE

purpose, for the teller of it received an addition to his income. As for Mrs. Fitzherbert, it was not long before her lover became unfaithful to her, and after they separated she had no little difficulty in getting her allowance paid regularly. In the autumn of 1788 there was a further Royal complication, for the King went mad. He had shown signs of madness for a few weeks in 1765, but on this occasion he went definitely out of his mind. George had been failing in health throughout the previous summer, and is said, while driving in Windsor Park, to have alighted and shaken hands with the branch of an oak tree under the impression that it was the King of Prussia.[1] Enough has been said in the present work to show that there was a streak of abnormality in the Guelphs. No normal man could have behaved as George I did to his wife, or George II to his son; sadism was the most prominent characteristic of the "Butcher" Duke of Cumberland; while the behaviour of the Queen of Denmark, the sister of George III, argues some degree of nymphomania. In the next generation few would describe George IV as completely balanced. There was a long struggle over the question of a regency, in which the Whigs took the ultra-Tory line that the Prince of Wales was entitled to it by right, while their opponents said that it lay with Parliament to define the Regent's powers. However, at the very moment when the Prince was about to assume the position, albeit with restrictions, his father recovered, to the obvious sorrow of the prospective Regent and his friends. The King was cured by one Willis, who had been a clergyman. When George heard that his doctor had been in Holy Orders he expressed his disapproval of the change, whereupon Willis remarked that Christ went about healing the sick, to this the King answered, "Yes, but I never heard that he had seven hundred pounds a year for doing so." The country was saved a great deal by the King's recovery, for the Prince was incorrigible. Three years later the running of his horse "Escape" was challenged at Newmarket, and the First Gentleman of Europe was warned off the Turf.

[1] *cf. A Page of the Presence: A History of the Royal Malady*, quoted by Rose, J. H.: *The Life of William Pitt*, Vol. I, p. 407.

The national finances were almost as complicated as the affairs of the Royal Family, as might have been expected in view of the methods adopted by North. There was a deficit of £6,000,000, which Pitt, who was Chancellor of the Exchequer as well as Prime Minister, had to face. There was also a floating debt of £14,000,000. One of his first acts was to throw open to public competition all tenders for Government loans, and the old jobbery was eliminated by having each proposal officially opened at the Bank of England. Pitt's measures were sound rather than sensational. He began by funding half the floating debt, and imposing taxes on such things as race-horses, men's hats, ribbons, and gauzes. Next year he completed the funding of the debt, but there was still a deficit, and it was met by fresh taxation, this time on shops and female servants. By 1786 there was a surplus of £900,000, and this was used as the basis of the sinking fund which was now established. Once a quarter £250,000 was to be paid to six commissioners for the purchase of stock, and the interest on this was to be invested in the same way. The fund thus created was to accumulate at compound interest, and so eventually extinguish the National Debt. In practice this scheme did reduce the National Debt by £10,000,000 by 1793, but when war came it meant that the Treasury, as income no longer balanced expenditure, had to borrow at a high rate of interest to pay off a debt contracted at a low one. Nevertheless, compound interest was one of the fetishes of the day, and the existence of the sinking fund created confidence in Pitt's finance by showing that the money raised by taxation was not being wasted. Perhaps the most convincing evidence of the nation's confidence is that when Pitt took office the three per cents were at 53⅞, while they had reached 97 when the war against France began.

The absence of the sensational from all that Pitt did has tended to blind posterity, as it blinded contemporaries, to the greatness of his achievements. Those who lived in the days of Chatham were clearly dazzled by the latter's brilliance, and the literature of the period abounds in references to his genius. The father was made to appeal to the heart, and the son to the head, which explains the different attitude of their fellow-countrymen. Yet nothing can minimize the debt which England owes to the younger Pitt. No one, in the spring of 1784, would have believed that in ten years France would be a bankrupt and regicidal republic, while Great Britain had a balanced Budget and a monarch more popular than any of his predecessors for a century. It seemed as if the long struggle between France and England was over, and that the latter would henceforth steadily decline after the manner of Sweden and Holland. That this did not happen was due to Pitt. He gave the country a feeling that while he remained at the helm all would be well, and the confidence thus gained stood him in good stead when the crisis came. In an age of somewhat flamboyant oratory, too, Pitt spoke in a business-like manner which appealed to the middle-class, while his scrupulous honesty secured their respect. If the Prime Minister was the most careful guardian of the nation's money, he could never look after his own, and he was generally in debt; indeed, on at least one occasion an execution in Downing Street itself was only avoided with difficulty.[1] Yet Pitt never attempted to use his official position for his own gain, as was the custom of his contemporaries, and he was too proud ever to have been made the subject of such a witticism as that which Selwyn perpetrated with regard to Fox. A sum of money was raised among the latter's friends to pay off his debts, and there was a certain amount over, which it was decided to invest for the benefit of the Whig leader. "How do you think Fox will take it?" Selwyn was asked. "Why, quarterly, of course," was the instant reply. No one would have made a remark of that sort about Pitt.

Few English statesmen have pursued so consistent a policy, for Pitt was not the man to allow the passage of measures that were mutually incompatible. He wished to effect all essential alterations within the framework of the Constitution, and if he was unsuccessful in persuading Parliament to reform itself he did much to ameliorate the lot of his fellow-citizens, and to soften the ferocity of their manners. The abolition of public

[1] cf. Pretyman MSS., quoted by Rose, J. H.: The Life of William Pitt, Vol. II, p. 473.

executions at Tyburn, the substitution of transportation of convicts to Australia for slavery in the tropics, and the admission of Roman Catholics to the Army and the Bar, were all measures of his administration.[1] Pitt was the first Prime Minister to take any interest in political economy, and that he had thoroughly mastered the principles put forward by Adam Smith in the *Nature and Causes of the Wealth of Nations* is proved by the treaty he concluded with France, when the duties were reduced on many of the principal articles of commerce of both countries. He even tried to get a clause for the limitation of armaments inserted in the treaty, but the French would not agree. A pleasant story is told of Pitt's personal relations with Adam Smith. The latter was one day asked to a certain house to meet the Prime Minister at dinner, but arrived late. The guests patiently waited for the economist and when he did appear, Pitt said, "Nay, we will stand until you are seated; for we are all your scholars."

---

[1] *cf.* Feiling, K.: *Sketches in Nineteenth-Century Biography*, pp. 3–15.

CHAPTER VI

THE STRUGGLE FOR EXISTENCE

ENGLAND was slow to appreciate the significance of the French Revolution, and those who took any interest at all in events on the Continent regarded it as analogous to what had been done in Great Britain a century before. Fox, indeed, showed himself enthusiastic from the beginning, and when he heard of the fall of the Bastille wrote to a friend who was going to Paris:

"How much the greatest event it is that ever happened in the world! and how much the best! If you go without my seeing you, pray say something civil for me to the Duke of Orleans, whose conduct seems to have been perfect: and tell him and Lauzun, that all my prepossessions against French connections for this country will be at an end, and indeed most part of my European system of politics will be altered, if this revolution has the consequences that I expect."[1]

For once Fox expressed the point of view of his fellow-countrymen, though he went far further than the vast majority of the latter were prepared to go, and his eulogy of Philippe Egalité showed his usual inability to judge character correctly. France under the Bourbons had been the persistent enemy of Britain, and anything that tended to weaken her or her ruling dynasty could not fail to be welcome on this side of the Channel. Any change in French policy, it was believed, must be for the better so far as this country was concerned. There was also to be detected a certain national pride in the fact that the French were apparently following in the footsteps of Britain, and limiting the power of their monarch.

The explanation of this slowness of appreciation of what was happening was largely due to the fact that events in France

[1] Hobhouse, C.: *Fox*, p. 223.

did not move by any means so rapidly as the reader of modern novels on the period (and still more the modern cinema-goer) might suppose. The storming of the Bastille took place on July 14th, 1789, but it was not until June 1791 that the French Royal Family attempted to escape, and another year elapsed before Louis XVI was suspended from the exercise of his functions. On more than one occasion during these years it appeared highly probable that the Revolution would be crushed (as it certainly would have been had Louis shown the firmness displayed by George during the Gordon Riots), or that France would settle down under a constitutional monarchy. That the infection might spread to his own country never at this stage occurred to the ordinary Englishman. Furthermore, there had been a crisis in the Near East, another in the Pacific, and a general election, so that there was plenty of excuse for not taking French politics too seriously. Anyhow, Pitt could be relied upon to know what he was doing; so the electorate gave him an increased majority, and continued to survey the progress of events in France with an air of detachment. The Government, too, saw no reason for alarm. As late as the beginning of 1792 the Army Estimates provided for the reduction of each regiment by seventy men, which left the total force in the British Isles at 13,701.[1] When Pitt introduced his Budget that same year he was only reflecting contemporary optimism in a speech which envisaged the state of the national finances in fifteen years. "I am not, indeed, presumptuous enough to suppose that, when I name fifteen years I am not naming a period in which events may arise which human foresight cannot reach, and which may baffle all our conjectures. We must not count with certainty on a continuance of our present prosperity during such an interval; but unquestionably there never was a time in the history of this country, when, from the situation of Europe, we might more reasonably expect fifteen years of peace than at the present moment."

---

[1] With all his efforts to reduce expenditure, Pitt had never economized on the Navy, and in 1790 there were no less than ninety-three line-of-battle ships ready for commission. The cost of building a 74-gun ship was £62,000, of which nearly half was for oak timber alone.

What caused indifference to change into horror, and then into hatred, was partly a growing comprehension of what was happening, and partly the sympathy shown by a small minority in the British Isles with the excesses of the revolutionaries. The nation was shaking off the effects of Walpole's narcotic, and beginning to take sides once more. The Enclosure Acts and the Industrial Revolution had completed the break-up of the old social and economic system, and had deprived a large number of people of any definite place in society. In some of the towns the demagogic utterances of Wilkes and Fox had not been without effect, while the Gordon Riots had shown what could be accomplished by an agitator. In Ireland, groaning under the Penal Laws, and in Scotland, where repression had been the order of the day ever since Culloden, there was even more inflammable material than in England. English revolutionaries always prefer a leader not of their own class, and this want, too, was supplied, for men like the Duke of Richmond, the Marquess of Lansdowne, and Earl Stanhope played at Jacobinism. The Duke of Norfolk went so far at a public dinner as to propose the toast of "Our Sovereign, the Majesty of the People", for which he was very properly dismissed from the command of a militia regiment, and from the Lord Lieutenancy of the West Riding of Yorkshire. Norfolk was an eccentric nobleman, for he could eat a rump of beef at a sitting, and could only be washed when he was drunk.[1] The movement also had its "intellectuals", of whom the most prominent was Tom Paine, author of *The Rights of Man*.[2] Yet it was in no sense popular, for there was little real discontent; when Pitt had brought forward a Bill for Parliamentary Reform in 1785 only eight petitions were presented in favour of it, and not one of these came from Birmingham or Manchester.

The vocal minority that desired a change began to form Corresponding Societies up and down the country, and there was also a Society for Constitutional Information in the capital. Most of these bodies were harmless enough, for their members

---

[1] *cf.* Fletcher, C. R. L.: *An Introductory History of England*, Vol. IV, p. 4.
[2] Paine finally fled to France, where he narrowly escaped the guillotine.

did little more than demand the reform of Parliament, and circulate *The Rights of Man*. Some of them, however, went further, and several united to send an address to the French Convention. When war with France broke out in February 1793 such action took on a different aspect, and came perilously near to treason.

"The outbreak of hostilities often tend to embitter the strife of parties. Those who oppose war find abundant cause for criticism in the conduct of Ministers, who in their turn perforce adopt measures alien to the traditions of Westminster. A system founded on compromise cannot suddenly take on the ways of a military State; and efforts in this direction generally produce more friction than activity. At such times John Bull, flurried and angry, short-sighted but opinionated, bewildered but dogged as ever, is a sight to move the gods to laughter, and his counsellors to despair."[1]

The reformers, however, had only themselves to blame, for such verses as those of Thelwall:

> But cease, ye fleeing Senators
> Your country to undo,
> Or know, we British *sans-culottes*
> Hereafter may fleece you,

were not calculated to reassure moderate opinion as to the aims of those who entertained such sentiments, and met in a so-called British Convention: nor were posters which expressed such sentiments as,

"You may as well look for chastity and mercy in the Empress of Russia, honour and consistency from the King of Prussia, wisdom and plain dealing from the Emperor of Germany, as a single speech of virtue from our Hell born Minister."[2]

The Press played a prominent part in this controversy, and there was a loud cry for reform in

[1] Rose, J. H.: *The Life of William Pitt*, Vol. II, p. 164.
[2] "H.O." Geo. III (Domestic), p. 36.

Couriers, and Stars, Sedition's evening host,
The *Morning Chronicle* and *Morning Post.*

The *Star* was the first evening daily paper, while the
Morning Chronicle and the *Morning Post* dated respectively
from 1769 and 1772; the latter only became Radical under
Daniel Stuart in 1795, and five years later had a daily circulation of 4,500 copies, which was considered enormous.
The *Morning Chronicle* owed much of its influence to its
editor, Perry, who mixed in the society of Fox and North,
and was a friend of Bellamy, wine merchant and doorkeeper
to the House of Commons, from whom he got a good deal of
information. Newspapers in those days were easy to start,
and changed hands frequently. The Government founded
two new ones, the *Sun* and the *True Briton,* to combat those of
their opponents, an act most displeasing to Mr. Walter of
The Times in view of his support of ministers.[1] The lack of
ordinary decency shown by the Press is well illustrated by a
quotation from the *Morning Post* recording the King's visit to
St. Paul's to return thanks for the victories of St. Vincent and
Camperdown, "The consequence of the procession to St.
Paul's was that one man returned thanks to Almighty God,
and one woman was kicked to death." As Leopold I of the
Belgians was to write to Queen Victoria:

"If all the editors of the papers . . . were to be assembled,
we should have a crew to which you would not confide a
dog that you would value, still less your honour and
reputation."[2]

Yet it is not difficult to understand the panic caused by
these activities on the part of the Radicals. Rumour exaggerated them to an absurd degree, and in the absence of an
effective police it was almost impossible to arrive at the truth.
From 1792 onwards the harvest was bad, and the discontent
to which this gave rise was confused with the results of Jacobin
propaganda. In the ports the activities of the Press Gang was
causing lively discontent, and at Liverpool the populace, in

[1] cf. *Bland Burges Papers*, pp. 227–229.
[2] *The Letters of Queen Victoria:* First Series, Vol. I.

1793, forced the election as Mayor of a Mr. Tarleton, who promised to keep it out of the town. At that time, too, troops were not quartered in barracks, but were billeted; and this made them peculiarly liable to seditious teaching. It is easy to read history backwards, and to scoff at the fears of contemporaries in the light of the information available for a later age, but it is not the way to arrive at the truth. Above all, ministers had a terrible example in the progress of events in France of the danger attendant upon letting matters slide. Nor did the French themselves behave in such a way as to allay the alarm, for a month before the declaration of war M. Monge,[1] the Minister for the Navy, issued a manifesto which left no doubt as to his country's intentions:

"The King and his Parliament mean to make war upon us. Will the English republicans suffer it? Already these free men show their discontent and the repugnance which they have to bear arms against their brothers, the French. Well! We will fly to their succour. We will make a descent in the island. We will lodge there 50,000 caps of Liberty. We will plant there the sacred tree, and we will stretch out our arms to our republican brethren. The tyranny of their government will soon be destroyed."

In the face of such language as this ministers would have been culpably negligent had they taken no action.

The measures enacted to strengthen the hands of the Government included an Aliens Act, which provided for the more effective supervision of foreigners; a Traitorous Correspondence Act, which attached the penalty of high treason to all who supplied arms to France or brought French paper money to Britain; the suspension of the Habeas Corpus Act, which made it possible to keep suspects in prison without trial; a Seditious Meetings Bill, by which no meeting of more than fifty people was lawful without the permission of a magistrate; and a Treasonable Practices Bill, which imposed severe penalties on those who attacked the Constitution. In consequence, a number of agitators were arrested, and in

[1] Under the Empire he became Count of Pelusium with a Westphalian estate bringing in 200,000 francs a year.

every case the trials were conducted with the utmost fairness; indeed, convictions were the exception rather than the rule, and Radical leaders such as Horne-Tooke, Hardy, Thelwall, and Holcroft were acquitted. In Scotland there were cases of real injustice, but that was due partly to the greater severity of the Scottish law, and partly to the presence on the Bench of MacQueen of Braxfield,[1] Stevenson's Weir of Hermiston, whose typical address to a jury was thus parodied in the *Morning Post:*

> I am bound by the law, while I sit in this place,
> To say in plain terms what I think of this case.
> My opinion is this, and you're bound to pursue it,
> The defendants are guilty, and I'll make them rue it.

Even so only one man was hanged, Robert Watt, whose trial "displayed to the public the most atrocious and deliberate plan of villainy which has occurred, perhaps, in the annals of Great Britain", as Walter Scott wrote to Miss Christian Rutherford.[2]

Generations of Whig historians have industriously created the legend of a reign of terror in Great Britain during the early years of the war against revolutionary France, but it will not stand investigation. If, too, Pitt and his colleagues were monsters of iniquity, what of their Whig predecessors in the reigns of the first two Georges who treated Jacobites little better than vermin, or of their Whig successors forty years later, who so savagely persecuted the wretched labourers of Wessex? In any event, those who shared the views of the victims had no right to complain, for their standard of justice can be gauged from the eulogies which they bestowed upon the authors of the terrible September Massacres in Paris. The truth is that the great majority of the nation welcomed the Government's repressive measures, and only criticized them because they did not go far enough. No one but his immediate circle agreed with Fox that Pitt had set up "a system of cruelty and oppression worse than any devised by the See of Rome, or the Spanish Inquisition, or any other tyrant, spiritual

---

[1] *cf.* Watt, F.: *Terrors of the Law.*
[2] *cf.* Lockhart, J. G.: *Life of Sir Walter Scott.*

or temporal". The so-called "friends of the people" were
often rough-handled by those whom they declared themselves
to be befriending. Dr. Priestley had his house at Birmingham
sacked by the mob because he chose to celebrate the anniversary
of the fall of the Bastille by a dinner to his Radical friends.
Indeed, Canning admirably parodied the attitude of these
"intellectuals" in *The Friend of Humanity and the Knife-
Grinder:*

Friend of Humanity:

> Needy Knife-Grinder! whither are you going?
> Rough is the road, your wheel is out of order—
> Bleak blows the blast; your hat has got a hole in't,
>   So have your breeches!
> Weary Knife-Grinder! little think the proud ones
> Who in their coaches roll along the Turnpike
> -Road, what hard work 'tis crying all day "Knives and
>   Scissors to grind, O!"

> Tell me Knife-Grinder how came you to grind knives?
> Did some great man tyrannically use you?
> Was it the squire? or parson of the parish?
>   Or the attorney?

> Was it the squire, for killing of his game? or
> Covetous parson, for his tithes distraining?
> Or roguish lawyer, made you lose your little
>   All in a lawsuit?

> (Have you not read the Rights of Man, by Tom Paine?)
> Drops of compassion tremble on my eyelids
> Ready to fall, as soon as you have told your
>   Pitiful story.

Knife-Grinder:

> Story! God bless you! I have none to tell, Sir,
> Only last night a-drinking at the Chequers,
> This poor old hat and breeches, as you see, were
>   Torn in a scuffle.

> Constables came up for to take me into
> Custody; they took me before the justice;
> Justice Oldmixon set me in the parish
>   -Stocks for a vagrant.

I should be glad to drink your Honour's health in
A pot of beer, if you will give me sixpence;
But for my part, I never loves to meddle
         With politics, Sir.

Friend of Humanity:

I give thee sixpence! I would see thee damned first—
Wretch! whom no sense of wrongs can rouse to vengeance—
Sordid, unfeeling, reprobate, degraded,
         Spiritless outcast!

(Kicks the Knife-Grinder, overturns his wheel, and exit in a transport of
Republican enthusiasm and universal philanthropy.)

When the news of the execution of Louis XVI reached
London in the late afternoon of January 23rd, 1793, there was
a feeling of universal horror; the theatres were closed, and all
who could afford it wore mourning, while in Paris

"the playhouses are open and the city is illuminated every
night, as if the French wished to make their wickedness
more visible".[1]

The spokesman of the anti-French reaction was Burke, who,
in 1790, published his *Reflections on the French Revolution.*
Few books have had so immediate a success, for although it
was published at five shillings no less than 7,000 copies were
sold in six days. The King was delighted, and told everyone,
"Read it; it will do you good; it is a book which every gentleman ought to read."[2] Yet the influence of Burke was greater
outside political circles than at Westminster, and when he
tried to persuade Pitt and Grenville, the Foreign Secretary,
nearly a year later to take action, he had to confess to his son,
"They are certainly right as to their general inclinations,
perfectly so, I have not a shadow of doubt; but at the same
time they are cold and dead as to any attempt whatsoever to
give them effect." No one denied the eloquence or genius of
Burke, but, as we have seen, he was regarded by the House of
Commons as something of a bore, but

[1] *The Times,* January 26, 1793.
[2] *cf.* Newman, B.: *Edmund Burke,* p. 228.

"it must be remembered that Burke was a pure-bred Irishman, and the Irish have never understood the literary effect of under-statement".[1]

His manner and appearance, too, were against him, for he had a very strong brogue; and Wilkes said of him that just as the Venus of Apelles suggested milk and honey, so Burke's oratory was reminiscent of whisky and potatoes. The dandies of Brooks's and White's laughed at his large spectacles, ill-fitting brown coat, and bob-wig. In office Burke was a definite liability, for he always allowed his heart to control his head, and during his second term at the Pay Office, in 1783, he caused the administration of which he was a member grave embarrassment by reinstating two officials who had been discharged by his predecessor for malversation.

The country knew nothing of all this. It read the *Reflections on the French Revolution,* then the *Appeal from New to Old Whigs,* and the *Letters on a Regicide Peace* with increasing approval. The romantic Irishman was saying exactly what the English thought, but could not express. By now they hated the French Revolution and all its works, and here was Burke telling them why they hated it. As his prophecies came true the ordinary man rallied to him, and even the politicians were affected. The Whigs broke up, and the Duke of Portland, Windham, and others crossed the floor, and Burke took his seat on the Treasury Bench. In 1797 he died, and when Canning heard what had happened, he wrote, "There is only one piece of news, but that is news for the world, Burke is dead." The fact that Britain entered the war against France at all was due, not to sentiment, but to the French invasion of the Low Countries; that she entered it with enthusiasm was due to Burke.

The work that had been begun by Burke was continued by another Irishman, George Canning, in the *Anti-Jacobin,* albeit on a more popular plane. Canning was one of those "new men" to whom the collapse of the Whig oligarchy was giving their opportunity. His immediate forebears were Ulster squires, but his father had been disinherited for his

[1] A. A. B.: *Burke: The Founder of Conservatism,* p. 13.

PROMISED HORRORS OF THE FRENCH INVASION

A caricature by James Gillray. The victorious Jacobins of Brookes's are shown attacking White's, while Fox, their leader, is scourging Pitt. Canning and Jenkison are srung up outside White's, while the Duke of Bedford is tossing Burke. Sheridan, the impecunious, is carting the revenue into the Whig stronghold.

THE SUBSCRIPTION ROOM AT BROOKS'S

marriage with a lady from Connaught. Canning's father died young, and his mother was left almost penniless; for a time she was on the stage, though in later life she was supported by her illustrious son. Hookham Frere had thus every justification for his picture of Canning:

> Born with an ancient name of little worth,
> And disinherited before his birth,
> A landless orphan, rank and wealth and pride
> Were freely ranged around him, nor denied
> His clear precedence . . .

Young Canning, through the care of an uncle, was educated at Eton and Christ Church, and at the age of twenty-three was returned to the House of Commons: two years later he was appointed Under-Secretary for Foreign Affairs. In his youth he had been a Whig, and his conversion had prompted Fox's friend, Fitzpatrick, to write of him:

> The turning of coats so common is grown
>   That no one would wish to attack it,
> But no case until now was so flagrantly known
>   Of a schoolboy turning his jacket.

It was Burke who had first shaken his allegiance to the Whigs, and now that Burke was gone Canning may well have felt that it was for him to expose to his fellow-countrymen the danger that threatened them from France.

The *Anti-Jacobin* was intended to appear every Monday morning while Parliament was sitting, and it did in fact last from November 1797 to July 1798. The editor was William Gifford, who afterwards edited the *Quarterly Review,* and among the chief contributors were Canning and Hookham Frere. The latter had already collaborated with Canning, when they were both boys at Eton, in an earlier journalistic venture, the *Microcosm,* and it is as a man of letters, particularly as the translator of Aristophanes, that Frere is now remembered. Yet for a time he was Under-Secretary for Foreign Affairs, and was British representative to the *Junta Central* in the early days of the Peninsular War: in the latter capacity he got on very badly with Sir John Moore, and Napier describes Frere as "a person of mere scholastic attainment",[1] of whom, of course, no British soldier could be expected to entertain any high opinion. The policy of the *Anti-Jacobin* was to implicate the whole Opposition in the doctrines of its extremists, and in this it was remarkably successful. Its appeal was primarily popular, and the cartoons of Gillray were by no means its least valuable asset. At the same time, the literary side of the revolutionary movement was by no means neglected, and Kotzebue, Schiller, and Goethe were hotly attacked for the advanced views which they then held. Most of the articles and poems were composite work, but Pitt occasionally contributed an article on finance.

The best-known metrical contribution of Canning, namely, *The Friend of Humanity and the Knife-Grinder*, has already been quoted, but in *The New Morality* occurred some verses that were destined to make Parliamentary history:

> Give me the avowed, the erect, the manly foe!
> Bold I can meet, perhaps may turn, the blow;
> But of all plagues, good Heaven, Thy wrath can send,
> Save, save, O save me, from the candid friend!

Years afterwards Peel, who had betrayed Canning during the last months of the latter's life, used this quotation in an attempt to crush Disraeli, but merely provided his antagonist with an opening of which he was not slow to take advantage:

"The right hon. gentleman knows what the introduction of a great name does in debate—how important is its effect, and occasionally how electrical. He never refers to any author who is not great, and sometimes who is not loved— Canning, for example. That is a name never to be mentioned, I am sure, in the House of Commons without emotion. We all admire his genius. We all, at least most of us, deplore his untimely end; and we all sympathize with him in his fierce struggle with supreme prejudice and sublime mediocrity—with inveterate foes and with candid friends. (Loud cheering.) The right hon. gentleman may be sure that a quotation from such an authority will always

[1] *History of the War in the Peninsula*, Vol. I, p. 288.

tell. Some lines, for example, upon friendship, written by Mr. Canning, and quoted by the right hon. gentleman! The theme, the poet, the speaker—what a felicitous combination! (Loud and long-continued cheers.)"[1]

After July 1798 the *Anti-Jacobin* changed its name to the *Anti-Jacobin Review and Magazine*, but its policy remained unchanged. One number contained an attack on Coleridge, Southey, Lloyd, and Lamb:

> See! faithful to their mighty dam,[2]
> C . . . . . dge, S . . th . y, L . . . d, and L . . be
> In splay-foot madrigals of love,
> Soft moaning like the widow'd dove,
> Pour, side by side, their sympathetic notes;
> > Of equal rights, and civic feasts,
> > And tyrant Kings, and knavish priests.
>
> Swift through the land the tuneful mischief floats.
> And now to soften strains they struck the lyre,
> > They sung the beetle, or the mole.
> > Thy dying kid, or ass's foal,
> By cruel man permitted to expire.

Lamb at any rate did not forget his satirists, and some years later he retaliated on Canning and Frere with the verses:

> At Eton School brought up with dull boys,
> We shone like men among the school-boys;
> But since we in the world have been,
> We are but school-boys among men.[3]

The efforts of Burke and the *Anti-Jacobin* bore fruit, and the minority which was opposed to the war became steadily weaker. The obvious determination of the French to establish a hegemony in Europe also opened the eyes of many who had hitherto been disposed to sympathize with the enemy, and in spite of a long series of disasters the country grew ever more determined to resist aggression. It is almost a commonplace that Pitt was a poor minister in time of war, and innumerable comparisons, all unfavourable to him, have been drawn between Pitt and Chatham. Those who take this view forget

---

[1] *The Times*, March 1, 1845. [2] *i.e. anarchy.*
[3] *cf.* Lucas, E. V.: *The Life of Charles Lamb*, Ch. XII.

that the son was faced with far greater difficulties than the father ever knew. In the Seven Years War the elder Pitt had the greatest soldier of his day, Frederick the Great, for an ally, and a France at the nadir of her fortunes for an enemy. Forty years later his son had one of the greatest soldiers not only of his day, but of all time, for an adversary, and as allies but the weak and shifty Cabinets of Vienna, Berlin, and Madrid. Such being the case, it can only be a matter for surprise that Pitt managed to hold his own, while his foresight is attested by the fact that while Napoleon was at the height of his power the British Prime Minister outlined the conditions upon which peace was ultimately made ten years later. In this connection it is interesting to note that Miranda, assuredly no mean judge of men, credited Pitt personally with such successes as England gained during his term of office.[1]

In spite of the support which Pitt enjoyed in the country, he was still the object of fierce denunciation in the House of Commons, and on one occasion he actually had to fight a duel as the result of words used there. During the course of a debate the Prime Minister accused Tierney, the "Friend of Humanity" in Canning's poem, of obstructing the defence of the country, and as he refused to withdraw or modify the expression Tierney sent him a challenge. The duel took place on Whit-Sunday, May 27th, 1798, and pistols were used. As Pitt was lean and his opponent was fat, the wits declared afterwards that in all fairness his figure should have been chalked out on Tierney's, and that no shot which took effect outside ought to count. The place chosen was a hollow near where the Portsmouth Road dips into Kingston Vale, and the two men met there in the early afternoon. Pitt brought Dudley Ryder, afterwards Lord Harrowby, as his second, while General Walpole came with Tierney. Addington, the Speaker, was also present. The first discharge left the duellists unhit, and at the second the Prime Minister fired his pistol into the air; neither was hurt, and honour was satisfied.[2] Public opinion was shocked at such a duel ever having taken

---

[1] *Archivo del General Miranda*, Vol. XIV, p. 368.
[2] *cf.* Pellew, C.: *Life and Correspondence of the first Viscount Sidmouth*, Vol. I, p. 206.

place, not least because it happened on a Sunday; while the King made no secret of his disapproval: "Public characters," he said, "have no right to weigh alone what they owe to themselves; they must consider what they owe to their country."

Eleven years later Canning and Castlereagh also fought on Putney Heath. Castlereagh thought that Canning, who was his colleague in the Cabinet, had been intriguing against him behind his back, and accordingly wrote three sheets of folio in which he stated his grievances, ending:

"Under the circumstances I must require that satisfaction from you to which I feel myself entitled to lay claim.
"I have the honour to be, Sir,
"Your obedient humble servant,
"CASTLEREAGH."

When Canning received the letter, he glanced at the last few lines, and exclaimed, "I had rather fight than read it, by God!" He then replied,

"Gloucester Lodge,
"*September* 20, 1809
"(half-past ten A.M.).

"MY LORD,
"The tone and purport of your Lordship's letter (which I have this moment received) of course precludes any other answer, on my part, to the misapprehensions and misrepresentations, with which it abounds, than that I will cheerfully give to your Lordship the satisfaction that you require.
"I have the honour to be, my Lord,
"Your Lordship's most obedient humble servant,
"GEO. CANNING."

The duel, also with pistols, took place at six a.m. on September 21st, and at the second discharge Canning was wounded in his thigh.

"The ball entered about eight inches below the hip, and, taking an outward direction, passed out again on the left side of the hinder part of the thigh. The wound, though a smart one, is, thank God, by no means dangerous; and your cousin is doing as well as he possibly can."[1]

Canning certainly took it all very coolly, for he was in bed when his second, Charles Ellis, came to tell him he must fight at six, whereupon he turned over and slept again until five.[2] Pitt was not the last British Prime Minister to fight a duel while in office, for that distinction belongs to the Duke of Wellington. In 1828 the Duke had presided at a meeting for the foundation of King's College, London, an institution which was to be wholly under the influence of the Church of England, and which was intended as a counterpoise to the recent and purely secular foundation of London University. The Earl of Winchilsea soon afterwards wrote a letter to the Standard describing the whole affair "as a blind to the Protestant and High Church party", and accusing the Prime Minister of insidious designs for the introduction of Popery in every department of the State. The Duke sent the then Sir Henry Hardinge, who was Secretary at War, with a letter couched in moderate language, but which demanded an apology. Winchilsea refused this, but offered to express his regret for having mistaken the motives ot the Prime Minister if the latter would give the assurance that when he took the chair at the meeting in question he was not contemplating any measure of Catholic Emancipation. On this the Duke demanded "that satisfaction which a gentleman has a right to require, and which a gentleman never refuses to give". The antagonists accordingly met in Battersea Fields on March 21st, 1829. Wellington deliberately fired wide, and Winchilsea discharged his pistol in the air, after which he gave a written apology for what he had done.[3]

The rump which still opposed Pitt and the prosecution of the war might be reduced in the matter of quantity, but in that of quality it left nothing to be desired. If the Whigs no

---

[1] Joseph Planta to Stratford Canning, quoted by Lane-Poole, S.: *Life of the Right Hon. Stratford Canning, Viscount Stratford de Redcliffe*, Vol. I, p. 74.
[2] *cf.* Petrie, Sir Charles: *Life of George Canning*, pp. 71–79.
[3] *cf.* Maxwell, Sir H.: *Life of Wellington*, Vol. II, pp. 231–236.

longer possessed political power, their social influence was greater than ever, and they looked down on those whom Disraeli was later to describe as "the plebeian aristocracy of Mr. Pitt".[1] Out of office they had little to do save pass from one country-house to another, while those they despised saved the nation from the French Revolution and the ambition of Napoleon. A letter written by Grey to his wife from Woburn in July 1800 throws an interesting light on the life of himself and his fellow-aristocrats:

"I did not find as large a party as I expected. It at present consists of Fox, Lord Robert (Spencer), Fitzpatrick, Lord John Townshend, (Philip) Francis, Dudley North, Richardson, and myself. Sheridan and Adair are expected to-day and Hare to-morrow. Fox is in the highest spirits. It is quite delightful to see such a man in the midst of a society which he appears to like, so unassuming, good-humoured, and cheerful. Everything seems to be a source of enjoyment to him, and I hardly know which to envy most—his amiable disposition or his unrivalled talents. When I descend from admiring him to think of myself, how I sicken at the contrast! He is enthusiastic about poetry, and admires Spenser as much as we do. You may remember how cheap Francis appeared to hold us for this taste at Woolbeding.[2] He is not stout enough to disparage Spenser as much as he did then, before Fox, but I assure you his opinions upon this subject, as far as he has ventured to express them, have gained him no applause.

"The room we inhabit is the Library, where we lounge over books or join in conversation as suits our inclination. In this manner the morning, or the greater part of it, passes, with perhaps a sauntering walk in the pleasure ground, or the Tennis Court, where Fox and Lord Robert generally play for an hour or two. We dine at four, and generally walk out after coffee, after which there is a Party of the good players, from which I am excluded, at Whist, in a room which opens into the Library, where the rest of the

---

[1] *Sybil*, Bk. I, Ch. III.
[2] Lord Robert Spenser's house, near Midhurst in Sussex.

party amuse themselves as in the morning. Supper is served in another adjoining room about eleven, after which we generally sit up pretty late."[1]

A few weeks before this Napoleon had won the battle of Marengo.

While the Whig leaders were either elegantly trifling in the country, or adopting obstructionist tactics in Parliament, Pitt was endeavouring to weather the storm. Like many another British statesman at the beginning of a war, he was unduly optimistic as to its duration. "It will be a short war," he said, "and certainly ended in one or two campaigns." "No, Sir," retorted Burke, "it will be a long war and a dangerous war, but it must be undertaken."[2] The poor harvests during the early years of the conflict caused widespread distress; in 1793 there were 1,926 failures, of which twenty-six were country banks. Pitt would have preferred to finance the war by loans rather than by taxation, but it was not long before he was compelled to have recourse to both. In 1792 the Funded Debt was about £238,000,000, whereas by 1801 it had risen to £574,000,000. Yet in spite of everything the country continued to prosper, and the balance of trade remained favourable. In 1796 the Government took the then unusual course of appealing direct to the public to meet a prospective deficit caused by the continually increasing demands for the public services. A "Loyalty Loan" of £18,000,000 was issued, bearing interest at 5⅝ per cent, and was subscribed within a few hours, so great was the confidence in the administration. Yet the very next year witnessed one of the worst financial panics in the nation's history such are the tricks played by fate at moments of crisis. An emergency meeting of the Privy Council was called, and an order was issued to empower the Directors of the Bank of England to refuse payments in cash until Parliament gave further orders on the subject. Twenty-two years elapsed before cash payments were resumed.

---

[1] Quoted by Trevelyan, G. M.: *Lord Grey of the Reform Bill*, pp. 107–108.
[2] *Life of William Wilberforce* (by his sons), Vol. II, p. 11.

In the last weeks of 1797 Pitt introduced what was then a novelty, the Income Tax. It was to be on a sliding scale; incomes under £60 were exempt, those between £60 and £65 paid at the rate of 2d. in the pound, and the proportion rose until it reached 2s. in the pound for incomes of £200 and more. There was at once an outcry that the country would be ruined, but Parliament duly voted the taxes. For some months Pitt was decidely unpopular: he was hooted in the City, and on one occasion had to be guarded by a squadron of horse. He was justified by events, for the trade returns in 1798 were distinctly better than those for the previous year. The next financial expedient was a "Patriotic Contribution", and that brought in no less than £2,300,000 in voluntary donations. Thus the Prime Minister was well justified in his statement in the House of Commons in December 1798. After paying a tribute to the Navy and Army, he went on to say:

"We must also do justice to the wisdom, energy, and determination of the Parliament who have furnished the means of employing the force whose achievements have been so brilliant; through the wisdom of Parliament the resources of the country have been called forth, and its spirit embodied in a manner unexampled in its history. By their firmness, magnanimity, and devotion to the cause, not merely of our own individual safety, but of the cause of mankind in general, we have been enabled to stand forth the saviours of the earth. No difficulties have stood in our way; no sacrifices have been thought too great for us to make; a common feeling of danger has produced a common spirit of exertion, and we have cheerfully come forward with a surrender of a part of our property as a salvage, not merely for recovering ourselves, but for the general recovery of mankind. We have presented a phenomenon in the character of nations."

Further taxation, it is true, soon proved necessary, but the corner had been turned, and confidence in British credit was restored.

The years 1797 and 1798 were probably the two most critical in the country's history, for in addition to the financial

panic they witnessed the naval mutinies at Spithead and the
Nore, as well as the rebellion in Ireland.

What is most remarkable about the mutinies is not that they
took place when they did, but that they had not happened
long before. The attack in Cartagena in 1741 revealed a
state of affairs in the Navy which was comparable only with
that existing in Newgate, and it would be unbelievable had not
Smollett been present to place on record the sufferings of the
sick and wounded.[1] The men were never allowed leave on
shore, and were thus often cut off from their families and
friends for years at a stretch. Their pay remained as it had
been fixed in the reign of Charles II, that is to say, at 22s. 6d.
per lunar month for able seamen and 19s. for ordinary seamen,
though the cost of living had risen 30 per cent, and the pay
of the Army had recently been increased. What they did
get was often hopelessly in arrears. The food was execrable.
Salt beef years old, rancid butter, and cheese alive with long
red worms were the staple articles of diet. Fresh vegetables
were not provided even in port, and the water was stored in
such a manner that by the time it reached the sailors it was
slimy. The surgeons were only too often either mere novices,
or drunken sots who never went near their patients, while in
an action wounds were patched up anyhow, sometimes with
the aid of the carpenter's tools, and it was by no means unknown
for the more badly wounded to be thrown overboard to save
trouble.[2]

Uncomfortable as were thus the circumstances of a sailor's
life, the latter was too often made unbearable by the brutality
of the officers. It is true that the principal method of re-
cruitment, namely the Press Gang, was hardly calculated to
provide a first-class personnel, but even so punishment of
offences was excessive. The regulations laid down that a
dozen strokes on the bare back was to be the maximum, but
they were honoured rather in the breach than in the observance.
Two or three dozen were the usual ration, a hundred was by

---

[1] cf. *Roderick Random*, Ch. XXXIV.
[2] cf. Manwaring, G. E., and Dobrée, B.: *The Floating Republic*, p. 15. To this
admirable work the curious reader is referred for further information.

no means uncommon, and two or three hundred not unknown.[1] In such a community, shut off from the civilizing influences of the outside world, sadism had full play. The most flagrant instance occurred in the West Indies, where Captain Pigot of the *Hermione* one day threatened to flog the last man down from the yards. Two sailors, in their anxiety to escape the ordeal, fell and broke their limbs, whereupon Pigot shouted, "Throw those lubbers overboard." That night there was mutiny, the officers were murdered, and the ship was handed over to the Spaniards. Another captain took a personal delight in being present at a flogging, and used to exclaim, "By God, I'll show them who's captain. I'll see the man's backbone, by God."[2] Most famous for his infamy was Captain Bligh of the *Bounty*, who so ill-treated his men that they turned him and a few others adrift in a boat in the Pacific. There were, needless to say, many officers who did all they could for the comfort of those who served under them, and foremost among these was Nelson.

What caused the mutinies of 1797 was the enlistment, owing to the needs of war, of large numbers of civilians whose standard of living was infinitely higher than that of the ordinary sailor, and who were not prepared to tolerate the state of affairs they found on shipboard. The muster rose from 16,000 in 1792 to 85,000 in 1794, and by 1802 it stood at 135,000. The mutiny at Spithead was ably organized, and the moderation displayed throughout reflected the greatest credit upon all concerned. It began when the fleet was ordered to put to sea, for, instead of weighing anchor, the crews manned the yards, cheered, and hoisted the red flag. No disrespect was shown to the officers, but the control of the ships was taken out of their hands. The demands of the mutineers were not excessive, for they only asked that pay should be raised to the Army level, and that officers accused of brutality should be dismissed their ships; they further required a promise that, unless the French put out, the fleet should not be sent to sea until the increase of pay had been voted by Parliament and the

---

[1] In Stuart times the code had been far milder.
[2] *cf.* Masefield, J.: *Sea Life in Nelson's Time*, p. 59.

King's pardon had been proclaimed. The Admiralty attempted to haggle, but finally gave way on all points. Unfortunately, a delay then ensued in presenting the necessary Bill to the House of Commons owing to official red-tape, and when it was introduced Fox and his friends could not resist the opportunity of making party capital out of the mutiny. This aroused the suspicions of the sailors, and there was further trouble, involving bloodshed, at Spithead. Finally Lord Howe was sent down to announce the King's pardon, and the passage of the Bill; over a hundred officers were removed from their ships, and the mutiny was at an end. One further incident calls for mention. During the height of the disturbance the Prince of Württemberg, who was about to marry the Princess Royal, came to Portsmouth to receive its freedom, and was duly taken round the fleet. "Who but Englishmen would have made a tour of state to show a foreign visitor their fleet in full mutiny? Or who but English sailors in mutiny would have turned out to salute the cruising dignitaries?"[1]

The revolt at the Nore was a much more unpleasant affair. It began just when the Spithead mutiny was finishing, and so the Nore mutineers had either to put forward further demands or return to duty. They chose the former course, and required, *inter alia*, that no officer who had been removed from his ship should be employed in her again without the consent of the crew. One Richard Parker was chosen as their leader, and when it became apparent that the authorities would not give way, the mutineers proceeded to carry matters with a very high hand. The mouth of the Thames was blockaded, farm-houses on the coast were sacked, and officers were tarred and feathered. The ships which were watching the Dutch actually left their station in face of the enemy. This had the effect of alienating public opinion on shore, which the mutineers at Spithead had been careful to cultivate, and the whole country was solidly behind the Government in the measures it took. The garrison at Sheerness was strongly reinforced, furnaces for heating shot were prepared in the forts on the Thames in case the ships attempted to come up the river, and

---

[1] Manwaring, G. E., and Dobrée, B.: *The Floating Republic*, p. 54.

the buoys at its mouth were removed to prevent the escape of the mutineers. This had the desired effect, and one ship after another hauled down the red flag. Parker was tried by court martial, and hanged, a fate which was also meted out to fourteen seamen and four marines. Parker was undeceived as to the virtues of ochlocracy before his death, for in a last letter he wrote to a friend:

"Remember, never to make yourself the busy body of the lower classes, for they are cowardly, selfish, and ungrateful; the least trifle will intimidate them, and him whom they have exalted one moment as their demagogue, the next they will not scruple to exalt upon the gallows. I own it is with pain that I make such a remark to you, but truth demands it. I have experimentally proved it, and am very soon to be made the example of it. There is nothing new in my treatment; compare it with the treatment of most of the advocates for the improvement of the conditions of the multitude in all ages."[1]

The mutinies were not without their effect, for conditions in the Navy began thenceforth to improve, but that they should have been necessary is a grave reflection upon the Admiralty.[2]

In the following year, 1798, England was threatened from another quarter, namely, by the outbreak of a rebellion in Ireland. The majority of the population of that country had lost rather than gained by the grant of Home Rule in 1782, for this measure did little but increase the power of the minority that controlled the kingdom. Pitt had attempted to establish freer trade between England and Ireland, but he had not been successful, and the grant to the Catholics of freedom of worship and the right to vote had done more harm than good, for their ineligibility to sit in Parliament had been retained. Government remained in the hands of those who were members of the Church of Ireland, and neither Protestant Dissenters nor Catholics had any part in it. The leading anti-English organization was called the "United Irishmen", because it

[1] Quoted by Manwaring, G. E., and Dobrée, B.: *The Floating Republic*, p. 275.
[2] There was an excellent account of the mutinies by Mr. D. Hannay in the *Saturday Review* in June and July, 1891.

worked for a union of the Dissenters in the North and the Catholics in the South. In these circumstances it was not surprising that the discontented began to look to France, with whom the Irish connection had always been strong, for help, and in 1796 a French expedition came within an ace of landing in Kerry. Unfortunately, the threat of danger impelled the loyalists to repression rather than conciliation, and the Orangemen, embodied in regiments of yeomanry, acquired a most unsavoury reputation for cruelty. These units were reinforced by others from Great Britain, including a regiment from Wales called the "Ancient Britons". The methods of the yeomanry can be gathered from an incident which took place near Newry. Information was received that arms were concealed in a certain house, and when this proved not to be the case, the building was set on fire by the Ancient Britons. The peasants in the neighbourhood, supposing the conflagration to be accidental, came to extinguish it, whereupon they were attacked by troopers, who killed thirty of them, including a woman and two children. An old man of seventy, who had fled from the scene of slaughter, was decapitated with a blow from a sabre while he was asking for mercy on his knees. In imitation of the Jacobins the United Irishmen wore their hair short, and it was a favourite pastime with the yeomen to torture "croppies" by affixing to their heads a "pitch-cap", a covering lined with hot pitch, which could not be removed without tearing the scalp. Torture and the lash were freely employed to extract information, but what, as ever, infuriated the Irish was the outrages perpetrated on women.

These measures, brutal as they were, broke the back of the separatist movement in the north, and a further blow was received by the United Irishmen when fifteen of their leaders were arrested in Dublin. The most prominent of them, Lord Edward FitzGerald, escaped for a time, and, when he was found, made so desperate a resistance that fire-arms were used on both sides, and he died soon after he had been captured. Deprived of their leaders and of immediate French support the rebels rose in May 1798, without any very definite plan. There was sporadic fighting in Kildare, Carlow, and Wicklow but the real centre of hostilities was in Wexford. Connaught remained quiet, Munster was scarcely affected, and two outbreaks in Antrim and Down were easily suppressed. The rebellion was marked by the most revolting atrocities, and there was little to choose between the two parties in point of savagery. The method of execution most favoured by the rebels was by means of pikes, possibly because gunpowder was scarce. There was a particularly revolting massacre of this nature on a bridge at Wexford town, when eighty-one prisoners were piked to death. The manner of piking was by thrusting two pikes into the front of the victim, and two into his back; in this state he was held up in the air until he died, when his body was thrown over the bridge into the river. Sometimes this procedure was varied by ripping open the belly of a prisoner, and making him run in that condition as far as he could, when he was duly piked. At Scullabogue, 180 people, including many women and children, were driven into a barn thirty-four feet long and fifteen wide, which was then set on fire, and the occupants burnt alive. A small child that managed to crawl under the door of the blazing building was piked by a rebel, and thrown back into the flames.

The rebellion was crushed on June 21st, when General Lake routed the insurgents at Vinegar Hill, and for some months afterwards a terrible vengeance was taken by the victors for the atrocities committed by the vanquished. At the same time, it is to be noted that the conflict was very largely in the nature of a civil war, for relatively few English soldiers were engaged. Hardly had the rising been suppressed than a detachment of French troops, under the command of General Humbert, landed at Killala in Mayo, and after occupying Ballina, defeated the British forces at Castlebar. The French were disappointed in finding that the rebellion was at an end, and after another victory at Collooney, they surrendered at Ballinamuck, near Granard in County Longford. The effect of these events upon the English people was considerable, and the impression they created was that Ireland would continue to be a danger until there was a legislative union between her and the other two kingdoms. Accordingly, in 1800 the

United Kingdom of Great Britain and Ireland came into being, and the opportunity was taken to drop the title "King of France" which had been used since the days of Edward III. As George III was in theory the ally of Louis XVIII against Republican France it was felt that the retention of the old formula would be invidious, and since that time all reference to the ancient claim to the throne of France has been omitted, save for the *fleurs-de-lys* which appear on the uniforms of the drummers of the Guards.

Thus, as on so many other occasions in her history, Britain pulled through in spite of her unpreparedness for war on the new scale introduced by the French Revolution. If the campaigns in Flanders ended in disaster, it was at least as much our allies' fault as our own, and at sea a long series of victories proved that whatever the hardships to which British sailors were subjected, the latter could give as good an account of themselves as ever in face of an enemy. The "glorious" First of June, Cape St. Vincent, Camperdown, and the Nile all awake memories that are among the most glorious in the national annals. Unhappily, at this juncture the obstinacy of George III deprived England for some years of the services of the great minister under whom she had weathered the storm.

Pitt realized that if the Union was to be a success equality of rights must be granted to Roman Catholics, but he had reckoned without the King and the treachery of at least one of his colleagues. The procedure he proposed to adopt was to secure the approval of the Cabinet for the necessary measure of relief, and then to discuss the matter with the Sovereign. Unfortunately, when the notices for the meeting of the Cabinet went out Lord Loughborough, the Lord Chancellor, was in attendance on the King at Weymouth, and he at once set to work to ingratiate himself with George by exciting his prejudices against Pitt's proposals. Loughborough was an extremely supple politician, and was admirably portrayed by Churchill:

> Adopting arts by which gay villains rise
> And reach the heights which honest men despise;
> Mute at the Bar and in the Senate loud.

Dull 'mong the dullest, proudest of the proud,
A pert prim prater of the Northern race,
Guilt in his heart, and famine in his face.

The line which Loughborough took was to advise the King that to consent to Catholic Emancipation would be a violation of his Coronation Oath, and thereafter this became an obsession with him. Dundas, who was loyal to Pitt, tried to allay the Royal scruples by explaining that the Oath referred, not to his executive actions, but only to assent to an act of the Legislature. Far from having the desired effect, this argument merely elicited from the King the retort, "None of your Scotch metaphysics, Mr. Dundas! None of your Scotch metaphysics!"

George II could always be relied upon to oppose any proposal that demanded breadth of vision, and the fact that it emanated from the man who had served him faithfully for seventeen years made not the slightest difference. At a *levée* at St. James's Palace he told Windham that he regarded all supporters of Catholic Emancipation as "personally indisposed" towards him. A little later he burst out to Dundas, "What is this that the young Lord[1] has brought over, which they are going to throw at my head? Lord C. came over with the plan in September. . . . I shall reckon any man my personal enemy who proposes any such measure. The most Jacobinical thing I ever heard of." Such an attitude of course encouraged all those who wished to stand well with the King to oppose Pitt, and George followed it up by making the Prime Minister's position impossible. Without waiting to find out whether the latter would resign if his advice was rejected, the King asked Addington to form a ministry; when that statesman demurred, his Royal master grew sentimental, and exclaimed, "Lay your hand upon your heart and ask yourself where I am to turn for support if you do not stand by me." On this Pitt resigned, but the matter was further complicated by the King's relapse for a short period into insanity. When he recovered he proceeded to lay the blame for his illness upon Pitt, and most unfairly extracted from the latter a promise that he would not again raise the question of Catholic Emancipation.

[1] i.e. Lord Castlereagh, who was Chief Secretary for Ireland.

By these manœuvres the King obtained what he wanted. He had once more a weak Prime Minister, and he had the assurance that the measure to which he so strongly objected would not be brought forward again. What weighed nothing with him was the fact that peace was about to be made with a France united under Napoleon, and that the country's interest demanded the strongest possible administration at the helm while the negotiations were in progress. George had broken the Whigs in the early days of his reign, and now he flattered himself that he had destroyed the national party so laboriously created by Pitt. He forgot that what might be good enough tactics in time of profound peace was highly dangerous in a crisis, and it was lucky for Great Britain that as a counterpart to her Royal destroyer of ministries she possessed a Nelson and a Wellington.

The new administration, although it contained some able men, was a joke. Addington was the son of a prominent physician, and the rapidity of his rise in the political world is attested by the fact that he was a Speaker at the age of thirty-two. He was Prime Minister in the early forties, and this seems to have turned his head, for Pitt described him as "without exception the vainest man he had ever met with".[1] Canning believed that Addington had been guilty of the blackest treachery to Pitt in taking office, and he attacked the new ministry, both in and out of Parliament, with a violence which has rarely been equalled, and never excelled, in British history. Some of Canning's quips have become immortal, such as the famous lines:

> Pitt is to Addington,
> As London is to Paddington.

When a proposal was made to defend the Thames estuary by means of block-houses, Canning wrote:

> If blocks can the nation deliver,
> Two places are safe from the French;
> The first is the mouth of the river,
> The second the Treasury Bench.

[1] Rose, J. H.: *The Life of William Pitt*, Vol. II, p. 477.

The new Prime Minister had appointed his brother, Hilery, Secretary at War, and his brother-in-law, Bragge Bathurst, Treasurer of the Navy, and this prompted Canning to the following lampoon:

> How blest, how firm the Statesman stands
> (Him no low intrigue can move)
> Circled by faithful kindred bands,
> And propped by fond fraternal love.
> When his speeches hobble vilely,
> What "Hear him's" burst from Brother Hiley;
> When his faltering periods lag,
> Hark to the cheers of Brother Bragge.
>
> . . . . .
>
> Each a gentleman at large,
> Lodged and fed at public charge,
> Paying (with a grace to charm ye)
> This the Fleet, and that the Army.

In more doubtful taste, not least because they came from one who was himself the son of an actress, were the attempts to discredit Addington on the score of his birth:

> My name's the doctor. On the Berkshire Hills
> My father purged his patients—a wise man,
> Whose constant care was to increase his store,
> And keep his eldest son—myself—at home.
> But I had heard of politics, and longed
> To sit within the Common's House and get
> A place; and luck gave what my sire denied.

On May 28th, 1802, Pitt's forty-third birthday, Canning organized a banquet at the Merchant Taylors' Hall in commemoration of the event, but neither Pitt nor Addington were present. The occasion was, however, made memorable by the recital of Canning's latest poem, *The Pilot that Weathered the Storm*. The last stanza is by far the best:

> And O! if again the rude whirlwind should rise,
> The dawning of peace should fresh darkness deform
> The regrets of the good and the fears of the wise
> Shall turn to the pilot that weathered the storm.

Nevertheless, in spite of these satires Addington continued in office. He secured a majority at a general election, and he

concluded the Treaty of Amiens with France; a peace, as
Sheridan said, "which all men are glad of, but no man can be
proud of". The Treaty soon proved to be no more than a
truce, and war began again in 1803, though in very different
circumstances from ten years before. Then, the British
Government had to contend with a noisy minority of uncertain
size which openly preferred the enemy to their own rulers, but
France was in a chaotic condition; now, Britain was united,
save for a handful of Whigs who persisted in believing that
Napoleon was more sinned against than sinning, but her rival
was at the very height of her power. Such being the case, it is
surprising how calmly contemporaries took the situation. Jane
Austen was writing at Chawton quite unmoved by events that
were transforming the world, and there is no reason to suppose
that she was in any way exceptional. Nearer the coast there
was more alarm, and Hardy, both in *The Trumpet-Major* and
The Dynasts, has shown how the shadow of a French landing
hung over his own county of Dorset.

When Napoleon assembled the *grande armée*, 115,000
strong, at Boulogne the threat of invasion became very real
indeed, and it was not rendered any less deadly by the lack of
an adequate defensive organization on this side of the Channel.
The coasts had never been properly fortified since the days of
Henry VIII, and that monarch's old castles were still being
patched up from time to time. Various ports, such as
Plymouth, Portsmouth, Sheerness, and Harwich, had received
attention under Charles II, and additional fortifications had
been added at intervals in the reigns of Anne and the first two
Georges, but there was no systematic *enceinte* of earthworks at
any British port before 1860. When war broke out in 1793
the Mayor and Corporation of each borough were still
theoretically responsible for its defence. As the "Army of
England" began to be marshalled opposite Dover, defensive
plans, many of them based on those of 1588, were hastily put
into operation. Martello towers appeared at the more exposed
points along the coast, and beacons ready for firing were
placed on all the heights. Sometimes these were lighted by
mistake, and a hasty mobilization was the result. Scott des-

cribes one such case in *The Antiquary*, and in the notes to that work he relates the readiness with which the Selkirkshire Yeomanry mustered on February 2nd, 1804, when a false alarm was given from Home Castle. In Dorset the news of a French landing became so frequent that it began to pall: as one of Hardy's characters put it:

". . . Never again do I stir my stumps for any alarm short of the Day of Judgment! Nine times has my rheumatical rest been broke in these last three years by hues and cries of Boney upon us. 'Od rot the feller; Now he's made a fool of me once more, till my inside is like a wash-tub, what wi' being so gallied, and running so leery!"[1]

The task of defending the coast was not made any easier by the partiality of the King for Weymouth, whither he went every year to Gloucester Lodge, a building which, although now an hotel, is but little altered. These visits necessitated a large concentration of forces, which could have been better employed elsewhere. To quote Hardy once again:

SECOND SPECTATOR:

Yes. I wonder King George is let venture down on this coast, where he might be snapped up in a moment like a minney by a her'n, so near as we be to the field of Boney's vagaries! Begad, he's as like to land here as anywhere. Gloucester Lodge could be surrounded, and George and Charlotte carried off before he could put on his hat, or she her red cloak and pattens!

THIRD SPECTATOR:

'Twould be no such joke to kidnap 'em as you think. Look at the frigates down there. Every night they are drawn up in a line across the mouth of the Bay, almost touching each other; and ashore a double line of sentinels, well primed with beer and ammunition, one at the water's edge, and the other on the Esplanade, stretch along the whole front. Then close to the Lodge a guard is mounted after eight o'clock; there be pickets on all the hills; at the Harbour

[1] *The Dynasts*, Part I, Act II, Scene V.

mouth is a battery of twenty four-pounders; and over-right 'em a dozen six-pounders, and several howitzers. And next look at the size of the camp of horse and foot up here.

FIRST SPECTATOR:

Everybody, however, was fairly galled this week when the King went out yachting, meaning to be back for the theatre; and the time passed, and it got dark, and the play couldn't begin, and eight or nine o'clock came, and never a sign of him. I don't know when 'a did land; but 'twas said by all that it was a foolhardy pleasure to take.

FOURTH SPECTATOR:

He's a very obstinate and comical old gentleman; and by all account 'a wouldn't make port when asked to.[1]

The King was a liability in the matter of defence in more ways than one, for he gave orders for the construction of extensive barracks at Weymouth without even consulting either the War Office or the Commander-in-Chief.

The enrolling of men to meet a possible invasion was somewhat haphazard, and in spite of their patriotic ardour it was probably just as well that they were not called upon to meet the French veterans. In any event, the population was only half that of France. Soon after the war broke out again 300,000 Volunteers, including no less a person than Fox himself, had been enrolled, but until June 1804 nearly half of them were without firearms of any sort, and the whole body was never fully equipped. An Act was also passed for the drawing up of lists of all men between seventeen and fifty-five, and the Lords-Lieutenant were instructed to see that it was enforced. In each parish which did not provide an adequate number of Volunteers, the inhabitants between these ages were called out, and drilled once a week for twenty weeks in each year. What regular troops existed were concentrated at Colchester, Chelmsford, Chatham, and Shorncliffe, and elaborate means of rapid communication were devised. By the system of semaphores called the "Aerial Telegraph" messages could be

[1] *The Dynasts*, Part I, Act II, Scene VI.

transmitted at the rate of about seven miles a minute, and there were also the numerous beacons to which allusion has already been made. The plan of campaign was to defend London at all costs, and the King announced that he would send the Queen and the Princesses beyond the Severn, while he himself headed the national resistance to the invader. Meanwhile there were collected in every creek along the coast hulks and flat-bottomed boats, which could be rapidly moved from place to place to resist landing-parties. The spirit of the nation could not have been better, and it was truly regrettable that when the immediate danger was over the ministry of the day refused to support a vote of thanks to the Volunteers for their services.[1]

Pitt played a very active part in organizing the local defences of Kent and Sussex in his capacity of Lord Warden of the Cinque Ports. He took up his residence at Walmer Castle, and was there joined by his niece, Lady Hester Stanhope, who was then twenty-seven. This lady has been severely handled by generations of historians, and because in her later days she was eccentric, it has been concluded that she was always slightly mad. If history was for long the peculiar preserve of the Whigs, so was Society, and Lady Hester suffered accordingly. She was the daughter of "Citizen Stanhope", but had early left the roof of her somewhat unbalanced parent[2] to live with her grandmother, old Lady Chatham, at Burton Pynsent; it was on the latter's death that she took up her residence with her uncle. Sir John Moore was at that time commanding at Shorncliffe, and Lady Hester fell in love with him, as a certain General Phipps discovered to his cost.

"She added that General Phipps had made a call one day, and the conversation turning upon Sir John Moore, that he had sought to disparage that officer in Mr. Pitt's estimation, and that she, perceiving his design, had said, 'You imagine, General, that Mr. Pitt does not greatly value Sir John's

[1] cf. Fletcher, C. R. L.: An Introductory History of England, Vol. IV, pp. 50–58, 234–235.
[2] Lord Stanhope had made her as a child regularly tend turkeys on a common.

abilities, but learn from me, you nasty kangaroo'—alluding to General Phipps' paralytic infirmity and imitating his manner of holding his hands—'that there is no one in the King's army whose services he appreciates more highly.' 'Lady Hester! Lady Hester! What are you saying?' exclaimed Mr. Pitt, with an ill-suppressed smile which betrayed his secret enjoyment of the scene."[1]

In later life Lady Hester certainly did betray a certain amount of eccentricity, or rather what was considered eccentricity in a woman in those days. She went out to the East, and the following extracts from one of her letters to Stratford Canning give a good idea of her life there:

"LATAKIA, 22 *Oct.* 1813.

"You must not be alarmed and fancy that I am going to keep up a correspondence with you, but I cannot avoid thanking you for your letter (which I received a few days ago), and also for the trouble you have taken about the poor victim, who has been driven by the plague from his retreat, but yet I hope has rather bettered his situation. All *you* say is very just, but to say the truth it does not quite please me to hear rich men complain of *poverty*: however, God will take care of his creatures in this and every other country. The English world are about as good-natured as I believed them to be; to ridicule a person said to be starving in a burning desert is very charitable, but poor souls their imagination is as miserable as their humanity is bounded, for it never I suppose entered their heads that I carried everything before me, and was crowned under the triumphal arch at Palmyra, pitched my tent amidst thousands of Arabs, and spent a month with these very interesting people. Let the great learn of them hospitality and liberality. I have seen an Arab strip himself to his shirt to give clothes to those he thought needed them more than himself. I have suffered great fatigue, it is very true, because all my people were such cowards, and they gave me a good deal of trouble, but yet

[1] Lane-Poole, S.: *Life of the Right Hon. Stratford Canning, Viscount Stratford de Redcliffe*, Vol. I, pp. 114–115.

I cannot regret past hardships, as it has given me the opportunity of seeing what is so curious and interesting, the manners and customs of the most free and independent people in the world. . . .

"In about a week I repair to a pretty convent at the foot of Lebanon for the winter. The Pasha of Acre is come into that neighbourhood to repair a castle, and the Prince of the Druses hunts within an hour of my habitation, so I shall often see him; we are great friends, he is a very agreeable man, and very popular in the mountain. I am quite at home all over the country; the common people pay me the same sort of respect as they do a great Turk, and the great men treat me as if I was one of them. In short I am very comfortable in my own odd way; part of this country is divine and I always find something to amuse and occupy my mind. Now the good people in England may imagine me forlorn and miserable, they are very welcome. I would not change my philosophical life for their empty follies. It would have been more friendly of you to have mentioned your own affairs, because you ought to know I am interested about them, but as I am in a perfect state of ignorance respecting all that concerns you since you left this country, I can only say I hope you prosper. . . .

"Mohammed Ali admitted me to the Divan and when at Acre I rode Soliman Pasha's parade horse, having the use of his own sword and khangar, all over jewels. My visit to the Pasha of Damascus in the night during the Ramadan was the finest thing possible. I was mounted on an Arab horse he had given me, my people on foot, and he surrounded with two thousand servants and picked guards, Albanians, Delibashis, and Mograbines. You see the Turks are not quite such brutes as you once thought them, or they never could have treated me with the degree of friendship and hospitality they have done."[1]

That was in 1813, and seven years later Stratford Canning noted in his diary,

[1] Lane-Poole, S.: *Life of the Right Hon. Stratford Canning, Viscount Stratford de Redcliffe*, Vol. I, pp. 120–121.

"Mr. Bankes had seen Lady Hester Stanhope in Syria; she was living in a small but comfortable house, at the foot of Mount Lebanon, in full persuasion of her being one day called to the assembling of God's chosen people, in the capacity of Queen of Jerusalem. This fancy, which Mr. B. represents as having taken full possession of her mind, arose (as she herself relates) from a prophecy which the famous Brothers made to her many years ago when her superstitious curiosity led her to try his oracular skill. He then predicted, she says, that she would pass some years in the East and reign at Jerusalem. She has already exceeded the probationary term by two years."[1]

She died in 1839 surrounded by thirty servants, and the same number of cats.

The sojourn of Pitt and his niece at Walmer was not destined to be of long duration, for much as Addington wished to retain office, his incapacity made the country turn once more to "the pilot that weathered the storm". When Pitt took office again it was clear that unless he had colleagues of ability his health would not stand the strain of conducting the entire government in time of war, and also of replying to the attacks of the Opposition in the House of Commons. He sought to include Fox in the ministry, but the King would not hear of it, and said he preferred civil war to that. So Pitt, with the hand of death on him, had to go forward alone.

"The two protagonists now stood face to face—Napoleon, Emperor of the French, President of the Italian Republic, Mediator of the Swiss Republic, controller of Holland, absolute ruler of a great military Empire; Pitt, the Prime Minister of an obstinate and at times half-crazy King, dependent on a weak Cabinet, a disordered Exchequer, a Navy weakened by ill-timed economies, and land forces whose martial ardour ill made up for lack of organization, equipment, and training."[2]

[1] Lane-Poole, S.: *Life of the Right Hon. Stratford Canning, Viscount Stratford de Redcliffe*, Vol. I, p. 292.
[2] Rose, J. H.: *The Life of William Pitt*, Vol. II, p. 505.

Pitt's second ministry was almost wholly occupied with efforts to curb the power of Napoleon, efforts that were brought to nothing by the French Emperor's great victory at Austerlitz. There was, however, to be one great British triumph before Pitt died—Trafalgar. Before Nelson sailed for the last time he had an interview with the Prime Minister at Downing Street, which is said to have been the only occasion on which they ever met, and Pitt paid Nelson the compliment of escorting him to his carriage. As they passed through the ante-room, they found there Arthur Wellesley, the future Duke of Wellington, who had recently returned from India. On November 9th, 1805, Pitt attended the Lord Mayor's banquet, and delivered the most impressive, as well as the shortest, speech that has ever been pronounced by a Prime Minister on this occasion: "I return you many thanks for the honour you have done me; but Europe is not to be saved by any single man. England has saved herself by her exertions, and will, as I trust, save Europe by her example." Within three months he was dead, at the age of forty-six.

Legend has been busy with the last days of Pitt. The most famous, which was immortalized by Hardy in *The Dynasts*, represents the worn Prime Minister at Shockerwick House, near Bath, receiving the news of Austerlitz, and, after locating that village on a map of Europe, bidding his host, "Roll up that map: it will not be wanted these ten years." Another version has it that the dying man uttered these words to Lady Hester Stanhope as he observed a map on the wall when entering his house at Putney. He had been to Bath in the hope of re-establishing his health, but all to no purpose, and he was brought home to die, though the seriousness of his condition was not realized. Ingenious theories have also been put forward concerning his last words, but there can be little doubt now as to the fact that they were "My country! How I leave my country!" Pitt did not know it, but the storm had been weathered, although another ten years were to elapse before the Ship of State was safely in port. The Opposition displayed all the old Whig rancour by dividing against the motion to bury him in Westminster Abbey, and it was only by the narrow majority of six that the Common Council of the City of London decided to erect a monument to his memory.

If contemporaries were forgetful of what they owed to the dead statesman posterity has been more appreciative.

"It is Pitt's supreme claim that he continued to govern England from the grave; that, while he suffered a bodily death in 1806, his spirit marched on for twenty-one years, to the death of Canning in 1827. . . . Ten years were to pass. Then, when the bells were ringing for victory; when the army which Pitt planned, under the leader whom Pitt chose, struck the hammer blows of the Peninsular War and withstood the reeling shock of Waterloo; when the statesman whom Pitt taught brought back from Vienna the pacification which Pitt had described, but did not live to see— then we may fancy that, as Castlereagh carried to the House of Commons tidings of 'peace with honour', long awaited and dearly bought, and the cheers volleyed forth, to a faithful few must have come a swift, transitory vision of a tall slender figure, with a little cocked hat above a tilted nose, walking stiffly to his seat, to a whisper like the rustle of autumn's leaves: 'Mr. Pitt, Mr. Pitt!'."[1]

[1] Lockhart, J. G.: *The Peacemakers, 1814–1815*, pp. 229–230.

CHAPTER VII

THE COMING OF THE MACHINE

WHILE George III was governing the country through North, and, later, while Pitt was battling with Fox and Napoleon, the face of Britain was being changed out of all recognition. The sparsely populated and agricultural land was becoming an industrial and urbanized civilization, and by the time that George IV was in his grave the link with the older England had in many cases been snapped. The changes of the early nineteenth century were so great that by the twenties and thirties the eighteenth century had to a great extent already been forgotten. As Francis Place rightly pointed out, this gulf between the two eras rendered the work of the early social reformers far more difficult. Side by side with this material transformation there was a change of outlook, and reform became the order of the day.

"Everyone started 'movements'. . . . Catholics were emancipated; national education began; trades unions were made legal; the penal code was made much more humane; and, finally, Parliament reformed itself, seeking, by a characteristic Whig compromise, to preserve the exclusive representation of property by a slight extension of the franchise, the extinction of rotten boroughs, the grant of representation to the new industrial towns, and much lip-service to the doctrine of popular government. . . . It all seemed remarkably successful. The devouring red flames of the gospel of humanity faded into the pale embers of humanitarianism, the sword was put back into the scabbard, and, with the refreshing alternatives of the factory or the workhouse before him, the working man turned to the task of building Sheffield and Middlesborough on the ruins of English agriculture. The country gentlemen went into the City and their tenants into the slums. Man was remembered at the polling booth. Society was forgotten in the mean streets. The age of freedom had begun."[1]

In effect, what happened was that the reformers were so busy correcting old abuses that they ignored the new ones which were growing up so rapidly under their eyes.

The first evidence of a more humane attitude of mind is to be seen in connection with the Slave Trade, which had continued for generations without arousing any strong opposition. In the earlier part of the century little black boys were frequently employed as pages to fashionable ladies, and Gainsborough painted the portrait of the negro butler of the Duke of Montague. These, of course, were slaves, and there seems to have been little prejudice against them on the ground either of race or colour. With the passage of time the number of negroes increased, and in 1772 the number of slaves in England was officially admitted to be in the neighbourhood of 14,000. In that year it was held, in Somersett's case, that "as soon as any slave sets his foot upon English territory he becomes free".[2] This put an end to legal slavery in England itself, but it also directed attention to the condition of the negroes thus emancipated. A Committee for relieving the Black Poor was formed, and many schemes were devised. Among them was a project for settling the negroes in question on the West Coast of Africa, and Pitt offered a Treasury grant of up to £14 a head for their transportation. Applications were accordingly invited from those who wished to profit "by this opportunity of settling in one of the most fertile and pleasant countries in the known world", and finally 441 blacks and 60 London prostitutes were shipped off to Sierra Leone.[3] Useless as such measures were to achieve their immediate purpose, they did at any rate direct attention to the fact of negro slavery, and as soon as the black ceased to be regarded as a mere animal in England itself the first step had been taken in his liberation in all British possessions.

It was less difficult to work up public opinion against the

---

[1] Jerrold, D.: *England*, pp. 79–80.
[2] *cf. State Trials*, Vol. XX, pp. 1–82.
[3] *cf.* George, M. D.: *London Life in the XVIIIth Century*, pp. 134–138.

Slave Trade, because only a small section of the population made money out of it. The centre of the traffic was Liverpool, and to it that port owed a large part of its commercial prosperity. Liverpool was only admitted to a participation in the Slave Trade in 1730, but she soon outdistanced her rivals, London and Bristol. Between 1783 and 1793 no less than 313,737 slaves were carried in Liverpool ships from Africa to the West Indies, and between 1795 and 1804, in spite of the fact that during the greater part of the period the country was at war, the number had risen to 323,777; this compared with 46,405 in London, and 10,718 in Bristol bottoms.[1] Before 1772 there had actually been sales of slaves in Liverpool itself.

> "To be sold at the Exchange Coffee House, in Water Street, this day, the 12th instant, September, at 1 o'clock precisely, eleven negroes imported by the *Angola*."[2]

The trade was very remunerative, for the average cost of a slave on the West Coast was about twenty-five pounds, whereas he or she would fetch twice that amount in the West Indies. The net profit worked out at 30 per cent, but that by no means represented the whole of the gain, for the ships returned to Liverpool with sugar, tobacco, rum, and the other products of Jamaica and Barbados. It was little wonder that the inhabitants of the Mersey-side opposed the abolition of the commerce upon which their very existence seemed to depend:

> If the slave trade had gone, there's an end to our lives,
> Beggars all we must be, our children and wives,
> No ships from our ports their proud sails e'er would spread,
> And our streets grown with grass, where the cows might be fed.[3]

The ships used for the Slave Trade were built on the Mersey, and they were constructed mainly with a view to speed, for it was of the first importance that their human freight should arrive at the American market in the best

---

[1] cf. Muir, J. R. B.: *A History of Liverpool*, p. 193 et seq.
[2] *Liverpool Advertiser*, September 12, 1766.
[3] cf. Roscoe, E. S.: *The English Scene in the Eighteenth Century*, pp. 114–116.

possible condition. The slave deck ran across the ship, and as its height was only 5⅔ feet it was impossible for most of the negroes to stand upright: an alley ran down the centre, and on either side were wooden benches clamped to the floor. To these the slaves were chained, the men on one side of the gangway, and the women on the other. A dead slave might remain with his or her fellows for some days, until the sailors had the time or the inclination to throw the body overboard. On leaving Liverpool for Africa a slaver carried a quantity of cheap trinkets which were exchanged for negroes, though the former usually had to be supplemented with cash. Deals were carried out at various places on the African coast with native chiefs, who collected the necessary merchandise from the interior. This was done by surrounding a village, and then rushing it by night, when the old people were knocked on the head; the rest of the inhabitants were stripped, and marched down to the coast. As soon as the purchase price had been fixed, the negroes were branded with hot irons, and thrust into the hold of the waiting slaver. There they had sometimes to remain for a considerable time until a full cargo had been obtained. It is satisfactory to know that on occasion these chiefs met with their just reward. One of them, for example, dined with a ship's captain, and got very drunk; when he came to his senses the vessel was at sea, whereupon he was promptly branded by the amused sailors, and thrown among his victims below. Thus began that "middle passage" which was one of the worst features of the traffic. It was essential that the slaves should be given some form of exercise to keep them alive (about 10 per cent usually died on the voyage), so they were paraded on deck from time to time, and made to leap about in their chains, the lash being freely applied to stimulate their activity. If they endeavoured to put an end to their miseries by refusing to eat they were forcibly fed, and iron contrivances for this purpose were to be seen in the Liverpool shops. In this way they reached their destination in the Americas, "prime negroes branded as per margin".

Even without discussing the ethical aspects of slavery, it is impossible to resist the conclusion that the social disadvantages both of the system and of the Slave Trade far outweighed any material profit. Few human beings are fit to be entrusted with absolute power over their fellows, and in the vast majority of cases such authority merely brings out a latent sadism or lust. Indeed, it is quite possible to argue that slavery did more harm to the masters than to the slaves. Contemporary literature bears eloquent testimony to the debauched habits of the white population in the West Indian islands, where European women were scarce, and negresses and half-castes could be enjoyed at will.[1] Only a society of saints could have escaped corruption in such circumstances, and Europeans in the Tropics have little encouragement to become saints. White men married old negresses for the sake of the money that had been left them by their former lovers, and young girls from Europe became, within a week of their arrival in America, as abandoned in their behaviour as the local prostitutes.[2] The sailors on the slavers were brutalized by having so many men to lash, and so many women to possess, at will, and Liverpool was in consequence troubled by an extremely turbulent element in her population. The rich merchants, a few of whose stately houses have escaped destruction in an age of "development", were not responsible for, or in many cases even conscious of, the horrors of slavery, and Gladstone palliated them with the reflection that the condition of the West Indian negro was paradise compared with that of the spinning-mill hands in Lancashire.[3] Wilberforce, with the powerful assistance of Pitt, was unremitting in his attacks on the Slave Trade, but it was not prohibited until 1807, and four years more elapsed before it was made a felony to engage in it. In 1833 slavery was abolished, though with compensation to those who had property in slaves.

The legislators who were so zealous on behalf of the slaves too often, *more Britannico*, forgot the miseries of those nearer home, as Byng, to his credit, fully realized.

" 'Has Meriden Common been long enclosed?' 'Ah,

---

[1] *cf. The Lady Nugent's Journal, passim.*
[2] *cf.* Vaucaire, M.: *Toussaint-Louverture*, p. 5.
[3] *cf.* Burdett, O.: *W. E. Gladstone*, p. 23, and pp. 24–25.

lackaday, Sir, that was a sad job; and ruined all us poor volk: and those who then gave into it, now repent it.' 'Why so?' 'Because, we had our garden, our bees, our share of a flock of sheep, the feeding of our geese; and could cut turf for our fuel. Now all that is gone. Our cottage, as good a one as this, we gave but 50 shillings a year for; and for this we are obliged to pay £9 10*s*.; and without any ground; and coals are risen upon us from 7*d*. to 9*d*. the hundred. My cottage with many others is pulled down; and the poor are sadly put to it to get a house to put their heads in!!! Heigh ho!'"

> Hear this, ye pitiers of money-begums.
> Hear this, ye freers of black slaves.
> Hear this, ye representatives of the people.[1]

The middle and later years of the reign of George III also witnessed the commencement of a reform of the prison system and the criminal code, and much of the credit for this must go to John Howard. The state of affairs which existed in the earlier part of the century has already been sufficiently indicated, and changes occurred slowly. When George III came to the throne no less than 160 crimes were capital felonies, and the theft, by pocket-picking, of any article worth more than a shilling was punishable with death. The severity of the law defeated its own ends, for the criminal was encouraged to commit a murder in the hope of covering up a robbery, since the punishment for both was death; the "one might as well be hanged for a sheep as a lamb" principle was the order of the day. As public opinion became more humane this resulted in injured parties refraining from prosecuting, juries refusing to convict, and judges recommending to mercy. In spite of this executions were very numerous, although only about a fifth of the capital sentences were ever carried out. In 1783, at two consecutive executions, twenty people were hanged together, and in ten months in 1785 no less than ninety-six prisoners were hanged at the Old Bailey. In the Lent assizes of the latter year there were 21 capital sentences at Kingston, 12 at Lincoln, and 16 at Gloucester; in each town 9 were put into effect.

[1] *The Torrington Diaries*, Vol. II, p. 108.

An execution had lost none of its popularity as a spectacle. The record attendance was probably reached in 1767, when 80,000 people are said to have been present at one in Moorfields, while the rarity of seeing a woman burnt alive (for the murder of her husband) took a crowd 20,000 strong to Tyburn six years later; in this instance, however, the onlookers did not get their full enjoyment, for the prisoner was strangled first. In 1783 executions ceased to be held at Tyburn, and in 1790 the burning of women was abolished. The punishment of the pillory also never failed to attract a crowd. If it had been inflicted for some act of which public opinion approved, such as libelling an unpopular minister, the victim was treated as a hero, but if the mob disliked what he had done his fate might be very different. Two men, in 1763 and in 1780 respectively were pelted to death in the pillory in London, and there was another case about the same time at Bury. After the Declaration of American Independence convicts could no longer be transported to America, so they were kept in hulks on the Thames and elsewhere; this was far worse, for transportation had few terrors for the felon with a little money, as Defoe shows in *Moll Flanders*. In 1787 the first shipload of convicts was sent to Australia, and for many years to come that country was used as a penal settlement.

If the harshness of the law and the publicity given to its punishments were expected to act as a deterrent, they failed completely of their object. Crime of every sort was rampant. At one time it was estimated that 40,000 people were engaged in smuggling, and two-thirds of the tea, and half the brandy, consumed in the country paid no duty. Smugglers enjoyed the sympathy of the mass of the population, as Mr. Kipling has so well said:

> If you meet King George's men, dressed in blue and red,
> You be careful what you say, and mindful what is said.
> If they call you "pretty maid", and chuck you 'neath the chin,
> Don't you tell where no one is, nor yet where no one's been![1]

The roads were little, if any, safer than they had been a generation before, and in London itself robberies were as

[1] *Puck of Pook's Hill.*

numerous as ever. What proportion of travellers were stopped by highwaymen it is impossible to say, and attention was naturally drawn to the minority who were attacked, rather than to the majority who escaped. Byng, at least, had little sympathy with the sufferers:

"I never was robbed; but I do not attribute this so much to luck, as to my observance of early hours. I neither see the use, or taste the pleasure of travelling in the dark! Modern young gentlemen, after dawdling away their day in London, think it polite to travel in the dark, and knock up inns; there they stop all the following noon, and they enjoy a subsequent night of clatter; wheels breaking, horses falling; then demanding applause or pity (which I shall never bestow) for the mischief they have sought; and for being encouragers of roguery!"[1]

As has already been mentioned, there was no effective system of police to deal with the criminal classes. With the exception of a few Bow Street officers and some mounted patrols, the only police in London were parish constables and the watchmen, many of whom were old and decrepit. In the event of serious trouble recourse was always had to the troops. As for the magistrates, with a few honourable exceptions such as the Fieldings, contemporaries could hardly find words strong enough to express their contempt. The magistracy of Middlesex had for the most part fallen into the hands of men described by Burke with pardonable exaggeration as "the scum of the earth" who used their office as a means of gain.[2] Smollett was even more emphatic,

"Many of the justices . . . were men of profligate lives, needy, mean, ignorant, and rapacious, and often acted from the most scandalous principles of selfish avarice."[3]

In 1792 a definite step forward was taken when Parliament established stipendiary magistrates appointed by the Crown for the London police courts, but another generation was to

[1] *The Torrington Diaries*, Vol. II, p. 79.
[2] *History of the Parliamentary Debates*, Vol. XXI, p. 592; and Vol. XXIX, p. 1034
[3] *History of England*, Vol. III, pp. 330–331.

elapse before they were supported by an efficient police, and not the least important reason for this delay was the widespread opposition to any measure calculated to increase the power of the authorities. The Tories remembered Cromwell, and the Whigs could not forget James II, so criminals remained at large in the sacred name of civil and religious freedom.

The long war with Revolutionary and Napoleonic France reduced the numbers of potential malefactors by augmenting the opportunities for gaining an honest living, and the situation was further improved by a mitigation in the severity of the law. In 1808 Sir Samuel Romilly secured the passage through Parliament of a measure abolishing capital punishment for the offence of pocket-picking, and this was the starting-point for further modifications. In 1819 a committee was appointed to consider the whole question of the Criminal Law, by which two hundred crimes were still nominally punishable with death,[1] and it reported in favour of sweeping changes. When Peel became Home Secretary in 1822 he gave effect to these recommendations, and within the next few years the system was transformed. By 1827 over 250 Criminal Statutes had been repealed or modified, and an Act had even been passed for the prevention of cruelty to horses and cattle,[2] when George IV died there were only thirteen crimes still punishable with death. Nor was this all, for Peel realized that his reforms would be ineffective unless based upon an adequate police force, and in 1829 the Metropolitan Police came into existence. This was to some extent modelled on the Royal Irish Constabulary which he had created a few years before, and it was in Dublin, rather than in London, that policemen were first called "Bobbies" and "Peelers".

These reforms were largely due to a revival of that religious feeling which had been deliberately repressed by Walpole and the Whig oligarchy. Enthusiasm of any sort, in their opinion, was to be deprecated as dangerous to the Revolution settlement, but religious enthusiasm was to be avoided like the

---

[1] It is to be noted that for only twenty-five of these had anyone ever been hanged.

[2] Cruelty to children did not attract the attention of Parliament until a later date.

plague. The methods employed to make Christianity safe for the Guelphs have already been discussed, and the consequence was that only the dwindling sect of the Non-Jurors remained to keep alive a religion uncontaminated by State control. The Presbyterians had mostly drifted to Unitarianism, and the other Dissenting bodies, where they still survived, were but shadows of their former selves. The Church of England was at its nadir during the reigns of the first two Georges, and during the early years of George III. Convocation remained silenced, and ecclesiastical preferments, invariably made to serve political ends, were regarded by clergy and laity alike as little more than desirable offices. Bishoprics and deaneries were solicited from the Prime Minister of the day with unblushing importunity. The effect of this was seen in the neglected condition of cathedrals and parish churches. *The Torrington Diaries*, for example, abound in references to rectors and vicars who scandalously neglected their duties; what their author says of Salisbury is typical:

> "The close is comfortable, and the divines well seated; but the house of God is kept in sad order, to the disgrace of our Church, and of Christianity. Whenever I see these things I wish for a return of the authority and Church government of the land. The church-yard is like a cow-common, as dirty and as neglected, and through the centre stagnates a boggy ditch."[1]

The reaction was initiated by John and Charles Wesley, and became known as Methodism. They came of a Puritan family, and were sons of the Rector of Epworth in Lincolnshire. It was not the original intention of either brother to break away from the Established Church, of which they were both ordained priests, but, given existing circumstances, the breach was inevitable. Although John Wesley was very far removed from being a hedgerow preacher, he laid great stress on enthusiasm; that this was unlikely to recommend him to his ecclesiastical superiors can be gauged from a charge by Bishop

---

[1] Vol. I, p. 106.

Secker, afterwards Archbishop of Canterbury, to the clergy of the diocese of Oxford:

> "Our liturgy consists of evening as well as of morning prayer, and no inconvenience can arise from attending it, provided persons are within tolerable distance of church. Few have business at that time of day, and amusements ought never to be preferred on the Lord's day before religion, not to say that there is room for both."[1]

Admirable advice, no doubt, but hardly couched in language calculated to rouse either clergy or laity to action. This attitude was in marked contrast with the zeal, sometimes excessive, of the Methodists. One step led to another in the direction of schism. The clergy would not lend their pulpits, and this meant open-air preaching, which in its turn was followed by lay preaching, until in the end lay ordination was reached. Contemporaries might scoff, as a later generation scoffed at the Salvation Army, but the Methodists gained ground, until Byng is found noting at Ashby-de-la-Zouch, as in no way exceptional,

> ". . . A Methodist chapel . . . to which there went five to the one that went to church; and no wonder, as here may be fervour, and devotion."[2]

On the conclusion of his tour in the Midlands in 1789 he wrote:

> ". . . About religion I have made some enquiry (having been in so many churches) and find it to be lodged in the hands of the Methodists; as the greater clergy do not attend their duty, and the lesser neglect it; that where the old psalm singing is abolished, none is established in its place; as the organ is inconvenient, and not understood; at most places the curates never attend regularly, or to any effect, or comfort, so no wonder that the people are gone over to Methodism."[3]

However regrettable it may be that Wesley and his followers

---

[1] Quoted by Roscoe, E. S.: *The English Scene in the Eighteenth Century*, p. 266.
[2] *The Torrington Diaries*, Vol. II, p. 69.   [3] *ibid*, Vol. II, p. 130.

could not find a sphere for their activities within the Establishment, as their prototypes had done in earlier centuries, it is satisfactory to note that there soon grew up in the Church of England the Evangelical Movement. At first it, too, was regarded with suspicion, and the story is told of one who was interested in it, and who was the guest of the Bishop of London at Fulham, wishing to see some member of the Clapham Sect; the episcopal carriage put him down at the "Plough", whence he was compelled to continue his journey on foot, since it was considered more fitting for the Bishop's equipage to be seen waiting outside that inn than at the door of the Evangelical. It is true that in the conflict of opinions uniformity was lost, but what is often forgotten is that those who became Methodists nevertheless remained Christians, and by his work among the new urban population Wesley probably saved the country from that rabid anti-clericalism which has been so distressing a feature in the recent history of many another country.

All this time there was another force at work which was ere long to exercise very great influence indeed, the Romantic Movement. Until George III had been for some years on the throne the classical tradition in both prose and verse was supreme. The heroic couplet, as perfected by Pope, was the object of every poet, while in prose Addison had handed on the torch of classicism to Johnson. The latter towered over his contemporaries like a Colossus.

"Nothing that was unlovely or of evil report, nothing that was pinchbeck or sham in the literary world, ever found favour with his pure, intrepid and clear-sighted judgment. He was a stalwart champion of what he liked, and a good hater of what he hated; he loved to knock down the idols of market-places. . . . That his own diction was, especially in his earlier work, both turgid and classical to a somewhat absurd degree is a small point; it was as a critic, not as a writer that he was super-excellent."[1]

Before Johnson was dead the Romantic Movement was born, and Gibbon was the last great master of the old Classical

---

[1] Fletcher, C. R. L.: *An Introductory History of England*, Vol. IV, p. 220.

school. The social and political influence of the Romantic Movement has rarely received in this country the attention which has rightly been paid to it abroad. M. Charles Maurras has shown how intimately the decay of the old classical spirit in literature was connected with the spread of democratic doctrines, and most of the leaders of the new movement, at any rate when they were exercising their greatest influence, held advanced views on political questions. This was fully realized by those who were responsible for the *Anti-Jacobin*, and is a tribute to their perspicacity. Sir Walter Scott was the exception that proved the rule. As Mr. Douglas Jerrold has so well put it:

"The classical tradition, still dominant at the end of the eighteenth century, has faded before the romantic movement, which derives its inspiration, not from that which, being common to all, unites all, but from that which, being individual to each, separates each man from his neighbour."[1]

The protagonists of the Romantic Movement were curiously unscientific in their attitude. They pretended to look to the Middle Ages for inspiration, but in thus appealing to the memory of a distant past, all they really sought was a weapon against the classical tradition which was associated with the existing order. If they had taken the trouble to investigate the conditions prevailing in the period they so much admired they would have found them infinitely more rigid than those of their own day, but Romanticism provided an excuse for loose thinking, and, in more than one case, for loose living as well. Others talked glibly about "noble savages", and followed Rousseau in depicting an age when mankind was innocent and free. The fact that savages, noble or otherwise, were and are subject to innumerable taboos and conventions was conveniently ignored, as was the judgment of Hobbes, which described the life of early man as "solitary, poor, nasty, brutish, and short".[2] The evil that the Romantics did lived after them, for not only did they seriously weaken that classical spirit which characterizes European civilization at its best, but the extremes to which they went precipitated the inevitable reaction of

[1] *The Criterion*, Vol. XII, No. XLVII, pp. 224–225.   [2] *Leviathan*, Ch. XIII.

Realism. This latter produced Zola, who, to quote M. Léon Daudet,

> "from the outset, made Truth his god and enshrined her, pen in hand, between the manure heap and the morgue".[1]

His influence upon the literature of the world is still very marked, and much to its detriment. The Romantic Movement has much for which to answer.

The immediate effects of Romanticism were not, however, wholly bad, for it fostered an affection for the monuments of the past, and also for the beauties of nature. Defoe took little or no interest in a ruin, and although the reverse was the case with Torrington, the latter's diary bears eloquent testimony to the fact that the normal eighteenth-century Englishman was a great deal of a Vandal; even Torrington himself was not above a little pilfering when opportunity offered. It is easy to laugh at "society" in the Victorian era with its elaborate picnics in ruined abbeys, at Beckford for his extravagances at Fonthill, and at the sham Gothic of Ashridge, but it is well to remember that they are evidence of a change of opinion which henceforth was to regard ancient monuments as treasures to be preserved, rather than as quarries to be developed. Formality, not least in dress, had gone too far, but there was both pathos and bathos in the "return to nature" school headed by Coleridge, Wordsworth, Blake, and Burns. Wordsworth wrote *Intimations of Immortality*, but he was also the author of *Peter Bell:*

> So from his pocket Peter takes
> His shining horn tobacco-box;
> And in a light and careless way,
> As men who with their purpose play,
> Upon the lid he knocks.

The criticism of Wordsworth might well be applied to the whole Romantic Movement:

> Two voices are there—one is of the Deep;
> . . . . .
> The other is an old half-witted sheep,
> . . . . .
> And, Wordsworth, both are thine.

[1] *Memoirs* (English translation), p. 20.

The middle and later years of George III, and the reign of his eldest son, thus witnessed the appearance of a humanitarianism to which the eighteenth century had previously been a stranger. The Slave Trade was abolished, the Criminal Law was overhauled, conditions in the Services were improved, and innumerable lesser reforms were put into operation. Yet all this was aimed at correcting the abuses of the past, and nothing was done for the victims of the Industrial Revolution which was so rapidly changing the whole face of the country. As Disraeli so aptly wrote:

"They come forth: the mine delivers its gang and the pit its bondsmen; the forge is silent and the engine is still. The plain is covered with the swarming multitude: bands of stalwart men, broad-chested and muscular, wet with toil, and black as the children of the tropics; troops of youth, alas! of both sexes, though neither their raiment nor their language indicates the difference; all are clad in male attire; and oaths that men might shudder at, issue from lips born to breathe words of sweetness. Yet these are to be, some are, the mothers of England! But can we wonder at the hideous coarseness of their language, when we remember the savage rudeness of their lives! Naked to the waist, an iron chain fastened to a belt of leather runs between their legs clad in canvas trousers, while on hands and feet an English girl, for twelve, sometimes for sixteen hours a day, hauls and hurries tubs of coals up subterranean roads, dark, precipitous, and plashy; circumstances that seem to have escaped the notice of the Society for the Abolition of Negro Slavery. Those worthy gentlemen too appear to have been singularly unconscious of the sufferings of the little trappers, which was remarkable, as many of them were in their own employ."[1]

The transformation of Great Britain from an agricultural into an industrial community was effected within the space of two generations, and to the rapidity of the change was in no small measure due the atrocities by which it was attended.

[1] *Sybil*, Bk. III, Ch. II.

About 1750 it was discovered that coal and coke could be used for smelting, and ten years later the Industrial Revolution may be said to have begun with the foundation of the Carron iron-works, which had blast furnaces for coal. One discovery succeeded another, until by 1796 the use of charcoal had almost ceased, and vast ironworks were established in the coal districts, which soon ceased to be agricultural. Inventions multiplied apace: Hargreaves invented the spinning jenny, Arkwright the water-frame, Crompton the muslin-wheel, Cartwright the power-loom, Bell the cylinder printing for calico, and Murray the new machines for spinning flax, while, above all, there was Watt's perfection of the steam-engine. Population became concentrated in those districts where the necessary power, either coal or water, was to be obtained, that is to say, in the North, which, hitherto the most backward part of the country, now became the chief seat of industrial life and commercial enterprise. The roads were improved out of all recognition by Telford and Macadam, and additional means of communication were supplied by the construction of canals. The Duke of Bridgwater played a prominent part in this work, and the new canal between Worsley and Manchester, with its later extension to Runcorn, reduced the carriage of goods from Liverpool to Manchester from 12s. to 6s. a ton, while by road it was 40s. For a time there was a veritable boom in the flota-tion of canal companies, and between 1790 and 1794 no less than eighty-one Acts of Parliament were passed for that purpose.

Contemporary evidence goes to prove that it would be difficult to exaggerate the terrible conditions which prevailed in these new manufacturing towns. In Manchester, in 1795, there were "nearly whole streets built of wood, clay, and plas-ter", and the town "unfortunately vies with, or exceeds, the Metropolis, in the closeness with which the poor are crowded in offensive, dark, damp and incommodious habitations, a too fertile source of disease".[1]

"The great majority of hand-loom weavers work in cellars, sufficiently lighted to enable them to throw the shuttle,

---

[1] Aiken, J.: *Description of the Country round Manchester*, p. 192.

but cheerless because seldom visited by the sun. The reason cellars are chosen is that cotton requires to be woven damp. . . . Unhappily, the medium which might be preserved without injury to the constitution and which is preserved in the best power loom factories, the impoverished hand loom weavers are often obliged to disregard. I have seen them working in cellars dug out of an undrained swamp; the streets formed by their houses without sewers and flooded with rain; and water therefore running down the bare walls of the cellars and rendering them unfit for the abode of dogs or cats. The descent to these cellars is usually by a broken step ladder. The floor is but seldom boarded or paved."[1]

Housing conditions had been steadily deteriorating both in town and country. The pulling down of cottages and the refusal to build new ones had resulted in several families crowding into the accomodation previously intended for one. Moreover, young people who in the days before the enclosures would have lived in the farms as servants in husbandry, or as apprentices, now remained in the cottages with their families.[2] In Sussex, for example, it was asserted:

"Many of them (i.e. labourers) have now got into one cottage; it was stated to me that forty years ago a cottage that only held a man and his wife and three children, now contained five families, consisting of nineteen persons."[3]

At Stourpaine, in Dorset, conditions were even worse. There is a room ten feet square, roofed with open thatch, and only seven feet high in the middle, with one window about fifteen inches square, slept a family of eleven in three beds; in one the father and mother and two young children; in the second two grown-up daughters and a younger girl; and in the third, four sons. It was further stated that his was no exceptional case, but represented the ordinary accommodation in

---

[1] *Report on Handloom Weavers*, 1840, XXIV, p. 7.
[2] *cf.* Pinchbeck, I.: *Women Workers and the Industrial Revolution, 1750-1850*, pp. 104-107.
[3] *Parliamentary Papers, Report on Emigration* (1826-17), V, p. 49.

the district.[1] Nor was this all, for it must not be forgotten that the inhabitants of the cottages were far worse off than in the days before the enclosures, when Cobbett estimated that the profit from a cow was equal every week to two days of the man's wage.[2]

In such circumstances it is not surprising that the standard of sexual morality in the villages was low, and that incest was by no means uncommon, particularly as the latter was not then a crime in the eyes of the law. The administration of the Poor Law was such that pre-marital pregnancy was the single woman's only means of escape from the inadequate dole supplied by the parish, for the latter then either provided her with a husband, or gave her an increased allowance for her child. In either case she was better off financially. An Act of 1733 compelled any man charged by a woman as the father of her illegitimate child either to contribute towards its maintenance, marry the woman, or go to prison. As few labourers could do the first, or were willing to do the last, the number of forced marriages was considerable, for the parish authorities would stop at nothing to prevent the woman or child becoming chargeable to them. Parson Woodforde quotes an instance of this:

"Rode to Ringland this morning and married one Robert Astick and Elizabeth Howlett by Licence . . . the man being in custody, and the woman being with child by him. The man was a long time before he could be prevailed on to marry her when in the churchyard; and at the altar behaved very unbecoming. It is a cruel thing that any person should be compelled by law to marry. . . . It is very disagreeable to me to marry such persons."[3]

Another clergyman, the Rev. Charles Lacy, said:

"I have repeatedly known instances of men being apprehended under a bastardy warrant, carried off immediately to surrogate for a licence, and brought to the church, all in

---

[1] *Parliamentary Papers, Report on Women and Children in Agriculture* (1843), XII, p. 19.
[2] *Cottage Economy*, pp. 105–106.
[3] Woodforde, Rev. J.: *The Diary of a Country Parson*, Vol. II, Jan. 25, 1787.

the same morning, to be married. . . . I have seen the hand-cuffs removed from the man at the church door as I approached; and then with the constable and overseer as witnesses to the marriage, I have been compelled in the discharge of my ministerial duty, to pronounce over such persons the words of a service, which breathes nothing but the spirit of a free and sanctified affection."[1]

Sometimes the determination of the local authorities to get rid of what they considered to be a surplus population led to surprising situations, and in 1815 a case occurred in which the parish officers actually induced a man to sell his wife.

"In 1814 Henry Cook of Effingham, Surrey, was forced under the bastardy laws to marry a woman of Slinfold, Sussex, and six months after the marriage she and her child were removed to the Effingham workhouse. The governor there, having contracted to maintain all the poor for the specific sum of £210, complained of the new arrivals, whereupon the parish officers of Effingham prevailed on Cook to sell his wife. The master of the workhouse, Chippen, was directed to take the woman to Croydon market, and there on June 17, 1815, she was sold to John Earl, for the sum of one shilling, which had been given to Earl for the purchase. To bind the bargain the following receipt was made out:

"5s. stamp.   "June 17, 1815.

"Received of John Earl, the sum of one shilling, in full for my lawful wife, by me, Henry Cook.

"Daniel Cook } Witnesses."
"John Chippen }

"In their satisfaction at having got rid of the charge-ability of the woman, the parish officers of Effingham paid the expenses of the journey to Croydon, including refreshments there, and also allowed a leg of mutton for the wedding dinner which took place in Earl's parish of Dorking.

---

[1] *Third Report Poor Law Commissioners* (1837), XXXI.

The ruse, however, was not successful. After some years, Earl, having ascertained that the marriage was invalid, deserted his wife, and she with a large family of children was again removed to be maintained by the parish of Effingham. In despair the officials now applied to the magistrates to compel Cook, the original husband, to support the whole family! The appeal, naturally, was dismissed."[1]

It was little wonder that the wretched peasants left the countryside to seek what they fondly hoped would prove to be their fortunes in the new manufacturing areas, but they were soon undeceived. Housing conditions might be bad in the rural districts, but the day's work was in the fresh air; in the factories and mines it was far otherwise. Mention has already been made of the conditions under which the hand-loom weavers worked, but the imagination can hardly grasp the state of affairs that existed in the mines. The task which employed a great number of workers was that of "hurrying", namely, conveying the coal won from the workings along subterranean passages either to the horseways or to the bottom of the shaft. In the better pits the wagons were mounted on wheels, and were pushed forward on small iron railways, but in thin seams, or in pits with little capital, the method still obtained of drawing by girdle and chain. In this case the hurrier buckled round his or her waist a broad leather belt, to which was attached a ring and about four foot of chain, the latter passing between the legs and being hooked on to a sledge shod with iron. Thus the hurrier, often a woman or girl, with candle in cap, crawled on hands and knees along the roads which sometimes had a gradient of one in three. Even this was an improvement on the days when the hurriers went on one hand and feet, pulling the sledge with the other hand. Children usually took up this employment at the age of seven or eight, for the smaller they were the better, as some of the roads were as low as 16 or 18 inches. It was declared to be impossible to clear the passages for men and horses as "the expense would be more than twice over what the coals would be worth after they

[1] Quoted by Pinchbeck, I.: *Women Workers and the Industrial Revolution, 1750–1850,* p. 83, from the *Second Report of the Poor Law Commissioners* (1836), XXIX, p. 311.

were got out."[1] It is regrettable that the cause of these poor
wretches did not come to the notice of Fox, Burke, and the
other Whig champions of liberty.

Similar examples could be cited from all the great industries,
and it is little wonder that the manners of those engaged in
them were uncouth in the extreme. Contemporaries were
unanimous on this point:

> "Three miles farther on the Wells road I perceived the
> same military way again approaching the turnpike, which it
> accompanies in a parallel direction for a considerable distance,
> sufficiently visible even to the eye not gifted with anti-
> quarian keenness. The village, indeed, at this spot receives
> its name from this venerable neighbour, Radstock being
> nothing more than 'the hamlet of the road'. Here a sudden
> alteration took place in the scene, which changed from rural
> simplicity and quiet to jargon and noise: the dingy tenants of
> the coal-mines in the vicinity were busily employed at the
> public-house, either in taking their 'morning rouse', or
> concluding the festivities of the preceding night, and the
> village rang with curses and vociferations. Like true tipplers,
> their courage had risen in proportion to the depth of their
> draughts; and when I saw them, they were
>
> > So full of valour, that they smote the air
> > For breathing in their faces; beat the ground
> > For kissing of their feet.
>
> I therefore climbed the opposite hill as rapidly as I could,
> not only to avoid the sounds of discord and confusion that
> distracted my mind, but also to escape some of the blows
> which I saw were dealt about with great activity amongst
> these early carousers."[2]

Wesley was no less emphatic. Of Huddersfield he wrote: "A
wilder people I never saw in England. The men, women and
children filled the street as we rode along, and appeared just
ready to devour us. They were, however, tolerably quiet

---

[1] cf. Pinchbeck, I.: *Women Workers and the Industrial Revolution, 1750-1850*,
pp. 248-255.
[2] Warner, Rev. R.: *A Walk through some of the Western Counties of England*, pp. 9-11.

while I preached; only a few pieces of dirt were thrown."[1] He described the colliers of Plessy, near Newcastle, as "such as had been in the first rank for savage ignorance and wickedness of every kind". On Sunday, "men, women and children met together to dance, fight, curse, and swear, and play at chuck, ball, span-farthing, or whatever came next to hand."[2]

Whitehaven, in 1813, was no better. A visitor in that year

"saw a horse drawing a long line of baskets driven by a young girl, covered with filth, debased and profligate, and uttering some low obscenity as she passed by us. We were frequently interrupted in our march",

he continues:

"by the horses proceeding in this manner with their cargoes to the shaft, and always driven by girls, all of the same description, ragged and beastly in their appearance, and with a shameless indecency in their behaviour, which awe-struck as one was by the gloom and loneliness around one, had something quite frightful in it, and gave the place the character of a hell. All the people whom we met with, were distinguished by an extraordinary wretchedness; immoderate labour and a noxious atmosphere had marked their counten-ance with the signs of disease and decay; they were mostly half naked, blackened all over with dirt, and altogether so miserably disfigured and abused, that they looked like a race fallen from the common rank of men, and doomed, as in a kind of purgatory, to wear away their lives in these dismal shades."[3]

The same authority goes on to say that the workers were regarded as

"mere machinery, of no worth or importance beyond their horse power. The strength of a man is required in excavating the workings, women can drive the horses, and children can open the doors; and a child or a woman is sacrificed, where a

---

[1] *Journal*, May 9, 1757.   [2] *ibid.*, April 1, 1743.
[3] Pinchbeck, I.: *Women Workers and the Industrial Revolution*, p. 243.

man is not required, as a matter of economy that makes not the smallest account of human life in its calculations."[1]

In these conditions it is hardly surprising that the morals of the workers were on a low plane, though, as the Report of the Factory Commission in 1833 stated, "there is no evidence to show that vice and immorality are more prevalent among these people, considered as a class, than amongst any other portion of the community in the same station, and with the same limited means of information". It was, indeed, in the end to prove an advantage to the industrial workers that their morals met with the disapproval of their superiors, for it was these, rather than the conditions in which they worked, that finally shook the complacency of the Victorian *bourgeoisie*, and so led to the passing of the first social legislation.

"Young girls 'hurrying' for men, working beside them in scanty garments, alone with them for hours of the day in an isolated part of the mine, were at their mercy."[2]

Contemporary literature is unanimous on the subject. Mrs. Tonna, in *Helen Fleetwood*, makes one of her characters state that but one girl in fifty kept her character after she went to the mills, and the heroine of that work suffered much persecution at the hands of her fellow mill-girls owing to their dislike of her purity. Mrs. Gaskell, in *Mary Barton*, shows a father as unwilling to have his daughter in the mills, while Esther leaves her work to become a man's mistress, and finally goes on the streets. Some employers and their sons are portrayed as definitely lecherous; young Carson in *Mary Barton* and Barnes Newcome in *The Newcomes* are cases in point; but that there were good men amongst them the novelists admit by giving us Thornton in *North and South*, Trafford in *Sybil*, and Rouncewell in *Bleak House*.

All revolutions bring a great deal of scum to the surface, and the Industrial Revolution was no exception. Even when employers were honourable and humane men they were only too often ignorant of the conditions of those who worked for

---

1 Ayton, R.: *Voyage round Great Britain*, Vol. II, pp. 155–160.
2 Neff, W. F.: *Victorian Working Women*, p. 73.

them, and they had little control over those who came between
them and their employees. It is always the men and women
half-way up who render any system, political or industrial,
intolerable. The moral anarchy, of which several instances
have been quoted, was also the result of the break-up of the
old system, and the uprooting of a large part of the population.
Nevertheless, it was chiefly the bad conditions of employment
that contributed to this result; as Mrs. Tonna said of Phoebe
Wright:

"Excluded from the free air, and almost from the pure
light of day; shut up in an atmosphere polluted by clouds
of fetid breath, and all the sickening exhalations of a crowded
human mass, whose unwashed, overworked bodies were also
in many cases diseased, and by the suffocating dust that rose
on every side; relaxed by an intensity of artificial heat which
their constitutions were never framed to encounter in the
temperate climate where God had placed them; doubly
fevered, doubly debilitated by excessive toil, not measured
by human capacity to sustain it, but by the power of
machinery obeying an inexhaustible impetus; badly clothed,
wretchedly fed, and exposed moreover to fasts of unnatural
length even from that miserable fare; who can marvel if,
under such a system, the robust adult speedily acquires a
sickly habit of body and morbid state of feeling, leading at
once to the most awful perversion of mind and corruption of
morals."[1]

It has generally been the case in political, economic, and
social revolutions in England that one or two classes of society
have remained unaffected by what is going on around them
until such time as the situation has once more composed itself,
and by this means the continuity of the national history has
remained unbroken. This was fortunately also the fact, thanks
in no small measure to the statesmanship of Pitt in avoiding
financial collapse, at the time of the Industrial Revolution. In
spite of the excessive simplicity of the Court, there was still a
great deal of pleasing ceremonial and pageantry in life, both

[1] *Helen Fleetwood.*

public and private. It is true that George III abandoned the custom of dining in public at Hampton Court to which even his grandfather had adhered, but in spite of his homeliness there was nothing of the *bourgeois* royalty of a Louis Philippe about him; for instance, every one knelt to the King on entering his chamber. The aristocracy, both new and old, also travelled in a great deal of state, and it was rare for a nobleman or a bishop to visit a country town save in a carriage and four.[1] The improvement in the means of communication was beginning to have its influence on manners, for so excellent was the system of coaches in the reign of George IV that all classes were commencing to use them, while the custom of having meals served in one's own apartments at an inn was giving place to the communal repast in the coffee-room. Still, that great leveller, the railway, was only in its earliest stages when the First Gentleman died.

Outward behaviour was still a great deal more rigid than it was later to become. Chatham, for instance, never in any circumstances allowed a permanent official to be seated in his presence, and he summoned his subordinates to his room as he would a footman, by ringing a bell. We have already noted the delight of Nelson at the condescension of Pitt in seeing him to his carriage. Canning was the first Foreign Secretary to relax somewhat the existing regulations, since he substituted a messenger for the bell, and did not require secretaries to remain standing except on official occasions. Yet in many ways there was what more recent generations would describe as an utter lack of formality. It would be difficult to imagine one of His Majesty's ambassadors or ministers to-day wrapping up a parcel in a letter to the Foreign Office, yet on one occasion Canning had to reprove the minister at Lisbon for the objectionable practice of packing tea in his official despatches, as well as for his "slovenly penmanship".

Nevertheless, it would be an insult to the memory of Canning to imagine him as a stern disciplinarian, who left his sense of humour behind him when he crossed the threshold

[1] *cf.* Lecky, W. E. H.: *A History of England in the Eighteenth Century*, Vol. VII, pp. 182–183.

of the Foreign Office; if proof of this be wanted it can be found in the famous despatch which he sent to Bagot at The Hague to inform him that in consequence of the obstinate attitude of Falck, the Foreign Minister of the Netherlands, a 20 per cent duty would be levied on Dutch shipping. The despatch was as follows:

"Decypher, Separate, Secret, and Confidential.

"FOREIGN OFFICE,
" SIR,   "*January* 31, 1826.
  In manners of commerce the fault of the Dutch
  Is offering too little and asking too much.
  The French are with equal advantage content,
  So we clap on Dutch bottoms just 20 per cent.
      (*Chorus*) 20 per cent, 20 per cent.
      (*Chorus of English Customs House Officers and
                French Douaniers.*)
      (*English*) We clap on Dutch bottoms just 20 per
      cent.
      (*French*)   Vous frapperez Falck avec 20 per cent.
"I have no other commands from His Majesty to convey to
  your Excellency to-day.
"I am with great truth and respect, Sir, Your Excellency's
  most obedient humble servant,
                                          "GEORGE CANNING.

"His Excellency the Rt. Honble, Sir Charles Bagot, K.B."

The humour of the situation was heightened by the fact that Bagot had not the necessary cypher, and wrote that he hoped the "circumstances will not be productive of any public inconvenience". Canning duly forwarded the cypher; and what ensued can best be gathered from Bagot himself:

"THE HAGUE,
"(*Private*)   "*Febry.* 13, 1826.
  "MY DEAR CANNING,—You have fretted me to fiddle-strings, and I have a great mind not to give you the satisfaction of ever knowing how completely your mystification of me has succeeded. It was more than you had a right to

expect when you drew from me that solemn and official lamentation which I sent you of my inability to decypher His Majesty's commands; but, as the Devil would have it, your success did not end here. The post which brought me the decyphers arrived at eleven o'clock at night, when I had only time before I sent off the other messenger to read your grave regret at what had occurred and to acknowledge the receipt of the mail. The next morning Tierney and I were up by cock-crow to make out *la maudite dépeche*, and it was not till after an hour of the most indescribable anxiety that we were put 'out of our fear' by finding what it really was, and that 'you Pyramus' were not Pyramus, but only 'Bottom the weaver'.

"I could have slain you! But I got some fun myself, for I afterwards put the fair decypher into Douglas's hands, who read it twice without moving a muscle, or to this hour discovering that it was not prose, and returned it to me, declaring that it was 'oddly worded; but he had always a feeling that the despatch must relate to discriminating duties'.

"C. BAGOT.

"The Right Hon. the Foreign Secretary."

This was Canning in his gentler moods, and well might Lord Strangford, who had just incurred a severe reprimand for a blunder at St. Petersburg, write to Bagot:

"Happy man, that you are, to swig your curaçoa in peace, and to be able to open your despatches without the fear of their actually exploding in your face."

The eighteenth century was not yet at an end.

CHAPTER VIII

THE FIRST GENTLEMAN OF EUROPE

THE death of Pitt only preceded by a few years the withdrawal of his master from the political arena, for in November 1810 the King finally relapsed into permanent insanity. For some years his sight had been failing, but in character he was as forceful as ever. Indeed, in 1807, he had compelled the resignation of a ministry which possessed a majority in the House of Commons, and replaced it by one more in accordance with his own views on one of the most important questions of the day. It was the last time that a King of England was to act in such a manner, for although at first sight William IV may appear to have behaved similarly in 1834, he had at least the excuse that the Chancellor of the Exchequer, who was the backbone of the administration in question, had succeeded to the peerage. The truth was that George had never been particularly partial to the ministry of "All the Talents",[1] which included Fox, that had been formed on Pitt's death; when it went to the country in the autumn of 1806 (Fox had died in September), he withheld the donation of £12,000 with which he was accustomed to assist his ministers for the time being at a general election. As soon as ministers proposed to grant commissions to Roman Catholics they were dismissed, and replaced by an administration, of which the Duke of Portland was the nominal head. Parliament was duly dissolved once more, and the King's Speech on that occasion was little more than a personal plea for a majority for the new ministry. For what was to be the last time it was proved once more that the King was a better judge of the temper of the country than was the House of Commons, and the Government was returned with a working majority in spite of the violent opposition of the Whigs.

[1] A misnomer in the absence of Canning, as Fox generously admitted.

In spite of this personal and political triumph the King suffered several shocks at this time, which probably had much to do with precipitating the final catastrophe. One was the death of his favourite daughter, Princess Amelia, and the other was the disgrace of the Duke of York. The latter had proved an incompetent commander in the field when called upon to face the armies of the French Revolution, but he had been a capable administrator, and it was due to his foresight that conditions in the Army had been improved without recourse to mutiny. Unfortunately, his mistress, a Mrs. Clarke, had received bribes to procure military appointments, and when his liaison with the lady came to an end, she determined to avenge herself on her late lover. Mrs. Clarke passed into the keeping of a Colonel Wardle, M.P., who raised the whole business in Parliament, basing his attack on the information with which she had supplied him. In the end the House of Commons acquitted the Duke not only of corruption but of connivance at corruption: the majority in his favour, however, was small, and he resigned. There was an almost immediate reaction in the Duke's favour, for an action was successfully brought against Colonel Wardle by a firm of upholsterers who had furnished a house for Mrs. Clarke by his orders in consideration of her services in giving hostile evidence against her former lover.

Another event which was a heavy blow to the King was the failure of the expedition to Walcheren. This latter was not at all badly conceived, for it constituted a serious threat to Napoleon's flank, but it was gravely mismanaged from the beginning. George insisted upon the military command being given to Lord Chatham, Pitt's elder brother, while the Navy was under the orders of Sir Richard Strachan. The result was delay and disunion:

> Great Chatham with his sabre drawn
> Stood waiting for Sir Richard Strachan;
> Sir Richard, longing to be at 'em;
> Stood waiting for the Earl of Chatham.

Chatham had been found wanting in various capacities over

a period of years, and he was one of the most indolent men alive. As an officer on his staff said,

> "We should not have known there was a Commander-in-Chief had we not seen in his garden, twelve miles away from our front, two turtles sprawling on their backs for his dinner. He never came down until two o'clock in the day."[1]

The same fatal division of command had, twelve months before, been largely responsible for the failure to gain the maximum advantage out of the Portuguese rising against the French. Sir Arthur Wellesley, Sir Hew Dalrymple, and Sir Harry Burrard shared the responsibility for the campaign in uncertain proportions:

> Sir Arthur and Sir Harry, Sir Harry and Sir Hew,
> Doodle, doodle, doodle, cock a doodle doo!
> Sir Arthur was a gallant knight, but for the other two,
> Doodle, doodle, doodle, cock a doodle doo!

So George III passed out of history, and spent the last years of his life at Windsor; he was still able to find some solace in music, especially in Handel, and he chose for the anthems in his chapel all the passages from that composer connected with blindness and madness.

At last the Prince of Wales had attained the coveted position of Regent, but the Whigs were disappointed of their hopes, for he had now turned against them, chiefly owing to the influence of his latest mistress, Lady Hertford. His manners had not improved. On one occasion he showed his sense of humour by getting the sheriffs of London drunk at his own dinnertable, and then presenting them in that condition to his aged mother.[2] The opinion of his contemporaries was overwhelmingly unfavourable. The Duke of Wellington, whose loyalty to the throne was above suspicion, said, "He speaks so like old Falstaff, that, damm me, if I was not afraid to walk into a room with him"; and in the year of his accession to the throne he declared him "degraded as low as he could be

---

[1] Quoted by Fletcher, C. R. L.: *An Introductory History of England*, Vol. IV, p. 264.

[2] cf. *The Diary and Correspondence of Charles Abbot, Lord Colchester* (edited by his son), Jan. 27, 1816.

already".[1] George also, especially in his later years, suffered from delusions, which at times were a source of considerable annoyance to those with whom he was brought into contact. He fancied that he had led the Heavy Dragoons at Salamanca, and that he had ridden "Fleur-de-Lys" at Goodwood. Nor were his habits any more attractive than his character. He was wont to give way on occasion to outbreaks of maudlin sentimentality, when he would weep on his ministers' shoulders, and even kiss the Duke of Wellington on the cheek. Canning, too, whom George never appreciated, was compelled to submit to these familiarities, and on at least one occasion he had to walk along the front at Brighton with the King's arm round his neck. Lady Bessborough gave an amusing account of George in moments of amorous enthusiasm:

"Such a scene I never went through. I stared and he went on, and after a long tirade threw himself on his knees and clasping me round kissed my neck. Then vows of eternal love, entreaties and promises of what he would do. He would break with Mrs. Fitzherbert and Lady Hertford. I should make my own terms. I should be his sole confidant, sole adviser. I should guide his politics."[2]

In the later years of his reign George IV withdrew from the public gaze, and became more indolent than ever, rarely rising before six o'clock in the evening, and receiving his ministers in night-attire. When Goderich resigned and the Duke of Wellington was summoned to form a ministry, the latter found the King in bed

"dressed in a dirty silk jacket and a turban night-cap, one as greasy as the other; for, notwithstanding his coquetry about dress in public, he was extremely dirty and slovenly in private".[3]

Such was the so-called "First Gentleman of Europe", a term that might have been applied with considerably more reason to either of the French monarchs who were his contemporaries,

---

[1] cf. Daudet, E.: L'Ambassade du Duc Decazes en Angleterre, p. 133.
[2] Quoted by Leslie, S.: George the Fourth, pp. 79–80.
[3] A Portion of the Journal kept by Thomas Raikes, 1831-47, Sept. 24, 1843.

and, so far as his character was concerned, it is difficult to resist the conclusion that a more contemptible monarch never wore the British, or any other, crown.[1]

In April 1795 George had been persuaded to marry his cousin, Caroline of Brunswick. The marriage was destined to failure from the beginning. Bride and bridegroom met for the first time at the Duke of Cumberland's house in Cleveland Row, and Lord Malmesbury, in his *Diary*, gives a graphic account of the incident. When the Prince entered the room Caroline went down on her knees to him:

> "The Prince raised her (gracefully enough) and embraced her, said barely one word, turned round, retired to a distant part of the apartment, and calling me to him, said, 'Harris, I am not well, pray get me a glass of brandy.' I said, 'Sir, had you not better have a glass of water?' Upon which he, much out of humour, said, 'No, I will go directly to the Queen.' And away he went."[2]

George also had recourse to something stronger than water before the wedding, and it was in no mere figurative sense that he was supported by the Dukes of Roxburghe and Bedford in the church. While the ceremony was in progress, and he was kneeling beside his bride, the Prince rose unsteadily to his feet, and turned towards the door, but the King persuaded him to kneel down again. Soon after the birth of their only child, Charlotte, in the following year husband and wife separated for good. George's letter on this occasion throws an interesting light on their character and relations:

> "Our inclinations are not in our power, nor should either of us be held answerable to the other because nature has not made us suitable to each other. Tranquillity and comfortable society is, however, in our power: let our intercourse, therefore, be restricted to that, and I will distinctly subscribe to the condition which you require through Lady Cholmondeley that, even in the event of any accident

---

[1] He had a sense of wit, and once when a waiter chaffed him, he said, "This is all very well between you and me, Sam, but beware of being equally familiar with Norfolk."

[2] Quoted by MacDonagh, M.: *The English King*, pp. 128–129.

happening to my daughter (which I trust Providence in His mercy will prevent) I shall not infringe the terms of the restriction by proposing, at any period, a connection of a more particular nature. I shall now finally close this disagreeable correspondence, trusting that, as we have completely explained ourselves to each other, the rest of our lives will be passed in uninterrupted tranquillity."[1]

After the separation Caroline lived at Blackheath, and by 1806 rumours of her indiscretions were so widespread that a secret inquiry into her conduct was instituted. She emerged from it with less stain on her character than had been anticipated, and as soon as peace came she went abroad, where she travelled for some years. Princess Charlotte was the true child of such ill-assorted parents, for she was both impetuous and undignified. At one time a marriage was arranged for her with the Prince of Orange. She demanded an assurance that she should not have to reside out of England, and also that after her wedding her mother should be received by her husband. She received neither; so when her father sent her a list of suggested wedding-guests with her mother's name omitted, she returned it after deleting that of her fiancé. In the end, she broke off the engagement, not least owing to the influence of Brougham.[2]

The Regent was now experiencing the common fate of the Guelphs, that is to say, the undutiful son in due course found he had undutiful children, but this reflection, if it ever occurred to him, did not reconcile him to the fact. He dismissed his daughter's household, and told her that she should never have an establishment until she married. The Princess thereupon walked out of Carlton House, hailed a cab, and drove to Oxford Street, where her mother was staying. A scene, in which many distinguished statesmen took part, followed, and it was not until dawn that she was persuaded to return to Carlton House with her uncle, the Duke of York. In the end she married Leopold of Saxe-Coburg-Gotha, later the

---

[1] Quoted by Fulford, R.: *George the Fourth*, pp. 75–76.
[2] *cf.* Aspinall, A.: *Lord Brougham and the Whig Party*, p. 102.

first King of the Belgians, and died in giving birth to a still-born child. Romance has been busy with Princess Charlotte, but what is known of her can only lead to the conclusion that it was well for England that she was never its Queen. She was too much like her father, and what was bad enough in a man would have been far worse in a woman.

The death of Princess Charlotte raised the whole question of the succession to the throne, for although George III had had seven sons and six daughters there was a dearth of legitimate heirs. For this the Royal Marriage Act was primarily responsible. Three of the Royal Dukes were rapidly married to German princesses in the hope that among them they might beget an English Sovereign, but they only entered the bonds of matrimony on terms. As the Duke of Kent wrote to Creevey:

"The Duke of Clarence demands the payment of all his debts, which are very great, and a handsome provision for each of his ten natural children. The next Prince in succession is myself, and although I trust I shall be at all times ready to obey any call my country may make upon me, God only knows the sacrifice it will be to make whenever I shall think it my duty to become a married man. It is now seven and twenty years since Madame St. Laurent and I have lived together."[1]

The Duke of Clarence lived in Bushey Park, of which he was Ranger, with Dorothea Jordan, a popular actress of the day. He allowed her £1,000 a year, but when his father remonstrated with him for his extravagance he suggested reducing the amount to £500. Mrs. Jordan sent him by way of reply the bottom of a playbill on which was printed, "No money returned after the rising of the curtain."[2] The marital experiences of the Duke of Sussex have already been related. In many ways he was the most attractive of the Royal brothers, and showed some interest in literature and art. The most unpopular was the Duke of Cumberland; his appearance was unattractive because he lost an eye in the Low Countries,

---

[1] Quoted by Leslie, S.: *George the Fourth*, p. 129.
[2] *cf.* MacDonagh, M.: *The English King*, p. 132.

and he was a fervent anti-democrat. He was certainly not as bad as he was often painted, and at one time was reported "going to church regularly and has left off swearing".[1] Cumberland eventually became King of Hanover when that country was separated from Great Britain on the accession of Queen Victoria.

In politics, the giants of the previous two or three decades had given place to men of smaller stature, with the notable exception of Canning and Castlereagh. Although from 1808 to 1814 the Peninsular War was being fought, there was no sort of political truce at home. The national movement which had arisen at the threat of invasion a few years before had spent itself, and the country was largely apathetic. There was also a great deal of distress owing to the interruption of trade with the Continent, and more than a little rioting. In Parliament the Whigs took advantage of every event at home or abroad that could be used as a handle against ministers, and the latter had to deal with criticism on its merits, for an appeal for a common front in the hour of crisis would not have met with any response from the England of George III. The London mob could always be relied upon to create trouble. In 1810, for example, that most aristocratic of Radicals, Sir Francis Burdett, M.P. for Westminster, was adjudged by the House of Commons guilty of a scandalous libel, and the Speaker accordingly issued a warrant for his committal to the Tower. Burdett defied arrest at his house in Piccadilly, and the mob rallied to his defence; the Riot Act was read, and the Life Guards called out, before he was duly incarcerated. Yet, this disunion at home did not prevent Wellington from winning victory after victory in the Peninsula; possibly it even stiffened the attitude of ministers, because as they knew that nothing would placate the Opposition there was no use attempting to pander to the latter.

The duel between Canning and Castlereagh had been followed by the formation of an administration with Perceval at its head. The new Prime Minister had been a favourite of

---

[1] He had a liaison with a Lady Graves at one time, and was caricatured as a "violator of graves".

Pitt ever since he had entered the House of Commons as M.P. for Northampton in 1796. Sir John Sinclair says:

"He spoke without the disagreeable cant of the Bar, was never tedious, was particularly distinct in matters of business, and explained his financial measures with clearness and ability. His style was singularly acute, bold, sarcastic, and personal."[1]

The same authority goes on to relate that when Pitt was asked, "If we lose you, where could we find a successor?" he at once replied, "Perceval". However that may be, the young man's rise was rapid, for he was Attorney-General in Pitt's second administration, and Chancellor of the Exchequer under Portland. He incurred the dislike of Canning and the bitter hatred of Napier, who wrote of his death, "That horrible crime was politically no misfortune to England or the Peninsula."[2] On May 11th, 1812, Perceval was assassinated by one John Bellingham as he was entering the lobby of the House of Commons. It subsequently transpired that the murderer hardly knew his victim even by sight, for the motive which prompted the crime was a grievance against the administration, Bellingham being a bankrupt merchant who believed the ministry responsible for his misfortunes.

After a good deal of somewhat unedifying intrigue the Earl of Liverpool succeeded Perceval, and remained Prime Minister until 1827. He had the misfortune to incur the contempt of Disraeli, who christened him the "Arch-Mediocrity", and thus described the unfortunate statesman.

"The Arch-Mediocrity had himself some glimmering traditions of political science. He was sprung from a laborious stock, had received some training, and though not a statesman, might be classed among those whom the Lord Keeper Williams used to call 'statemongers'. In a subordinate position his meagre diligence and his frigid method might not have been without value; but the qualities that he possessed were misplaced; nor can any character be con-

---

[1] Quoted by Rose, J. H.: *The Life of William Pitt*, Vol. II, p. 466.
[2] *History of the War in the Peninsula*, Vol. IV, p. 155.

THE PROJECTED WEST FRONT OF THE ROYAL PAVILION AT BRIGHTON

GEORGE CANNING

From the portrait by Sir Thomas Lawrence in the National Portrait Gallery

ceived less invested with the happy properties of a leader.
In the conduct of public affairs his disposition was exactly
the reverse of that which is the characteristic of great men.
He was peremptory in little questions, and great ones he
left open."[1]

This is good invective, but it is no more true than the same
author's criticism of the ministry of which Liverpool was the
head:

"They fell into a panic. Having fulfilled during their lives
the duties of administration, they were frightened because
they were called upon, for the first time, to perform the
functions of government. Like all weak men, they had
recourse to what they called strong measures. They
determined to put down the multitude. They thought they
were imitating Mr. Pitt, because they mistook disorganiza-
tion for sedition."[2]

Ministers certainly made mistakes, but they knew their own
minds, and they did not give way to opposition. That was
left for the Duke of Wellington, but by then the eighteenth
century was moribund, and a new ideology was coming into
fashion.

Liverpool brought the country through the last years of
the war, the difficult task of making peace, and the post-war
decade; he managed to retain in the same Cabinet statesmen
as opposed in temperament as Canning, Castlereagh, Sidmouth,
and Wellington; and in spite of the follies of the King, and the
fury of the mob, there was no revolution. Professor Trevelyan
is more to the point:

"England could organize herself for no social purpose, and
allowed her millions to become the economic prey of the
blind forces of war and of the unguided Industrial Revolution."[3]

That is the real charge against the post-war administration
and marked its departure from the social policy of Pitt, who
had conceded the principle of outdoor relief, wished to abolish

[1] *Coningsby*, Bk. II, Ch. I.   [2] *ibid.*   [3] *Lord Grey of the Reform Bill*, p. 119.

the rule that applicants for it should be totally destitute, and advocated compulsory arbitration in industrial disputes. Mr. Feiling's estimate of Liverpool is surely the just one:

"The Judaic rule of our older historians, that one man should die for the people, must be relaxed in the new-found study of mass opinion. This overworked Prime Minister has been pilloried long enough for the faults of millowners and justices; for severities in which he was overborne by Eldon, for omissions which he shared with Peel. If any new epitaph is to be carved on his tomb, it is like to condemn, not the man, but the party that raised and restrained him; the Tory passing by may reflect, that within this narrow ground of intelligence and achievement lies all the power for good conceded by his forerunners to this Prime Minister, for fifteen years chosen leader of a great Parliamentary majority, a man of good will."[1]

Almost as many tears have been shed over the repressive measures adopted after Waterloo as over those of Pitt, which, in retrospect, do not seem so very terrible after all. As in the earlier instance, it is necessary to bear in mind that Peel had not yet created a police force, and that order had to be preserved by the armed forces of the Crown; these latter had, in accordance with the invariable British custom, been cut to the bone almost before the ink was dry on the treaty of peace. As a young man Liverpool had witnessed with his own eyes the storming of the Bastille, and, like Pitt, he fully appreciated the fact that had the government of Louis XVI shown any firmness the situation would have been saved. It was only forty years before that the Gordon Riots had devastated London, and contemporary foreign opinion was far from taking the complacent view of the British situation which has been expressed by many later historians. Louis XVIII, as shrewd a critic as any in Europe, wrote to Decazes, then French ambassador in London, in 1820 that the progress of events formed a close parallel with what had happened in France in the summer of 1789,[2] and he was certainly not alone in holding this point of

---

[1] *Sketches in Nineteenth Century Biography*, p. 31.
[2] *cf.* Daudet, E.: *L'Ambassade du Duc Decazes en Angleterre*, p. 129.

view. The facts were such as to justify the gravest apprehensions.

The Government was "not called upon to deal merely with merry peasants and innocuous idealists",[1] for there were desperate schemes afoot in some quarters. There can be little doubt that the influence of Cobbett, exerted through *The Weekly Register*, had much to do with fanning the flames of revolt, though it must be admitted that Cobbett himself never advocated recourse to actual violence, and some of his opinions were definitely Tory in character. Yet his plea for sweeping reforms reached the ears of many who were none too scrupulous as to the means by which they might be attained. All over the country there were revolutionary clubs which demanded universal suffrage and annual Parliaments, and they were assisted by the slump that began soon after the war came to an end. Rioting began in the late spring of 1816. The disturbances were particularly numerous in the counties of Cambridge, Essex, and Suffolk, and at Littleport, in May, the troops were obliged to open fire; two men were killed, while five were afterwards executed for their share in the outbreak. Before the end of the year the spirit of discontent had spread to London, where a rising took place with the seizure of the Tower for its object; it failed owing to the personal courage of the Lord Mayor, but not until some blood had been spilt. In the following January the Prince Regent was insulted in the streets on his return from the opening of Parliament.

In 1818 the centre of disturbance was temporarily transferred to the North of England, and in particular to Manchester. Towards the end of that year there was a cotton strike, which was accompanied by considerable violence and some bloodshed, while in August 1819 there took place the so-called "Manchester Massacres". A monster reform meeting was convened for the 16th of that month, and the magistrates foolishly decided to arrest the ringleaders in the middle of the demonstration. For this purpose they had at their disposal several companies of infantry, six troops of the 15th Hussars, and a body of Yeomanry, as well as a number of special con-

---

[1] Feiling, K.: *Sketches in Nineteenth Century Biography*, p. 27.

stables. The Chief Constable declared that he could not effect the necessary arrests without the aid of the military, and a detachment of Yeomanry was ordered to advance, only, however, soon to be isolated in the middle of a surging crowd. At this point one of the magistrates, who thought that the Yeomen were in danger, asked the officer in command of the Hussars to rescue them, and to disperse the mob. Four troops of Hussars, and a few of the Yeomanry, thereupon charged, and people fled in all directions. Some of the demonstrators were cut down, and others were trampled on, but the talk of "several mounds of human beings" lying where they had fallen was mere political propaganda. In actual fact the loss of life did not exceed five or six, and there were a number of injured. The affair did much to aggravate panic in one quarter, and resentment against the existing order in another, but the responsibility must rest with the local authorities who lost their heads at the critical moment.

The echo of these events in Manchester had hardly begun to die away than the Cato Street conspiracy took place. Its author was one Arthur Thistlewood, and his plan was to murder the entire Cabinet in a private house; when this had been accomplished, a Provisional Government was to have been proclaimed. Happily, the Government found out what was afoot, but wisely determined to catch the plotters in the act. Accordingly, twenty-four conspirators armed themselves in Cato Street, near Edgware Road, with the intention of assassinating the ministers as they sat at dinner in Lord Harrowby's house, 39 Grosvenor Square, while some of their associates were posted near the door of that house to summon them when all the guests were assembled. At the critical moment both the revolutionaries and the authorities bungled badly. As a result of the information which had been given the ministerial dinner was not held, but the watchers were deceived by the arrival of carriages for a party next door, and thus failed to warn their co-conspirators in Cato Street. On the other hand, the Coldstream Guards, who were to have supported the police, did not arrive in time,[1] so Thistlewood and a good many

---

[1] The officer in command did not know the district, and was unprovided with a guide.

of his men escaped, though he himself was captured the next morning. In the following April an outbreak in Scotland was put down without much difficulty at Bonnymuir, though not before a treasonable proclamation had spread consternation in Glasgow. These events bore so marked a resemblance to the Cato Street conspiracy that they served to increase the alarm which that attempt had aroused among those who had anything to lose.

The violence of the extreme reformers defeated its own ends, for it frightened moderate people, and gave the authorities no alternative but to use force. Much ink has been spilt over the Six Acts, by which Sidmouth, as Home Secretary, sought to strengthen the forces of law and order, but in retrospect they do not appear very drastic. Two of them, against illegal and military training and the traversing of indictments, have since become part of the ordinary law. One, which enabled magistrates in certain localities to search for arms, was only in force for two years; another, aimed at blasphemous and seditious libels, was a dead letter so far as its penalties were concerned, though no one who has the slightest knowledge of contemporary political literature can deny that some check was greatly needed; another was at least equitable, for it submitted the cheap pamphlet Press to the duty already paid by newspapers. The only one of the Six Acts which can be said to have been really drastic was that which forbade public meetings unless convoked by five justices of the peace, but this only continued in force for five years. If the authorities were mistaken in confusing legitimate grievances with Jacobinism, they were only committing an error very common in governments, and their attitude was at least as venial as that of the numerous agitators who endeavoured to exploit the prevailing misery for their own ends. The decade that followed Waterloo is not a very creditable one in the domestic annals of Great Britain, but the blame must be distributed far more widely than has always been the case.

It is not without interest to note that the ministers of the post-war period were complaining of the amount of work that was thrown upon them.

"They (i.e. the members of the Cabinet) shrink from no just responsibility" (Canning declared) "they neglect no attendance . . . but it ought to be borne in mind how great a change has taken place of late years in the business of the House of Commons—a change which has thrown a burden of business upon ministers, which no physical or mental constitution can adequately sustain. I call upon those members of the House of Commons who recollect the good old times when the destinies of the Empire were swayed by Mr. Pitt, or Mr. Fox, to say whether the labours of an administration in those days were to be compared with what they are now. The Ministers were not then harassed and perplexed by a complication of daily business, with the whole of the details of which, however trifling, it was expected that they should be intimately and accurately acquainted."[1]

Yet Lady Hester Stanhope said of her uncle:

"Ah, Doctor, what a life was his! Roused from sleep (for he was a good sleeper) with a despatch from Lord Melville; then down to Windsor; then, if he had half an hour to spare trying to swallow something; Mr. Adams with a paper, Mr. Long with another; then Mr. Rose: then, with a little bottle of cordial confection in his pocket, off to the House until three or four in the morning; then home to a hot supper for two or three hours more, to talk over what was to be done next day:—and wine, and wine. Scarcely up next morning, when 'tat-tat-tat', twenty or thirty people one after another, and the horses walking before the door from two till sunset, waiting for him. It was enough to kill a man—it was murder."[2]

In the midst of these disturbed years George III died, and the Regent became King in name as well as in fact. This change, although it necessitated a general election, would have had little political effect had it not been for the complication of the new monarch's matrimonial position. Upon hearing of

---

[1] Petrie, Sir Charles: *Life of George Canning*, pp. 119-120.
[2] Rose, J. H.: *Life of William Pitt*, Vol. II, p. 531.

her husband's accession to the throne, Caroline announced her
intention of returning to England, and she was confirmed in
this attitude by the exclusion of her name from the Prayer
Book. From the beginning she was used by the Opposition as
a stick with which to beat the Government, for, as Canning
put it, "Faction had marked her for its own"; even her legal
adviser, Brougham, did not believe in her. Brougham, indeed,
had no other object but his own advancement, and he was as
ready to sell Caroline to the Cabinet as the Cabinet to Caroline.
When the King fell ill, and it was clear that his death would
be followed by a settlement, Brougham wrote: "I never
prayed so heartily for a prince before."[1] Theodore Hook
expressed the general attitude towards Brougham very well:

> There is he whom they call
> Squire Brougham of Brougham Hall
>   Who would pass for a man of condition;
> In blood, to be sure,
> He may match Peter Moore,
>   But the Hall is a mere imposition;
> The fellow's a hack politician,
> A tailor in all but ambition,
> Who offer'd to bilk
> For a gown of black silk
> The Queen—and her whole Opposition.

Hook edited *John Bull*, a paper which espoused the cause of
the King, and never neglected an opportunity of attacking
Caroline and her supporters.

The man-in-the-street had no great respect for the Queen,
but he had still less for George, so he gave her an uproarious
welcome. She received an ovation at Dover, and her journey
to London was in the nature of a triumph. As the palace was
denied to her, she took up her residence with Alderman Wood
in South Audley Street. Two years before a secret commission
had gone out to Milan to investigate her conduct, and now,
since she refused any compromise, its report was the basis for
the proceedings taken against her by command of the King.
On July 8th, 1820, a Bill of Pains and Penalties was introduced
by the Prime Minister into the House of Lords to deprive her

[1] *Creevey Papers*, Vol. I, p. 297.

of her title, and to dissolve the marriage. For weeks the discussion of this measure continued, while the Lords heard the evidence of the Milan commission, and the country was deluged with its squalid details. The crux of the question was whether the Queen had slept on the deck of a yacht under an awning with Bergami, but the witnesses on both sides seemed equally unsatisfactory. What was far more important than Caroline's morals was the effect of her trial upon the populace. The Duchesse Decazes gives a lively account of what was happening:

"*La princesse Thérèse (Esterhazy) et moi, nous sommes imaginé l'autre jour qu'il fallait aller voir passer la reine se rendant au Parlement. Nous voici, moi avec lord Carrington auquel j'avais demandé une fenetre chez son père, et elle avec lord Francis. Il faut concevoir que celui-là était bien choisi: le fils de la maîtresse du roi! Nous montons dans ma voiture et nous voilà partis, emmenant chacune un secrétaire d'ambassade. Arrivés assez loin encore de Westminster, la voiture ne put aller plus loin et nous voilà à la porte de lady Carrington, sans avoir été insultés. J'avais bien peur. Nous trouvâmes un déjeuner excellent et tout plein de petits soins.*

"*Après avoir attendu deux heures, on nous dit que le cortège commençait à passer. Thérèse et moi nous nous mîmes à une fenetre. Mais, à peine y étions-nous que la foule commence à proférer des injures. Chacune de nous se jetait la balle et disait que c'était pour l'autre. Je me retirai la première. Les cris continuèrent. On lança à Thérèse des écailles d'huître. Elle se cacha. Quand la reine parut, les long life to the queen furent si multipliés qu'on ne fit plus attention à personne. Thérèse avait dit à ses gens de venir la chercher. Mais, sa voiture avait été tellement huée qu'elle fut obligée de s'en retourner. La mienne avait été mieux traitée; je ne sais si c'est parce qu'on ne la connaissait pas ou qu'on croit que les Français sont mieux pour la reine. Le soir, nous dinions chez Thérèse. Le prince Paul voulut se fâcher contre nous parce que sa femme ne lui avait pas dit que nous irions chez lady Carrington. Moi, j'avais prévenu mon mari et obtenu la permission. Je dis au prince:*

"*Si vous continuez à faire le grognon, je raconterai partout que vous avez eu votre redingote crottée et déchirée et que vous avez été obligé de vous cacher.*

"*Effectivement, il avait voulu aller à pied et on l'avait insulté en lui jetant de la boue. Je ne sais pourquoi les gens d'ici en veulent tant aux Autrichiens. Nous sommes restés jusqu'à deux heures chez Thérèse à jouer des charades. Son cousin, le prince de Lichtenstein, a un vrai talent de comédien.*

"*Il y a eu toute la nuit grand tapage dans les rues de Londres, des rassemblements de milliers de personnes qui cassaient des vitres dans la cité. En France, cela ferait beaucoup d'effet. Le lendemain, on a l'air de n'y plus penser et chacun retourne à sa besogne comme si de rien n'était.*"[1]

The last sentence explains why there was no revolution—the public did not think the Queen worth one.

On November 12th the third reading of the Bill was carried by the small majority of nine, and the Prime Minister announced that the Government would not proceed further with the measure. It had, indeed, little chance of passing the House of Commons, where the best speaker on the ministerial side, Canning, was shortly to resign sooner than support the attitude of his colleagues towards the Queen.

Caroline was by no means satisfied with this victory, and refused to abate any of her pretensions. She went to St. Paul's to return thanks, and London was illuminated for three nights in her honour. Nevertheless, the public was becoming tired of her, and its attitude in the early months of 1821 was reflected in the lines:

> Gracious Queen, we thee implore,
> Go away and sin no more;
> But if that effort be too great,
> Go away at any rate.

At the Derby she met with a cold reception, and the last act of the drama was played at the coronation, for she was determined to be crowned with the King. She wrote to him to ask what she should wear, and the wits suggested he should

---

[1] Daudet, E.: *L'Ambassade du Duc Decazes en Angleterre*, pp. 130–132.

reply that a white sheet in the middle aisle would be most suitable. At five o'clock in the morning on the coronation day the Queen appeared at Westminster Abbey in a coach and six, and the Guards duly presented arms, while mingled groans and cheers came from the spectators. On reaching the door she was denied admission on the ground that she was without the necessary ticket, and after trying all the entrances in turn with the same result she drove away. Shortly afterwards she died, but even in death she was destined to be a nuisance. She had latterly been living at Brandenburg House, Hammersmith, and by her will she ordered that her body should be buried in Brunswick with the inscription, "Here lies Caroline of Brunswick, the injured Queen of England", on the coffin. The authorities were determined to get the corpse to Harwich without taking it through the centre of London, in order to avoid a riot, but the mob thought otherwise. Great crowds met it at St. Mary Abbot's Church: the pavement was torn up, trees were thrown across the road, and the procession was forced into Hyde Park. At Cumberland Gate it attempted to make for Edgware Road, and a conflict took place in the course of which two people were killed. The funeral was then allowed to proceed along Edgware Road, Marylebone Road, and Euston Road as far as Tottenham Court Road; there the mob overcame all opposition, and forced it to pass through the City. Napoleon, too, died that summer, and it is said that when the King was informed that his greatest enemy was dead he remarked, "Is she?"

The coronation itself was one of the most spectacular ever held. The abbey was full by six, although the King himself did not arrive until ten. The ceremony lasted for four hours, and during it George retired now and again for rest and refreshment to the Chapel of St. Edward, where the altar had conveniently been converted into a bar, and was covered with bottles and plates of sandwiches; on these occasions the service was suspended until his return. The coronation was followed, for the last time in English history, by the traditional banquet in Westminster Hall, at which covers were laid for three hundred people, exclusive of those who were at the Royal table. As soon as the King was seated the Duke of Wellington, the Marquess of Anglesey, and Lord Howard of Effingham, each by virtue of an office in the Household, rode on horseback in mediaeval attire into the hall, and waited there while the pages placed the dishes on the table; they then performed the by no means easy feat of backing their horses out again. Hardly had those who were present recovered from this spectacle than a trumpet sounded, and the hereditary champion rode in dressed in complete armour; he was preceded by a herald who read his challenge defying to single combat any who dared to dispute the King's title to the throne. The champion then threw down his gauntlet, which was at once returned to him, and this procedure was repeated three times. Finally, he was presented with a gold cup for his services. The whole ceremony did not finish until eight o'clock in the evening. The King had not been too well received by the crowd, which had cheered Alderman Wood and hooted Castlereagh, but towards evening there was a change for the better in the temper of the mob. For the future George enjoyed greater popularity with the masses, though the upper and middle classes abated none of their dislike.

As soon as the coronation was over the King proceeded to visit Ireland, Scotland, and Hanover. No British monarch had set foot in Ireland since James and William fought at the Boyne, or in Scotland since the middle of the seventeenth century, unless the *de jure* James III and VIII be excepted. The first two Georges had spent much time in Hanover, but George III had never left England. Both Dublin and Edinburgh gave the new King the warmest of welcomes; Daniel O'Connell presented him with a laurel crown, and urged the building of a palace in Ireland. George crossed in one of the earliest steam-packets, and John William Ward, afterwards fourth Viscount Dudley, describes him as having behaved like a popular candidate on an election campaign, and says that

"if the day before he left Ireland, he had stood for Dublin, he might have turned out Shaw or Grattan."[1]

[1] *Letters to Coplestone*, p. 295.

The visit to Scotland took place in 1822, and was followed by the reversal of the attainders on many of those who had fought for the Stuarts. There can be no doubt that it was a happy thought of the King to go to his other kingdoms, and it is to be regretted that so far as Ireland was concerned this display of sympathy on the part of the Royal Family proved to be merely a passing incident. With all his faults, George was no fool; what he lacked was the application to pursue any consistent line of action long enough to achieve success.

It is not easy for a later generation to understand the position of George IV, for the last hundred years have witnessed a trans-valuation of political values. When his personal character is considered it seems difficult to resist the conclusion that the ministers who treated him with such respect must have done so with their tongues in their cheeks; yet such was by no means the case. To them the office was everything, and the man nothing; it was to the former that they owed allegiance as convinced believers in the monarchical system. Time and time again throughout the eighteenth century the occupant of the throne thwarted his ministers, and encouraged opposition to their schemes, but with hardly an exception they defended him from the consequence of his own folly. It is true that for many years it was for the King and his advisers a case of hanging together or hanging separately, for any serious disunion would have meant the return of the Stuarts; but even when this danger no longer existed, as in the reign of George IV, the statesmen behaved correctly towards the Crown. Canning was a notable example of this. He believed so implicitly in the monarchy as an effective piece of the machinery of the Constitution that he would do nothing to lower its prestige even when it was in the wrong, and he was the victim. He realized to the full how extremely unstable was the British throne, but he preferred to suffer in silence, even when the King publicly insulted him to a foreign diplomat, rather than, by vindicating himself, run the risk of overturning the monarchical system altogether. This should be remembered to his credit when Canning is denounced as an opportunist.

There was never any suggestion that George IV should not interfere in politics; all that his ministers demanded was that such interference should be within the limits of the Revolution settlement, and that he should not seem to utilize his position as King of Hanover to oppose the official policy of his British advisers. Actually, he exercised more direct influence upon the progress of events than the first two monarchs of his dynasty had done. Furthermore, he kept the prerogatives of the Crown intact, namely, that of mercy, the dissolution and convocation of Parliament, the dismissal and selection of ministers, the cession of territory, the creation of peers, and the nomination to official appointments. George left them as he found them, though it must be admitted that this is a tribute to the loyalty of his ministers rather than to his own skill.

The King went to Scotland by sea, but he travelled overland to Hanover, and at Calais there was awaiting him the once-famous Beau Brummell. The Beau had fallen far since the days when he told "Wales" to ring the bell, called for "Mistress" Fitzherbert's carriage, and asked "Who's your fat friend?" That Beau Brummell was intolerable judged by any ordinary standard of behaviour can hardly be denied, but George had tolerated him. Both were vulgar, but Meredith, in *Evan Harrington*, drew a distinction between them: "George, for instance, possessed a port; Beau Brummell wielded a Presence." Even if later generations find it hard to forgive the man who introduced starched neckcloths, that does not excuse his treatment by George. He was ignored at Calais, and several years were yet to pass before he even obtained the Consulate at Caen. Yet George kept everything save his word and his friends. He never disposed of his old clothes, and when he died his wardrobe was sold for £30,000. He was always in debt, though careless of money, and before the sale took place there were found in the pockets of the various suits no less than £10,000 in notes. When he was lying dead the Duke of Wellington saw round his neck an old black ribbon, much the worse for wear; attached to it was a jewelled locket containing a minature of Mrs. Fitzherbert. The Duke ordered it to be buried with his master.

The scenes that marked the funeral of Caroline were the closing ones of the eighteenth century, for although it is convenient to date the end of that period at the death of the First Gentleman, it had been moribund for some years. Whig propaganda has obscured the fact that reform began, not with Lord Grey, but with Lord Liverpool. Grants from the Exchequer for the building of churches and for relief works, wholesale reduction of duties and the establishment of free trade between Great Britain and Ireland, and the institution of an effective system of police, all look to the age that was beginning, while, if further evidence be required, it is surely to be found in the combination laws of 1824–1825, which guaranteed, for the first time in any country, freedom of collective bargaining. Abroad, Canning was calling "the New World into existence to redress the balance of the Old"; Byron was dying for the independence of Greece at Misso-longhi; and a young pamphleteer of twenty-one, named Benjamin Disraeli, was declaring that if the leaders of the revolt against Spain in the Americas were

"not pure and practical patriots, we know not what names should be inscribed on the illustrious scroll of national gratitude."[1]

Above all, the Surrey Iron Railway, with its four-foot gauge, which ran between Wandsworth and Croydon, was finding imitators, and two months after the death of George IV the line from Liverpool to Manchester was officially, if tragically, opened. The contrast between what had gone and what was to come was as great as that between the old voluptuary hiding from the gaze of his subjects at Windsor, and his niece playing on the lawn in front of Kensington Palace for any passer-by in the Gardens to watch.

It was at this time, too, that the Press began to assume its modern importance. In 1802 the *Edinburgh Review* made its appearance, and soon exercised a far-reaching influence both upon literature and politics. It was the virulence of its literary

[1] *cf.* Monypenney, W. F.: *The Life of Benjamin Disraeli, Earl of Beaconsfield*, Vol. I, pp. 59–60.

criticisms that called forth a rejoinder from Byron in *English Bards and Scotch Reviewers*. The *Edinburgh Review* was strongly Whig, and in 1807 John Murray, the publisher, wrote to Canning pointing out the harm it was doing to the Tory cause, and suggesting that the time had come to found a rival, which he declared himself ready to finance. Canning put Murray in touch with Gifford, the late editor of the *Anti-Jacobin*, and so the *Quarterly Review* was born. Ministers did not hesitate to write for the Press even while in office, as we have seen in the case of Pitt, and Sir Walter Scott certainly did not disapprove of the practice, for he wrote to Charles Ellis with reference to the new venture:

"As our start is of such immense consequence, don't you think Mr. Canning, though unquestionably our Atlas, might for a day find a Hercules on whom to devolve the burden of the globe, while he writes for us a review? I know what an audacious request this is, but suppose he should, as great statesmen sometimes do, take a political fit of the gout, and absent himself from a large ministerial dinner which might give it him in good earnest—dine at three on a chicken and pint of wine, and lay the foundation of at least one good article? Let us but once get afloat, and our labour is not worth talking about; but, till then, all hands must work hard."[1]

The position of the Press was still, however, very far removed from what it has since become. In the reign of George IV the cost of producing a daily newspaper was relatively little, and the result was that a proprietor did not depend upon the revenue from advertisements, so that his interest was not confined to the circulation of the particular organ which he owned. The Press really did influence public opinion, for it never hesitated to take a strong line upon the important political questions of the hour. It was certainly more scurrilous than it is now, and probably more venal; but in an age when it was still somewhat of a novelty the Press was a power with which it behoved statesmen to deal cautiously. One of the

[1] Lockhart, J. G.: *Memoirs of the Life of Sir Walter Scott*, Vol. II, p. 214.

chief weaknesses of the Liverpool administration was that it had but little newspaper support, and Canning, in particular, was anathema to a large section of the Press, not least because he refused to communicate information to particular editors. He stated his own attitude quite clearly when he said of the Press:

"I acknowledge its power, I submit to its judgment, but I will not be summoned to its bar."

One by one the survivors of the eighteenth century passed away. Castlereagh died by his own hand in 1822, and five years later Liverpool's servants found the Prime Minister unconscious and paralysed beside his breakfast-table. The Cabinet which thus found itself so suddenly deprived of its chief was a very different body from that which had taken office with him fifteen years before. Of the more important ministers, only the Lord Chancellor, the Lord Privy Seal, the First Lord of the Admiralty, and the Secretary of State for War remained the same as in 1812. Canning had succeeded Castlereagh at the Foreign Office and as Leader of the House of Commons, while at the Home Office the self-satisfied Sidmouth had given place to Robert Peel. Huskisson and Wynn had also brought fresh blood into the administration during recent years, though it would be an exaggeration to apply the same observation to the substitution of Robinson for Vansittart as Chancellor of the Exchequer. On the whole, however, the personnel of the ministry was a great deal more imposing than it had been in 1812, and its debating strength in both Houses of Parliament was formidable in the extreme.

The two burning questions of the day were Roman Catholic Emancipation and Parliamentary Reform, and upon the former the Cabinet was hopelessly divided. Reform was the real line of demarcation between Whigs and Tories, and none of the latter would hear of it; but so far as Emancipation was concerned there was considerable difference of opinion within the ranks of those who supported the administration. Canning, Huskisson, Melville, and Robinson were in favour of concessions to the Catholics, while the rest of the Cabinet, including the Prime Minister, was opposed to such a cause. In the country the Tory strongholds, such as the Church and the Universities, were centres of opposition to any alteration in the existing laws. Whenever the subject was debated in Parliament it was left to a free vote of the House, as was still the custom in the case of all save a few measures of exceptional importance, but although the Commons usually showed a majority in favour of emancipation, the Lords were decidedly of the other way of thinking. The King had by now completely shed the Radicalism of his youth, and was as "Protestant" as his father had been, but the stress which he placed upon the dictates of conscience failed to impress either the politicians or the public.

After an interval of intrigue Canning was appointed Prime Minister. The King, who had never quite forgiven his support of Caroline, was inclined to be influenced by the Tory extremists, until Canning said to him, "Sir, your father broke the domination of the Whigs. I hope Your Majesty will not endure that of the Tories." To this the "First Gentleman" replied, "No, I'll be damned if I do," and the statesman left the room Prime Minister at last, to preside over a coalition of Whigs and Tories. Wellington threw up all his offices in disgust, which prompted Tom Moore to write:

> Great Captain, who takest such pains
> To prove—what is granted—*nem. con.*
> With how moderate a portion of brains
> Some heroes continue to get on.

"The Hundred Days of Canning," as Metternich termed his Premiership, lasted until August, when the Prime Minister died at the Duke of Devonshire's house at Chiswick, where Fox, too, had breathed his last. For a few weeks Goderich, as Robinson had become, "the transient and embarrassed phantom" of Disraeli's gibe, attempted to hold the ministry together.

"Nothing can give an idea of the scene under Goderich. No order at the Cabinet. A most ludicrous scene. Nothing ever done. Anglesey sitting with a napkin round his head from the tic, but the only one who seemed to exert himself. ... In a few days Goderich sent for Lyndhurst to Downing Street—walking up and down the room in great agitation, wringing his hands and shedding tears."[1]

Before long Goderich did resign, weeping on the King in the act, and was succeeded by the Duke of Wellington, who promptly executed a *volte face* by granting Catholic Emancipation, not as an act of justice, but in response to threats of violence in Ireland. When such things could happen the eighteenth century was clearly tottering on the brink of the grave, and on June 26th, 1830, it died with the Fourth George.

[1] Monypenny, W. F.: *The Life of Benjamin Disraeli, Earl of Beaconsfield*, Vol. I, pp. 387-388. Yet Goderich had once been known as "Prosperity" Robinson.

APPENDIX

BRITISH ADMINISTRATIONS, 1711–1830

HARLEY, 1711

Lord Treasurer	Robert Harley, May 29, 1711
	D. of Shrewsbury, July 30, 1714
Chancellor of Exchequer . .	Robert Benson, June 1711
Lord President	D. of Buckinghamshire, June 1711
Lord Keeper	Sir Simon Harcourt
Lord Chancellor . . .	Lord Harcourt, April 7, 1713
Secretary of State (Northern Dept.)	Henry St. John (cr. Visc. Bolingbroke 1712)
Secretary of State (Southern Dept.)	E. of Dartmouth
	Wm. Bromley, succ. Aug. 1713
Lord Privy Seal . . .	John Robinson, Bishop of Bristol, April 23, 1711
.	E. of Dartmouth, succ. Aug. 1713
Lord-Lieutenant of Ireland . .	D. of Ormonde
	D. of Shrewsbury, succ. Sept. 1713
First Lord of Admiralty . .	Sir John Leake
	E. of Strafford, succ. 1712
Secretary at War . . .	Geo. Granville (afterwards Ld. Landsowne)
	Sir Wm. Wyndham, succ. June 1712
	Francis Gwynn, succ. Aug. 1713, dismissed Sept. 1714

TOWNSHEND, September 1714

First Lord of Treasury . .	E. of Halifax, d. 1715
	E. of Carlisle, succ. May 1715
	Robt. Walpole (also Chanc. of Exchequer), succ. Oct. 1715
Lord Chancellor . . .	Ld. Cowper
Lord President	E. of Nottingham
	D. of Devonshire, succ. July 1716

TOWNSHEND, September 1714 *(contd.)*

Lord Privy Seal . . .	M. of Wharton, d. 1715
	E. of Sunderland, succ. Aug. 1715
	D. of Kingston, succ. Dec. 1716
First Lord of Admiralty . .	E. of Orford
Secretary of State (Northern Dept.)	Visc. Townshend
	James Stanhope, succ. Dec. 1716
Secretary of State (Southern Dept.)	James Stanhope
	Paul Methuen, succ. 1716
Lord-Lieutenant of Ireland . .	E. of Sunderland
	Visc. Townshend, succ. 1716
Secretary for Scotland . . .	D. of Montrose
	D. of Roxburghe, succ. 1716
Captain-General . . .	D. of Marlborough
Paymaster-General of Forces .	Robt. Walpole
	E. of Lincoln, succ. Oct. 1715
Secretary at War . . .	Wm. Pulteney (afterwards E. of Bath)

STANHOPE, APRIL 1717

First Lord of Treasury and Chancellor of Exchequer	Lord Stanhope
Lord Chancellor . . .	Ld. Cowper
Lord President	D. of Devonshire, res. April 16. In abeyance
Lord Privy Seal . . .	D. of Kingston
First Lord of Admiralty . .	E. of Berkeley
Secretary of State (Northern Dept.)	E. of Sunderland
Secretary of State (Southern Dept.)	Joseph Addison
Lord-Lieutenant of Ireland . .	D. of Bolton
Secretary for Scotland . . .	D. of Roxburghe
Paymaster-General of Forces .	E. of Lincoln
Secretary at War . . .	James Craggs, junr.

STANHOPE, MARCH 1718

First Lord of Treasury . .	E. of Sunderland
Chancellor of Exchequer . .	John Aislabie
Lord Chancellor . . .	Lord Parker

STANHOPE, 1718 (*contd.*)

Lord President	E. of Sunderland
	D. of Kingston, Feb. 1719
	Visc. Townshend, June 1720
Lord Privy Seal . . .	D. of Kingston
	D. of Kent, Feb. 1719
	D. of Kingston, June 1720
First Lord of Admiralty . .	E. of Berkeley
Secretary of State (Northern Dept.)	E. Stanhope
Secretary of State (Southern Dept.)	Jas. Craggs
Lord-Lieutenant of Ireland . .	D. of Bolton
	D. of Grafton, June 1720
Secretary for Scotland . . .	D. of Roxburghe
Paymaster-General of Forces .	E. of Lincoln
	Robert Walpole, 1720
Secretary at War . . .	Visc. Castlecomer
	Robt. Pringle, succ. May 1718
	Geo. Treby, succ. Dec. 1718

WALPOLE, 1721

First Lord of Treasury and Chancellor of Exchequer	Robt. Walpole
Lord Chancellor . . .	E. of Macclesfield
	Ld. King, succ. 1725
Lord President	Ld. Carleton, d. 1725
	D. of Devonshire, succ. 1725
Lord Privy Seal . . .	D. of Kingston, d. 1726
	Ld. Trevor, succ. March 1726
First Lord of Admiralty . .	E. of Berkeley
Secretary of State (Northern Dept.)	Visc. Townshend
Secretary of State (Southern Dept.)	Ld. Carteret
	D. of Newcastle, succ. April 1724
Lord-Lieutenant of Ireland . .	D. of Grafton
	Ld. Carteret, succ. 1724
Secretary for Scotland . . .	D. of Roxburghe, res. 1725
Paymaster-General of Forces .	Ld. Cornwallis, d. 1722
	Hon. Spencer Compton (cr. E. of Wilmington, 1730)
Secretary at War . . .	Geo. Treby
	Henry Pelham, succ. 1724

WALPOLE, 1727

First Lord of Treasury and Chancellor of Exchequer	Sir Robt. Walpole
Lord President	D. of Devonshire
	Ld. Trevor, succ. May 1730
	E. of Wilmington, succ. Dec. 31, 1730
Lord Privy Seal . . .	Ld. Trevor
	E. of Wilmington, succ. May 1730
	D. of Devonshire, succ. June 1731
	Visc. Lonsdale, succ. May 1733
	E. of Godolphin, succ. May 1735
	Ld. Hervey, succ. April 1740
Lord Chancellor . . .	Ld. King
	Hon. Chas. Talbot, succ. Nov. 1733
	Ld. Hardwicke, succ. Feb. 1737
First Lord of Admiralty . .	Visc. Torrington
	Sir Chas. Wager, succ. Jan. 1733
Secretary of State (Southern Dept.)	D. of Newcastle
Secretary of State (Northern Dept.)	Visc. Townshend
	Ld. Harrington, succ. June 1730
Lord-Lieutenant of Ireland . .	Ld. Carteret
	D. of Dorset, succ. Sept. 1731
	D. of Devonshire, succ. 1737
Secretary for Scotland . . .	D. of Newcastle
	E. of Selkirk, succ. 1731
Paymaster-General of Forces .	Hon. Sir Spencer Compton (cr. E. of Wilmington 1730)
	Hon. Henry Pelham, succ. 1730
Secretary at War . . .	Hon. Henry Pelham
	Sir William Strickland, succ. June 1730
	Sir Wm. Yonge, succ. May 1735

CARTERET, FEBRUARY 1742

First Lord of Treasury . .	E. of Wilmington, d. 1743
	Henry Pelham, succ. Aug. 1743
Chancellor of Exchequer . .	Samuel Sandys
	Hon. Henry Pelham, succ. Dec. 1743

CARTERET, February 1742 (*contd.*)

Lord President	E. of Harrington
Lord Privy Seal . . .	Ld. Gower, till Dec. 1743
	E. of Cholmondeley, succ. Dec. 1743
Lord Chancellor . . .	Ld. Hardwicke
Secretary of State (Northern Dept.)	Ld. Carteret, res. Nov. 1744
Secretary of State (Southern Dept.)	D. of Newcastle
First Lord of Admiralty . .	E. of Winchilsea
Lord-Lieutenant of Ireland .	D. of Devonshire
Secretary for Scotland . .	M. of Tweeddale
Paymaster-General of Forces .	Hon. Henry Pelham
	Thos. Winnington, succ. 1743

PELHAM, NOVEMBER 1744

First Lord of Treasury and Chancellor of Exchequer	Hon. Henry Pelham
Lord President	D. of Dorset
Lord Privy Seal . . .	Ld. Gower
Lord Chancellor . . .	Ld. Hardwicke
Secretary of State (Northern Dept.)	E. of Harrington
Secretary of State (Southern Dept.)	D. of Newcastle
First Lord of Admiralty . .	D. of Bedford
Lord-Lieutenant of Ireland .	D. of Devonshire
	E. of Chesterfield, succ. Dec. 1744
Secretary for Scotland . .	M. of Tweeddale
Paymaster-General of Forces .	Thos. Winnington, d. April 1746
	Wm. Pitt, May 6, 1746

PULTENEY, FEBRUARY 10–12, 1746

In February 1746 Pelham and his friends tendered their resignation to the King, whereupon the Earl of Bath, guided by Granville, undertook the formation of a ministry, which expired, however, in two days while yet incomplete. The members actually appointed were as follows :

First Lord of Treasury . .	E. of Bath
Secretary of State . . .	E. Granville
Lord Privy Seal . . .	E. of Carlisle
First Lord of Admiralty . .	E. of Winchilsea

PELHAM, February 1746

First Lord of Treasury and Chancellor of Exchequer . .	Hon. Henry Pelham, d. March 6, 1754
Lord President	D. of Dorset
	E. Granville, succ. 1751
Lord Privy Seal	Ld. Gower
Lord Chancellor	Ld. Hardwicke
Secretary of State (Northern Dept.)	E. of Harrington, Feb. 14, 1746
	E. of Chesterfield, Nov. 4, 1746
	D. of Newcastle, succ. Feb. 6, 1748
Secretary of State (Southern Dept.)	D. of Newcastle, till Feb. 6, 1748
	D. of Bedford, Feb. 12, 1748, till June 13, 1751 [1751
	E. of Holdernesse, succ. June 21,
First Lord of Admiralty . .	D. of Bedford, till Feb. 6, 1748
	E. of Sandwich, succ. 1748
	Ld. Anson, succ. 1751
Lord-Lieutenant of Ireland . .	E. of Chesterfield, Dec. 1744
	E. of Harrington, succ. Sept. 1747
	D. of Dorset, succ. Sept. 1751
Secretary at War . . .	Sir Wm. Yonge
	Henry Fox, succ. May 1746
Paymaster-General of Forces .	William Pitt

DUKE OF NEWCASTLE, April 1754

First Lord of Treasury . .	D. of Newcastle
Chancellor of Exchequer . .	Hon. Henry Bilson Legge
	Sir Geo. Lyttleton, succ. Nov.
Lord President	E. Granville [1755
Lord Privy Seal . . .	E. Gower, d. 1754
	D. of Marlborough, succ. Jan. 1755
	E. Gower, succ. Dec. 1755
Lord Chancellor . . .	E. of Hardwicke
Secretary of State (Northern Dept.)	E. of Holdernesse [1755
Secretary of State (Southern Dept.)	Sir Thos. Robinson, till Nov. 15,
	Henry Fox, succ. Nov. 15, 1755
First Lord of Admiralty . .	Ld. Anson
Lord-Lieutenant of Ireland . .	D. of Dorset
	M. of Hartington, succ. 1755

DUKE OF NEWCASTLE, April 1754 (*contd.*)

Paymaster-General of Forces	. Wm. Pitt
	E. of Darlington and Visc. Dupplin, jointly, succ. 1755
Secretary at War . . .	. Henry Fox, till Nov. 15, 1755 .
	William Wildman Barrington, Visc. from Nov. 1755

PITT, NOVEMBER 1756

First Lord of Treasury .	. D. of Devonshire
Chancellor of Exchequer .	. Hon. Henry Bilson Legge
Lord President . . .	. E. Granville
Lord Privy Seal . .	. E. Gower
Lord Chancellor . .	. Great Seal in Commission
Secretary of State (Northern Dept.)	E. of Holdernesse
Secretary of State (Southern Dept.)	Wm. Pitt
First Lord of Admiralty .	. E. Temple
Lord-Lieutenant of Ireland .	. D. of Bedford
Paymaster-General of Forces	. Visc. Dupplin and Thos. Potter, jointly

PITT, JUNE 19, 1757

First Lord of Treasury .	. D. of Newcastle
Chancellor of Exchequer .	. Hon. Henry Bilson Legge
Lord President . . .	. E. Granville
Lord Privy Seal . .	. E. Temple
Lord Keeper . . .	. Sir Robt. Henley
Lord Chamberlain . .	. D. of Devonshire
Secretary of State (Northern Dept.)	E. of Holdernesse
Secretary of State (Southern Dept.)	Wm. Pitt
First Lord of Admiralty .	. Ld. Anson
Lord-Lieutenant of Ireland	. D. of Bedford
Paymaster-General of Forces	. Henry Fox
Secretary at War . .	. Visc. Barrington
President of Board of Trade and Plantations	E. of Halifax

NEWCASTLE, NOVEMBER 1760

First Lord of Treasury .	. D. of Newcastle
Secretary of State (Northern Dept.)	E. of Holdernesse
	E. of Bute, succ. Oct. 1761

NEWCASTLE, November 1760 (*contd.*)

Secretary of State (Southern Dept.)	Wm. Pitt
	E. of Egremont, succ. March 1761
Lord President	Ld. Granville
Lord Keeper and Lord Chancellor	Ld. Henley
Lord Privy Seal . . .	E. Temple
Lord Chamberlain . . .	D. of Devonshire
Groom of the Stole . . .	E. of Bute
	E. of Huntingdon, succ. Oct. 1761
President of Board of Trade .	E. of Halifax
	Ld. Sandys, succ. March 1761
Chancellor of Exchequer . .	Hon. Henry Bilson Legge
	Visc. Barrington, succ. March 1761
First Lord of Admiralty . .	Ld. Anson
Master-General of Ordnance .	Visc. Ligonier
Lord-Lieutenant of Ireland . .	D. of Bedford
	E. of Halifax, succ. 1761
Unofficial	Ld. Hardwicke
Unofficial	Ld. Mansfield
Secretary at War . . .	Visc. Barrington
	C. Townshend, succ. 1761

BUTE, MAY 1762

First Lord of Treasury . .	E. of Bute
Secretary of State (Northern Dept.)	G. Grenville
Secretary of State (Southern Dept.)	E. of Egremont
Lord President	Ld. Granville
Lord Chancellor . . .	Ld. Henley
Lord Privy Seal . . .	D. of Bedford
Chancellor of Exchequer . .	Sir F. Dashwood
First Lord of Admiralty . .	E. of Halifax
	G. Grenville, succ. Oct. 1762
Master-General of Ordnance .	Visc. Ligonier
Lord-Lieutenant of Ireland . .	E. of Halifax
Secretary at War . . .	C. Townshend
	W. Ellis, succ. Dec. 1762

GRENVILLE, MAY 1763

First Lord of Treasury and Chancellor of Exchequer	G. Grenville

GRENVILLE, May 1763 (*contd.*)

Secretary of State (Northern Dept.)	E. of Halifax
Secretary of State (Southern Dept.)	E. of Egremont
	E. of Sandwich, succ. Sept. 1763
Lord President	Ld. Granville
	D. of Bedford, succ. Sept. 1763
Lord Chancellor . . .	E. of Northington
Lord Privy Seal . . .	D. of Marlborough
First Lord of Admiralty . .	Ld. Egmont
Master-General of Ordnance .	M. of Granby
Lord-Lieutenant of Ireland . .	E. of Northumberland
	Visc. Weymouth, succ. 1765
Secretary at War . . .	W. Ellis

ROCKINGHAM, JULY 1765

First Lord of Treasury . .	M. of Rockingham
Secretary of State (Northern Dept.)	D. of Grafton
	D. of Richmond, succ. May 1766
Secretary of State (Southern Dept.)	H. S. Conway
Lord President . . .	E. of Winchilsea
Lord Chancellor . . .	E. of Northington
Lord Privy Seal . . .	D. of Newcastle
Chancellor of Exchequer . .	W. Dowdeswell
First Lord of Admiralty .	Ld. Egmont
Master-General of Ordnance .	M. of Granby
Lord-Lieutenant of Ireland . .	M. of Hertford
Secretary at War . . .	Visc. Barrington

CHATHAM, AUGUST 1766

First Lord of Treasury . .	D. of Grafton
Secretary of State (Northern Dept.)	H. S. Conway
Secretary of State (Southern Dept.)	E. of Shelburne
Lord President	E. of Northington
Lord Chancellor . . .	Ld. Camden
Lord Privy Seal . . .	E. of Chatham
Chancellor of Exchequer . .	C. Townshend
	Ld. North, succ. Sept. 1767
First Lord of Admiralty . .	Sir C. Saunders
	Sir E. Hawke, succ. Dec. 1766

CHATHAM, August 1766 (*contd.*)

Master-General of Ordnance .	M. of Granby
Lord-Lieutenant of Ireland . .	E. of Bristol
	Visc. Townshend, succ. Oct. 1767
Secretary at War . . .	Visc. Barrington

GRAFTON, DECEMBER 1767

First Lord of Treasury . .	D. of Grafton
Secretary of State (Northern Dept.)	Visc. Weymouth
	E. of Rochford, succ. Oct. 1768
Secretary of State (Southern Dept.)	E. of Shelburne
	Visc. Weymouth, succ. Oct. 1768
Secretary of State (Colonies) .	E. of Hillsborough, apptd. Jan 1768
Lord President	E. Gower
Lord Chancellor . . .	Ld. Camden
	C. Yorke, received great seal Jan. 17, d. 20th, 1770
Lord Privy Seal . . .	E. of Chatham
	E. of Bristol, succ. Oct. 1768
Chancellor of Exchequer . .	Ld. North
First Lord of Admiralty . .	Sir E. Hawke
Master-General of Ordnance Unofficial	M. of Granby
	H. S. Conway
Lord-Lieutenant of Ireland .	Visc. Townshend
Secretary at War . . .	Visc. Barrington

NORTH, JANUARY 1770

First Lord of Treasury and Chancellor of Exchequer	Lord North
Secretary of State (Northern Dept.)	E. of Rochford
	Visc. Weymouth, succ. Nov. 1775
	E. of Hillsborough, succ. Nov. 1779
Secretary of State (Southern Dept.)	Visc. Weymouth
	E. of Sandwich, succ. Dec. 1770
	E. of Halifax, succ. Jan. 1771
	E. of Suffolk, succ. June 1771
	Visc. Stormont, succ. Oct. 1779

NORTH, January 1770 (*contd.*)

Secretary of State (Colonies)	. E. of Hillsborough
	E. of Dartmouth, succ. Aug. 1772
	Ld. G. Germain, succ. Nov. 1775
	W. Ellis, succ. March, 1782
Lord President . . .	. E. Gower
	E. Bathurst, succ. Nov. 1779
Lord Chancellor . .	. Great Seal in Commission. Ld. Apsley, 1771
	Ld. Thurlow, succ. June 1778
Lord Privy Seal . .	. E. of Halifax
	E. of Suffolk, succ. Jan. 1771
	D. of Grafton, succ. June 1771
	E. of Dartmouth, succ. Nov. 1775
First Lord of Admiralty .	. Sir E. Hawke
	E. of Sandwich, succ. Jan. 1771
Master-General of Ordnance	. M. of Granby
	Visc. Townshend, succ. Oct. 1772
Lord-Lieutenant of Ireland .	. Visc. Townshend
	E. Harcourt, succ. 1772
	E. of Buckinghamshire, succ. 1777
	E. of Carlisle, succ. 1780
Secretary at War . .	. Visc. Barrington
	C. Jenkinson, succ. Dec. 1778

ROCKINGHAM, MARCH 1782

First Lord of Treasury .	. M. of Rockingham
Secretary of State (Home) .	. E. of Shelburne
Secretary of State (Foreign) .	. C. J. Fox
Chancellor of Exchequer .	. Ld. J. Cavendish
Lord President . . .	. Ld. Camden
Lord Chancellor . .	. Ld. Thurlow
Lord Privy Seal . .	. D. Grafton
First Lord of Admiralty .	. Visc. Keppel
Master-General of Ordnance	. D. of Richmond
Lord-Lieutenant of Ireland .	. D. of Portland
Secretary at War . .	. T. Townshend

SHELBURNE, July 1782

First Lord of Treasury . .	E. of Shelburne
Secretary of State (Home) . .	T. Townshend
Secretary of State (Foreign) .	Ld. Grantham
Lord President	Ld. Camden
Lord Chancellor . . .	Ld. Thurlow
Lord Privy Seal . . .	D. of Grafton
Chancellor of Exchequer . .	W. Pitt
First Lord of Admiralty .	Visc. Keppel
Master-General of Ordnance .	D. of Richmond
Lord-Lieutenant of Ireland . .	E. Temple
Secretary at War . . .	Sir G. Yonge

COALITION, FOX and NORTH, April 1783

First Lord of Treasury . .	D. of Portland
Secretary of State (Home) . .	Ld. North
Secretary of State (Foreign) .	C. J. Fox
Lord President	Visc. Stormont
Lord Chancellor . . .	Great Seal in Commission
Lord Privy Seal . . .	E. of Carlisle
Chancellor of Exchequer . .	Ld. J. Cavendish
First Lord of Admiralty .	Visc. Keppel
Master-General of Ordnance .	Visc. Townshend
Lord-Lieutenant of Ireland . .	E. of Northington
Secretary at War . . .	R. Fitzpatrick

PITT, December 1783

First Lord of Treasury and Chancellor of Exchequer	W. Pitt
Secretary of State (Home) . .	E. Temple
	Lord Sydney
	W. W. Grenville, succ. June 1789
	H. Dundas, succ. June 1791
	D. of Portland, succ. July 1794
Secretary of State (Foreign) .	M. of Carmarthen
	Ld. Grenville, succ. June 1791
Secretary of State (War) . .	H. Dundas, apptd. July 1794

PITT, December 1783 (*contd.*)

Lord President	E. Gower
	Ld. Camden, succ. Dec. 1784
	E. Fitzwilliam, succ. July 1794
	E. of Mansfield, succ. Dec. 1794
	E. of Chatham, succ. Dec. 1796
Lord Chancellor . . .	Ld. Thurlow
	Ld. Loughborough, succ. Jan. 1793
Lord Privy Seal . . .	D. of Rutland
	E. Gower, succ. Nov. 1784
	E. Spencer, succ. July 1794
	E. of Chatham, succ. Dec. 1794
	E. of Westmorland, succ. Feb. 1798
First Lord of Admiralty . .	Visc. Hood
	E. of Chatham, succ. July 1788
	E. Spencer, succ. Dec. 1794
Master-General of Ordnance .	E. of Richmond
	M. Cornwallis, succ. Feb. 1795
Lord Lieutenant of Ireland . .	D. of Rutland
	M. of Buckingham, succ. 1787
	E. of Westmorland, succ. 1790
	E. Fitzwilliam, succ. 1794
	E. Camden, succ. 1795
	M. Cornwallis, succ. 1798
Secretary at War . . .	Sir G. Yonge
	W. Windham, succ. July 1794

ADDINGTON, MARCH 1801

First Lord of Treasury and Chancellor of Exchequer	H. Addington
Secretary of State (Home) . .	D. of Portland
	Ld. Pelham, succ. July 1801
	C. P. Yorke, succ. Aug. 1803
	Lord Hawkesbury
Secretary of State (Foreign, War, and Colonies)	Ld. Hobart
Lord President	E. of Chatham
	D. of Portland, succ. July 1801
Lord Chancellor . . .	Ld. Eldon
Lord Privy Seal . . .	E. of Westmorland

ADDINGTON, March 1801 (*contd.*)

First Lord of Admiralty . .	E. St. Vincent
Master-General of Ordnance .	E. of Chatham, apptd. June 1801
Board of Trade	Lord Auckland
Board of Control . . .	Visc. Lewisham
	Visc. Castlereagh, succ. July 1802
Lord-Lieutenant of Ireland .	E. of Hardwicke
Secretary at War . . .	C. P. Yorke
	C. Bragge, succ. Aug. 1803

PITT, MAY 1804

First Lord of Treasury and Chancellor of Exchequer	W. Pitt
Secretary of State (Home) . .	Ld. Hawkesbury
Secretary of State (Foreign) .	Ld. Harrowby
	Ld. Mulgrave, succ. Jan. 1805
Secretary of State (War and Colonies)	E. Camden
	Visc. Castlereagh, succ. July 1805
Lord President	D. of Portland
	Visc. Sidmouth, succ. Jan. 1805
	E. Camden, succ. July 1805
Lord Chancellor . . .	Ld. Eldon
Lord Privy Seal . . .	E. of Westmorland
First Lord of Admiralty . .	Visc. Melville
	Ld. Barham, succ. May 1805
Master-General of Ordnance .	E. of Chatham
Board of Trade . . .	D. of Montrose
Board of Control . . .	Visc. Castlereagh
Duchy of Lancaster . . .	Ld. Mulgrave [1805
	E. of Buckinghamshire, succ. Jan.
	Ld. Harrowby, succ. July 1805
Lord-Lieutenant of Ireland .	E. of Hardwicke
	E. Powis, succ. Nov. 1805
Secretary at War . . .	W. Dundas

GRENVILLE, FEBRUARY 1806

First Lord of Treasury . .	Ld. Grenville
Secretary of State (Home) . .	E. Spencer
Secretary of State (Foreign) .	C. J. Fox
	Visc. Howick, succ. Sept.

GRENVILLE, February 1806 (*contd.*)

Secretary of State (War and Colonies)	W. Windham
Lord President	E. Fitzwilliam
	Visc. Sidmouth, succ. Oct.
Lord Chancellor . . .	Ld. Erskine
Lord Privy Seal . . .	Visc. Sidmouth
	Ld. Holland, succ. Oct.
Chancellor of Exchequer . .	Ld. H. Petty
First Lord of Admiralty . .	C. Grey (April, Visc. Howick)
	T. Grenville, succ. Sept.
Master-General of Ordnance .	E. of Moira
Chief Justice, King's Bench .	Ld. Ellenborough
Lord-Lieutenant of Ireland . .	D. of Bedford
Secretary at War . . .	R. Fitzpatrick

PORTLAND, MARCH 1807

First Lord of Treasury . .	D. of Portland
Secretary of State (Home) . .	Ld. Hawkesbury
Secretary of State (Foreign) .	G. Canning
Secretary of State (War and Colonies)	Visc. Castlereagh
Lord President	E. Camden
Lord Chancellor . . .	Ld. Eldon
Lord Privy Seal . . .	E. of Westmorland
Chancellor of Exchequer and Duchy of Lancaster	S. Perceval
First Lord of Admiralty . .	Ld. Mulgrave
Master-General of Ordnance .	E. of Chatham
Board of Trade . . .	E. Bathurst
Board of Control . . .	R. S. Dundas
	E. of Harrowby, succ. July 1809
Lord-Lieutenant of Ireland . .	D. of Richmond
Secretary at War . . .	Sir J. Pulteney [1809
	Ld. G. Leveson Gower, succ. June

PERCEVAL, OCTOBER 1809

First Lord of Treasury, Chancellor of Exchequer and Duchy of Lancaster	S. Perceval

PERCEVAL, October 1809 *(contd.)*

Secretary of State (Home) . .	R. Ryder
Secretary of State (Foreign) .	E. Bathurst
	M. Wellesley, succ. Dec. 1809
	Visc. Castlereagh, succ. March 1812
Secretary of State (War and Colonies)	E. of Liverpool
Lord President	E. Camden
	Visc. Sidmouth, succ. April 1812
Lord Chancellor . . .	Ld. Eldon
Lord Privy Seal . . .	E. of Westmorland
First Lord of Admiralty . .	Ld. Mulgrave
	C. P. Yorke, succ. May 1810
Master-General of Ordnance .	E. of Chatham
	Ld. Mulgrave, succ. May 1810
Board of Trade . . .	E. Bathurst
Lord-Lieutenant of Ireland . .	D. of Richmond
Secretary at War . . .	Visc. Palmerston

LIVERPOOL, June 1812

First Lord of Treasury . .	E. of Liverpool
Secretary of State (Home) . .	Visc. Sidmouth
	R. Peel, succ. Jan. 1822
Secretary of State (Foreign) .	Visc. Castlereagh
	G. Canning, succ. Sept. 1822
Secretary of State (War and Colonies)	E. Bathurst
Lord President	E. of Harrowby
Lord Chancellor . . .	Ld. Eldon
Lord Privy Seal . . .	E. of Westmorland
Chancellor of Exchequer . .	N. Vansittart
	F. J. Robinson, succ. Jan. 1823
First Lord of Admiralty . .	Visc. Melville
Master-General of Ordnance .	Ld. Mulgrave
	D. of Wellington, succ. Jan. 1819
Board of Trade . . .	E. of Clancarty
	F. J. Robinson, succ. Jan. 1818
	W. Huskisson, succ. Jan. 1823

LIVERPOOL, June 1812 (*contd.*)

Board of Control . . .	E. of Buckinghamshire
	G. Canning, succ. June 1816
	C. B. Bathurst, succ. Jan. 1821
	C. W. Wynn, succ. Feb. 1822
Master of the Mint . . .	E. of Clancarty
	W. W. Pole, succ. Sept. 1815
	T. Wallace, succ. Oct. 1823
Duchy of Lancaster . . .	C. B. Bathurst
	N. Vansittart, succ. Feb. 1823
Without office . . .	E. Camden
Lord-Lieutenant of Ireland .	D. of Richmond
	Visc. Whitworth, succ. Aug. 1813
	E. Talbot, succ. Oct. 1817
	M. Wellesley, succ. Dec. 1821
Secretary at War . . .	Visc. Palmerston

CANNING, APRIL 1827

First Lord of Treasury and Chancellor of Exchequer	G. Canning
Secretary of State (Home) . .	W. S. Bourne
	M. of Lansdowne, succ. July
Secretary of State (Foreign) .	Visc. Dudley
Secretary of State (War and Colonies)	Visc. Goderich
Lord President	E. of Harrowby
Lord Chancellor . . .	Ld. Lyndhurst
Lord Privy Seal . . .	D. of Portland
	E. of Carlisle
Lord High Admiral . . .	D. of Clarence
Board of Trade and Treasurer of Navy	W. Huskisson
Board of Control . . .	C. W. Wynn
Master of the Mint . . .	T. Wallace
	G. Tierney, succ. May
First Commissioner of Woods and Forests	C. Arbuthnot
	E. of Carlisle, succ. May
	W. S. Bourne, succ. July
Duchy of Lancaster . . .	Ld. Bexley
Without office . . .	M. of Lansdowne
Lord-Lieutenant of Ireland .	M. Wellesley
Secretary at War . . .	Visc. Palmerston

GODERICH, September 1827

First Lord of Treasury . .	Visc. Goderich
Secretary of State (Home) . .	M. of Lansdowne
Secretary of State (Foreign) .	E. Dudley
Secretary of State (War and Colonies)	W. Huskisson
Lord President	D. of Portland
Lord Chancellor . . .	Ld. Lyndhurst
Lord Privy Seal . . .	E. of Carlisle
Chancellor of Exchequer . .	J. C. Herries
Lord High Admiral . . .	D. of Clarence
Master-General of Ordnance .	M. of Anglesey
Board of Trade and Treasurer of Navy	C. Grant
Board of Control . . .	C. W. Wynn
Master of the Mint . . .	G. Tierney
First Commissioner of Woods and Forests	W. S. Bourne
Duchy of Lancaster . . .	Ld. Bexley
Lord-Lieutenant of Ireland . .	M. Wellesley
Secretary at War . . .	Visc. Palmerston

WELLINGTON, January 1828

First Lord of Treasury . .	D. of Wellington
Secretary of State (Home) . .	R. Peel
Secretary of State (Foreign) .	E. Dudley
	E. of Aberdeen, succ. June 1828
Secretary of State (War and Colonies)	W. Huskisson
	Sir G. Murray, succ. May 1828
Lord President	E. Bathurst
Lord Chancellor . . .	Ld. Lyndhurst
Lord Privy Seal . . .	Ld. Ellenborough
	E. of Rosslyn, succ. June 1829
Chancellor of Exchequer . .	H. Goulburn
First Lord of Admiralty . .	D. of Clarence
	Visc. Melville, succ. Sept. 1828
Board of Trade and Treasurer of Navy	C. Grant
	W. V. Fitzgerald, succ. June 1828
Board of Control . . .	Visc. Melville
	Ld. Ellenborough, succ. Sept. 1828

WELLINGTON, January 1828 (*contd.*)

Master of the Mint . . .	J. C. Herries
Duchy of Lancaster . . .	E. of Aberdeen
	C. Arbuthnot, succ. June 1828
Lord-Lieutenant of Ireland . .	M. of Anglesey, Feb. 1828
	D. of Northumberland, succ. Feb. 1829
Secretary at War . . .	Visc. Palmerston
	Sir H. Hardinge, succ. May 1828

INDEX

Date Due